Dear Guests:

Beware of Wild Monkeys

Tips and Tales from a Family World Odyssey

By Joe Tash

AuthorHouse™
1663 Liberty Drive
Bloomington, IN 47403
www.authorhouse.com
Phone: 1-800-839-8640

First published by AuthorHouse 8/2/2010

ISBN: 978-1-4520-4446-0 (sc)
ISBN: 978-1-4520-4445-3 (e)

Library of Congress Control Number: 2010911400

Printed in the United States of America
Bloomington, Indiana

This book is printed on acid-free paper.

authorHOUSE®

To Ava and Salome, the best traveling companions ever, whether it's a journey around the world or over the peaks and valleys of life.

Do something every day that scares you.

I once read that piece of advice, and it stuck with me. I'm a "play it safe" person by nature. So I have to push myself to take risks.

Recently, I put that principle into action with the biggest risk I've ever taken – quitting my job, putting my stuff in storage and taking off on a round-the-world trip. And that's not all – I convinced my wife to join me with our 8-year-old daughter.

Since our return, I've attempted to set down the highs and lows of our family adventure in the following pages.

The book features advice on planning and executing an extended family world trip, such as choosing an itinerary, purchasing round-the-world tickets, selecting the right clothing and gear, arranging for home-schooling, and finding the best travel and health insurance. It also covers the ins and outs of renting the family house and handling finances from the road. Mixed in with the practical tips and examples are tales of our travel experiences in South America, Western and Eastern Europe, India, Thailand, Cambodia, Hong Kong and Tokyo.

During our trip, we came within 10 feet of a wild tiger while riding in an open jeep in India, and sat on a jetliner that experienced a serious "electrical malfunction" at 35,000 feet. We ate roasted guinea pig and fried crickets, and dined on a floating restaurant in a bay in southern Thailand. We hiked through the cloud forest along Peru's Inca Trail, and rode in a motor boat to the base of the Garganta del Diablo, or Devil's Throat, at the spectacular

Iguazu Falls between Brazil and Argentina. We traveled by van on a dirt road from Thailand to Cambodia to see the Angkor Wat ruins, and were stranded in the middle of Lake Titicaca, between Peru and Bolivia, when the engine died on our dilapidated excursion boat.

When it was over, we'd visited 20 countries on four continents and snapped 5,000 photos, the best of which are included here. Excerpts from my daughter's travel journals provide a unique family perspective of the trip. In telling this story, I've drawn on my 20-plus years' experience as a journalist, and attempted to include a fair dose of the laughter, tears and insights gained during our nine months on the road, in some of the strangest and exotic places we'd ever been.

I hope you enjoy this compilation of travel tidbits and lessons learned from our family's "trip of a lifetime," which we call, DEAR GUESTS, BEWARE OF WILD MONKEYS: Tips and Tales from a Family World Odyssey.

Table of Contents

Chapter 1   **'You Must Really Love That Man'** 8
Overview, Itinerary, RTW air tickets, tours
and accommodations

Chapter 2   **Guinea Pig for Dinner** 18
Ecuador, Peru, Bolivia

Chapter 3   **Real Estate Tycoons** 43
What to do with your house and your stuff

Chapter 4   **Tango, Samba and Everything In Between** 49
Chile, Argentina, Uruguay, Brazil

Chapter 5   **Book Smarts** 86
Homeschooling on the road

Chapter 6   **Mind the Gap** 93
London, Western Europe

Chapter 7   **Say Aaaaah!** 134
Staying healthy

Chapter 8   **Life after the Iron Curtain** 141
Austria and Eastern Europe

Chapter 9   **Dollars, Reales or Rupees, It's all Money** 198
How much the trip cost, and how to care
for your money while you're away

Chapter 10   **Hungry Monkeys and Sacred Cows** 204
Mumbai to Delhi, India

Chapter 11   **Where Do I Plug In My Blow-Dryer?** 274
What to take, and what to carry it in

Chapter 12   **India High and Low** 282
From the Himalayas to the Arabian Sea

Chapter 13   **Angkor What?** 333
Thailand, Cambodia, Hong Kong and Tokyo

Chapter 14   **Home at Last** 391
Re-entry, lessons learned

Chapter 1

"You Must Really Love That Man"

Overview, itinerary, RTW air tickets, tours and accommodations

"Remember what Bilbo used to say: It's a dangerous business, Frodo, going out your door. You step onto the road, and if you don't keep your feet, there's no knowing where you might be swept off to."

J.R.R. Tolkien

I looked straight ahead and saw red – hundreds of tail lights shining and flashing in the pale morning light.

My car sat at a dead stop on Interstate 5 on a Monday morning, surrounded by an army of fellow rush-hour commuters. That's when a crazy thought popped into my brain: Why not get away from all of this, really far away? Why not travel around the world?

Prudence argued against such a risky endeavor. I had a good job, bills to pay and a retirement plan to follow. I had a wife and daughter, with their work and school to consider. Finally, we had the house, mortgage payments, cars, furniture and pets.

Maybe the whole idea was just too far-fetched. But.... it sure would be great to get away from all these red lights, I thought. My mind began working like a calculator, figuring out how much cash we had on hand and how much we could raise by refinancing or selling our house. I thought about what it would cost for three people to circle the globe on a budget, and how we would deal with schooling, health insurance and family finances.

All that day at work, I turned the idea over in my mind, thinking about how I would convince Ava, my wife, to go along for the ride. But that night, she quickly agreed to the idea, almost as if she had been thinking the same thing.

We both love to travel. We've been doing it ever since we got together, more than 25 years ago. We've backpacked all over Mexico and hiked to waterfalls in Hawaii. We even quit our jobs and hit the road once before, in the mid-1990s, when we toured the western U.S. while living in my red Nissan pickup with its black camper shell.

Having a kid didn't slow us down. We went to Europe for the first time when Salome was 18 months old. That trip wasn't all wonder and awe – we ran out of diapers on the overnight flight to Paris, and didn't even know the French word for "diapers" when we landed. The taxi driver held his breath and quickly drove us to a drug store.

After that, we traveled many times as a family, to Germany, France and the Netherlands, to Greece and Turkey, to Mexico and Hawaii. While there are some things you can't do when traveling with a young child, such as staying out all night in dance clubs, kids can also open doors in foreign lands. Over the years, Salome has served as a kind of ambassador, introducing us to many wonderful people and places, experiences we would certainly have missed otherwise.

We were convinced from the beginning that traveling around the world would be a good thing for our daughter, and for our entire family. Salome would be out of school for a year, but the education she gained from visiting the many countries on our itinerary would more than make up for the missed classroom time. We knew she would learn about world history, cultures, languages and even math (Salome turned out to be a whiz at currency conversion) in a way she could never have done in school.

Unfortunately, we didn't count on some of the complications that arose. Being away from her friends and teachers was harder than we had expected, intensifying Salome's natural feelings of homesickness.

We also hit a serious obstacle due to Salome's diagnosis with a medical condition the year before we left on our trip.

Doctors said she suffered from trichotillomania, defined as an urge to pull one's own hair, eyelashes or eyebrows. Breaking the habit is tough, and we know several adults – including one of Salome's teachers – who struggle with the condition.

A doctor prescribed medication to help Salome resist the urge to pull her lashes, which worked fine for a while. About a month into our trip, though, she had an adverse reaction to the medication, which caused her to fly into a rage with little or no provocation. We came to call these episodes "meltdowns," and they almost derailed our trip. We stopped giving her the medication, and gradually, her moods returned to normal, which allowed us to carry on.

Once we made up our minds to travel around the world, we enjoyed talking about our upcoming trip with each other - and anybody else who would listen.

The actual work of planning our adventure was another matter. At first, we were like wanderers in a vast desert with no idea where to turn. Our heads were full of romantically vague ideas of places we wanted to see, based on books and movies and our friends' travel tales. But stitching those destinations together into a coherent plan for a yearlong family journey was so much different than daydreaming about lying on a remote tropical beach or standing inside the Sistine Chapel.

In the two years before our trip, I devoured guidebooks and travelogues about the countries we wanted to see, how-to guides for globetrotters, even books about getting the best deal on round-the-world air tickets. I read titles like The Frugal Globetrotter, 100 Places to See before You Die, and Adventuring with Children.

I put a map of the world on the wall of my home office, and we stuck colored pins into the countries and cities we wanted to visit.

I tried to absorb it all, hoping as I did so, our path would become clear in my head like a glowing line on my world map. It didn't. The more I read, the more confused I became. There were so many places to see and so many ways to see them. Such choices depend greatly on a traveler's personal style, the size of his or her bank account and personal goals for the trip.

Ava and I spent hours turning the pages of guidebooks and world atlases. We kept a running list of countries we wanted to visit on a yellow legal pad, adding destinations and scratching them off as we went along. At the kitchen table and in coffee shops, we debated the pros and cons of various countries. I went online to the U.S. State Department's Web site, researching the safety of countries we were considering.

Slowly, over a period of weeks and months, our itinerary took shape. Based on places we had heard and read about, and gut feelings about our own travel desires, we settled on two months in South America, a side trip to Morocco, another two months in both Western and Eastern Europe, two months in India, a month in Thailand, Cambodia and Vietnam, two months in China and one month in Japan. Give or take, about 10 months total, on a trip covering four continents, including North America.

Our itinerary set, the next task was shopping for round-the-world air tickets. My initial plan was to use a "consolidator," a type of travel agent who specializes in discount air tickets. Airlines sometimes sell blocks of seats to consolidators, who act as middlemen and sell them to travel agencies, or directly to passengers. A number of consolidators who specialize in round-the-world tickets are based in San Francisco; Air Treks and Air Brokers International are a couple of examples.

These agents shop for one-way, discount tickets that can be strung together to get a traveler where he or she wants to go. This often means flying on a number of different airlines, many of them lesser-known and smaller carriers, during the course of a round-the-world journey. While this can be a cheaper way to go, it is sometimes difficult to find tickets for the exact cities on a traveler's itinerary. Also, there may be restrictions, some quite onerous, regarding changes to dates, flights or destinations. Refund policies on such tickets also vary widely.

We settled on a ticket issued by Oneworld Alliance, a consortium of airlines including industry giants American, British Air and Cathay Pacific. The consolidators could not beat the price or flexibility of the Oneworld Alliance tickets. Our tickets allowed us to take 18 flights on four continents over a one-year period, starting from the date of the first flight. Date changes were free, although there was a charge for changing departure or destination cities. Another plus was the ability to go to the office of any alliance partner as we traveled, if we needed to make any changes to our itinerary. This turned out to be a great convenience, as we adjusted our route and flight dates from the road. Round-the-world airfare for the three of us cost about $11,000, including a 25 percent discount for Salome's ticket.

For those researching round-the-world airfares, United and Lufthansa head a similar consortium called the Star Alliance.

Our next step was to drill down into our itinerary and determine which events and activities within the countries we planned to visit would require advance planning. While it would have been both impossible and inadvisable to book out the whole trip ahead of time – we needed flexibility as we traveled and didn't want to carry a filing cabinet full of reservations with us on the road – certain things had to be booked in advance.

For example, in Ecuador, our first international destination, I wanted to study Spanish and live with a local family. Ava was set on a boat trip through the Galapagos

Islands, which turned out to be one of the highlights of our entire trip. Both of us wanted to hike the Inca Trail to the ancient citadel of Machu Picchu. In India, we were tantalized by the Pushkar Camel Fair, a colorful, crowded amalgamation of religious pilgrimage, livestock market and traveling carnival.

With the help of guidebooks and the Internet, I found a language school in Quito that could arrange both our homestay and our Galapagos cruise. I used a "call-around" number for international calls, which involves dialing a code before entering the international number you want to call, but for a fraction of the price of phone company rates. The charges show up on your regular phone bill. Since we planned our trip in 2004-2005, online services such as Skype have come into existence, making international calls even cheaper – and sometimes free!

Booking the Inca Trail hike in advance is also imperative because the Peruvian government rations the hiking permits it issues each season.

Finally, although the Pushkar Camel Fair is open to all comers, I had read that hotels in the northern Indian town book up early for the festival period. I reserved a hotel room in Pushkar by email, then sent the required deposit by Western Union money-gram. When we arrived in Pushkar, we found that rooms were indeed available a mile or so from the fairgrounds, at a far lower price than we had paid. That said, our "expensive" Pushkar booking cost $75 a night, for a place in the center of town with an extremely helpful and friendly staff.

Even though we had been thinking about, researching and discussing our trip for at least two years, by necessity the bulk of our planning and preparation took place in the spring of 2005, a few months before our June departure date. We decided to leave as soon as Salome finished third grade, which would give us maximum time for travel and allow us a few months to get settled back at home before she was due to start fifth grade. Salome's fourth-grade year would be spent on the road, with her parents and the world as her teachers.

Along with finalizing the details of the trip itself, we had many other matters to attend to, such as arranging for Salome's independent study program, obtaining travel and health insurance, storing our belongings, renting out our house, and hiring a property manager. We also researched the types of bags and clothing we would take, the electronic gear we'd need, and how to handle our finances while we were away. All of these subjects will be covered in depth later in the book.

Once we landed in South America, I knew the hard work and stress leading up to the trip had been worth it. My anxiety never completely dissipated – I always found something to worry about – but it receded into background noise as we swam with sea lions and giant sea turtles in the Galapagos Islands and met interesting people from around the world.

You'll have to read on for a full account of our adventures, but here is just a taste:

- In India, we came within 10 feet of a tiger while riding in an open jeep; we also stalked wild rhinos from the back of an elephant. We sat on a jetliner, hearts pounding, as the airplane experienced a serious "electrical malfunction" at 35,000 feet.

- We gazed in wonder at the Taj Mahal, Stonehenge and the Coliseum. We toured the British Museum in London and the Prado in Madrid.

- The strangest foods we ate were roasted guinea pig and fried crickets, and followed the Ecuadorian custom of putting popcorn in our soup. Vegetarian cuisine took on a new, delightful dimension in India.

- We listened to mournful Belarusian folk songs in a restored Tsarist-era train station in eastern Poland while downing shots of iced vodka with new friends.

- We hiked through the rain over Peru's Inca Trail, dragging ourselves up the steep rock stairway known as the Inca Elevator, and rode in a motor boat to the base of the Garganta del Diablo, or Devil's Throat, at the spectacular Iguazu Falls on the border between Brazil and Argentina.

- We traveled by van on a dirt road from the Thai border to Siem Riep in Cambodia to see the Angkor Wat ruins, and were stranded near dark in the middle of Lake Titicaca, between Peru and Bolivia, when the engine died on our dilapidated excursion boat.

Some of these experiences were intentional, and others, of course, quite accidental. But they all had one thing in common – while they were happening, we felt extraordinarily alive, with all senses on high alert and our minds taking in everything with absolute clarity.

When it was over, we had traveled in 20 countries on four continents, snapped 5,000 photos and gathered memories to last a lifetime.

In the months and weeks before our trip, friends and family alternated between envy and suspicion about our sanity. One friend, a soccer mom, told Ava, "You must really love that man." It's true, we do love each other deeply. It's also true that our journey, while occasionally testing our devotion, brought our family closer together than ever before, bonds that will last the rest of our lives, like the memories of our fantastic travels to some of the most fascinating places on Earth.

Chapter 2

Guinea Pig for Dinner

Ecuador, Peru and Bolivia

"It is not true that people stop pursuing dreams because they grow old, they grow old because they stop pursuing dreams."

Gabriel Garcia Marquez

The plane touched down in Quito, the capital of Ecuador, around 10 p.m. on a Sunday in late June 2005. Finally, after two years of planning and anticipation, we were standing on South American soil, three gringos who'd never been south of Mexico City. The flight to Quito was short, sweet and uneventful.

Inside the Quito airport, the lines for passport control and customs were long, but fast-moving. Soon we were walking with our luggage through the airport lobby, dazed by the late hour and strange surroundings. Hundreds of people pressed against barriers on either side of us, shouting and waving to catch the attention of friends and relatives. The crowd spilled outside onto the pavement, where the air was chilly on what was a winter night in Ecuador, even though it was summer where we'd come from.

Ava was the first to spot Hernan, the father of our Ecuadoran host family. Hernan was mild-mannered, gray at the temples, with a thin, friendly face. He wore wire-rim spectacles and a smile, and held a small paper sign with our names on it. After grabbing Salome's bag and leading us to his compact car, he put us at ease, chatting in English as we drove through the densely populated neighborhood around the airport. Quito sits in a long, wide valley with steep hills along two sides; a snow-capped volcano towers above the city. Many homes have been built up on the sides of the valley, and Hernan, his wife, Paulina, and their two teenage daughters have a home with a spectacular view of the city. Obstructing the view, though, were the bars on all the doors and windows, and the wall that surrounded their property. A private security guard with an automatic rifle stood at the end of their street.

Paulina also greeted us warmly; for more than 10 years, the family has hosted foreign students, mostly from Europe and the U.S., who study Spanish at the language school around the corner. The two girls, Maria Jose, 18, and Maria Elena, 15, ("My husband likes the name Maria," Paulina explained) nonchalantly went about their business in spite of a family of strangers turning up late at night. The welcome committee included the family's two hyper-friendly dogs: Tom (a cocker spaniel) and Cookie (a toy terrier.)

We were shown to our rooms, and tried to sleep. It had been more than a week since we'd left home, which we had spent in New York City and Miami. It felt like the past eight days had been a warm-up, and only now had our round-the-world adventure truly begun.

The next morning we were up early for our first Spanish

classes. Paulina and Hernan laid out a breakfast of toast, fruit, cereal and coffee. We walked to the Academia Kolumbus school, which is German-owned. Class began promptly at 8:30 each morning. Ava and I were in one classroom, and Salome, being the only child at the school, had one-on-one sessions with her own teacher. I was nervous about letting her out of our sight for two hours at a time, but it seemed safe enough. While we studied, Salome's teacher would sometimes take her to a little park across the street to play.

We began by learning verbs, conjugation and vocabulary. The teachers were experienced and spoke English well. We would study for a couple of hours, take a break (the school had a swing set for Salome in its tiny backyard) and then hit the books until lunchtime. We usually ate at the home of Paulina's parents, who lived at the end of the street. Their four-story home was elegantly appointed with heavy wooden furniture, and lunch was at a large table in the kitchen, with Paulina, Hernan, Paulina's mother and father, the teenage girls and several foreign students. They served chicken, rice, salad and often, the meal began with soup, which was garnished with popcorn. The food was tasty, but not spicy as we had expected. It was nothing like the Mexican food we were used to.

Paulina's parents owned a small clothing store, and they also took in foreign students. The parents had a good friend in Southern California, whom they occasionally visited. As we chatted at lunch, trying our best to keep up with the conversation in Spanish, they smiled and pulled out their Costco cards, saying they loved to shop at the warehouse store when visiting the U.S.

When classes were finished In the afternoon, the school often had a special program. One day, we practiced salsa dancing; another day we learned how to make mojitos with sugar, fresh mint, soda water and rum. (Salome got a virgin mojito.) Instead of hitting the books one morning, we piled into a van for a tour of Quito, including the city's cathedral, historic district and a hilltop statue of the Virgin Mary that afforded sweeping views of the city. When we weren't in class, we rambled around, checking out the mall (of course), which was very modern and had a terrific crepe and waffle restaurant. There was a huge supermarket at the bottom of the hill from where we were staying and we often went there to stock up on groceries for the house. We made sure to buy instant coffee, because it only took a day or two for Ava and I to go through the small jar that Hernan and Paulina provided. Taxis back up the hill with our groceries cost less than a dollar.

Our plan was to spend a week in Quito studying Spanish, then fly to the Galapagos Islands for a weeklong boat cruise, and return to Quito for one more week of Spanish lessons. We'd then depart for Cuzco and Machu Picchu in Peru.

The week passed pleasantly enough as we got our bearings in Quito and adjusted to life in a foreign country. I ran in the mornings, a challenge because of the steep hill where our host family lived. One morning I ran down to the valley floor of central Quito, which is covered by the greenery of Carolina Park. In the morning it was full of joggers and soccer players in shorts and sweatsuits, but Hernan told us to avoid the place after dark. He said he'd been mugged while taking a shortcut through the middle of the park one evening, then was mugged again when he made the mistake of taking the same path home.

Salome was adjusting well and enjoying herself, although she continued to pull her hair and eyelashes, and had a few small bald patches on her scalp. As this point, we were still giving her the medication and rewarding her when she resisted the temptation to "pull."

Acclimating to Ecuador, the first foreign country on our itinerary, was relatively painless because the national language is Spanish, which was familiar to us since we live on the border with Mexico. Also, Ecuador adopted the U.S. dollar as its national currency in 2000 as part of a program to stave off massive inflation and stabilize its economy. Within a few days, our bodies had adjusted to Quito's breath-taking altitude of 9,300 feet.

On our first weekend in Quito, we navigated the local bus system and rode about an hour out of town to the equator, known locally as la Mitad del Mundo, or middle of the world.

We visited a quirky museum near the equator, the imaginary dividing line between the Earth's northern and southern hemispheres. The best part was a demonstration of how water in a basin circles the drain in a clockwise direction when it is placed south of the equator, and in a counterclockwise direction when it is placed on the north side of the equator. (Amazingly, the water ran straight down when the basin was perched directly over the dividing line!) The demonstration was low-tech: two young men carried the metal basin across a red line painted on the cement walkway indicating the precise location of the equator. The water drained into a white plastic bucket, which the guys had to re-position each time they moved the basin.

Scientists dismiss such displays as pure hokum. They contend the phenomenon known as the Coreolis Force, which causes hurricanes to swirl either clockwise or counterclockwise (depending on their position relative to the equator) is much too weak to affect the tiny amount of water held in a basin. Whether the demonstration was based on fact or fiction, we'll never know, but it made for great theater.

After a week in Quito, it was time for our flight to the Galapagos Islands. The trip took several hours because of a layover in Guayaquil, Ecuador's most populous city.

Due to construction, the main airport was closed, and all flights were routed to the islands' secondary airport. This tiny airport was ill-equipped to handle the thousands of tourists who fly to the islands each day, and as we disembarked from our plane, a jet screamed past on a runway just a couple of hundred feet away with a mind-bending roar.

Our eight-day cruise was well-organized, and we were met in the terminal by our guide, Jorge. We were soon bumping down the road in a van on the way to our first destination: a lookout point that would have provided spectacular views if it hadn't been overcast and foggy. It was just the first of several fog banks we would encounter at key points during our travels in South America. We also visited a sanctuary for some of the Galapagos' oldest residents, the famous tortoises.

While at the tortoise reserve, we first noticed what I can only call a personality change in Salome, an angry streak we had never seen before. It took us several weeks to figure out that her mood swings were triggered by the medication she was taking for trichotillomania (the condition that caused her to pull out her hair and eyelashes) but at first we were baffled by these outbursts.

Later that afternoon, we were ferried out to the Floreana, the 16-passenger ship that would be our home for the next week. The two-person cabins were tiny, with private bathrooms and air conditioners, and sometimes they reeked of diesel fumes from the ship's engines. But they were generally clean and comfortable, even if it was hard for a six-footer like me to move around in them. The ship had a dining room below deck, and a covered area on the top deck laid out with lounge chairs.

The cast of characters on the small ship could have populated a sit com minus the Professor, Ginger and the Millionaire.

Jorge, the guide, was short, stocky and had a professorial manner when he described features of the islands' geography, animals and plant life in reasonably good English. He had a sense of humor, but came across as a bit standoffish. He spent a month at a time on the Floreana separated from his wife and two sons in Guayaquil, and then got a week off to return home.

The passengers included Olaf, the owner of a tattoo and piercing shop in Zurich, who was a walking advertisement for his business. He had numerous tattoos on his arms, legs and torso, and multiple piercings in his ears and who knew where else. He traveled with his 8-year-old daughter, Geneva, and his elderly parents, who didn't speak English. Salome became good friends with Geneva, who spoke Swiss-German and Spanish, and was one of the few kids Salome's age we met during our trip.

Also on board was an English couple, Paul and Abbie, who were wrapping up a six-month trip through South America; and Ilan, an English financial analyst who, between jobs, had spent a month or so in Columbia before arriving in the Galapagos. Paul often joked around with Salome, and nick-named her "shark bait." The passenger roster was rounded out by a French honeymooning couple who spent most of their time nuzzling in a lounge chair on the upper deck, and an Italian woman and her teenage son, Cesar, who seemed less than thrilled at the prospect of an eight-day cruise – and bunking with his mom.

Midway through the week, at our one and only port of call, the French couple disembarked and we were joined by four eager, young American medical students.

The ship's crew included Raul, the waiter, bartender and sometimes boat driver, who had a quick smile and would often drop what he was doing to dance or play cards with Salome and Geneva. The captain was an affable man who didn't speak much English. He displayed a wicked left-footed shot, playing in stocking feet, during the traditional crew vs. passengers soccer match on the last day of the cruise. (Final score: crew 6, passengers, 4.)

Each evening, Jorge would go over the next day's itinerary, which usually included a wake-up bell at the ungodly hour of 6:30 a.m., followed by breakfast and then a morning hike or snorkel at whichever island we were visiting that day.

The Galapagos are a string of islands 600 miles off the coast of Ecuador, accessible for most visitors only by air. The islands are famous as the living laboratory where Charles Darwin formulated his theories on evolution. The islands' animal species have no natural predators, so even today, with thousands of tourists visiting the islands every week, most of the animals are unafraid of humans and appear to be as curious about us as we are about them.

On the second day of the cruise, we donned wetsuits, masks, snorkels and flippers for a swim with dozens of young sea lions. The Floreana pulled into a cove at one of the islands and dropped anchor, so we were able to dive right off the side of the boat. The water was cold, even with wetsuits, but I was mesmerized by the sight of dozens of sea lion pups swimming under and around us as we paddled face-down a few dozen yards away from the boat. I could see their curious faces, with their whiskers and large brown eyes, very clearly through my face mask. Most of the pups kept a respectful distance of a foot or two, but one large sea lion caused trouble. He kept nipping at the end of my flipper and followed me no matter where I swam. When I noticed scratches and gouges in his flesh, I wondered if he had been in fights with other animals and I started to get nervous. As much as I enjoyed swimming among the sea lions, I worried that the aggressive pup might try to take a bite of me (instead of just my flipper), so I swam back to the boat.

Salome's Journal

7/3/05 Galapagos Islands, Ecuador

We just arrived to the Golopogos where our journey begins. We have spent one night on the boat but 7 more to go. We just got back from swimming with sea lions in the ocean. It was incredible. The boat is like I can't say in words. So that is where our journey begins.

During our daily island excursions, we walked among the animal inhabitants, from the famous blue-footed boobies to marine and land iguanas and giant tortoises, and also enjoyed the underwater sea life during many snorkeling sessions.

Each island had its own unique topography, physical characteristics (such as white, black or brown sand) and varieties of plants and animals. The animals – from tiny finches to iguanas and sea lions – were more likely to ignore us or approach with curiosity than to run or fly away.

At one white-sand beach, we shuffled our feet as we waded into the surf to avoid stepping on dozens of black rays lurking in the shallows. At another beach, I snorkeled into the water and was lucky enough to come face-to-face with a sea turtle that must have been three feet across.

Our ship would usually anchor during the daytime and then set off for our next destination after dinner. During one of the calmer evenings, after Salome fell asleep in her bunk, six of us hunkered down in the dining room and polished off three liters of alcohol – one each of rum, vodka and tequila. I think we even talked politics, with us Americans joining in the Europeans' Bush-bashing. We were sure our alcohol consumption had set some kind of record, and we paid a heavy price when Jorge started ringing his little bell about 6 o'clock the next morning.

Although the food on the Floreana was excellent and

varied, the portions were modest, especially for the hearty appetites of the young English guys, Paul and Ilan. Because Salome didn't always finish her portion, they were quick to volunteer, which was fine with me, especially when we were having spaghetti or fried fish. On the night when Raul served plates of giant prawns, however, I quickly let them know that Salome's leftovers were already spoken for.

Most of us enjoyed the food, except for Cesar's mom, a brunette with long, wavy hair who had issues with the cuisine.

"This is terrible," she complained when the cook served macaroni salad with mayo. "When you come to Rome, you will never see this. I promise you will never eat pasta with mayonnaise."

During our eight days in the Galapagos, we visited numerous islands, including Santa Fe, North Seymour, Espanola, Santiago, Bartolomeo and Santa Cruz. All too soon, it was time to fly back to Quito.

We spent our remaining time in the Ecuadoran capital studying Spanish and exploring the city. One day, we rode the newly opened tram – called the Teleflorico – up to an altitude of 12,000 feet near the top of Pichincha, the volcano. Feeling the altitude, we nevertheless hiked and enjoyed the panoramic views of the Quito far below. We also went to a mall to see the new Tom Cruise movie War of the Worlds. A blackout during the film eerily echoed the plot, in which aliens interrupt the power supply on Earth as a prelude to their reign of terror. As they say in Quito, "Se fue la luz," or "Out go the lights."

During our stay with Hernan and Paulina, we often

enjoyed playing with their dogs. Tom was one of those dogs who never tired of chasing a ball or a stick. One afternoon when we returned to the house after class, everyone was gone, and Cookie was locked outside on the balcony. Salome begged us to let her in and we relented. The little dog immediately jumped up on Hernan and Paulina's bed and peed on the comforter. We were horrified and quickly tried to blot up the mess and hustle Cookie back outside.

When Paulina returned, we felt very guilty, but too embarrassed to say anything. Soon, we heard yelling, and Paulina marched out of her room, holding Cookie before her. "Cookie is a very naughty dog, she go pee-pee on the bed." We never did 'fess up, and weren't sure if our hostess realized Cookie's little mistake had actually occurred before she got home.

Salome's Journal

7/17/05 Cuzco, Peru

Our second stop starts in Peru. In just about two days we will be climbing an enormous mountain called Machu Picchu. We are going on the two day hike. (That is long enough) but there is also a 7 day hike. Which I am so glad not to be going on! We will be staying in Peru for about a week. We still have a while left. This is going to be a great hike to Machu Picchu.

Then it was time to move on to Peru and the ancient Inca citadel of Machu Picchu. Flights into Cuzco, the jumping-off point for visits to Machu Picchu, can only land in the morning, before the wind picks up over the Andes and makes the landing too dangerous. The airline had scheduled us to arrive in Lima about midnight, with our connecting flight for Cuzco departing at 5:30 a.m. In spite of the many travelers who regularly wait for hours in the dead of night for their connecting flights, the airport has done little to make the wait more comfortable. Many people were stretched out on concrete floors using their backpacks as pillows. We tried to catch a few winks in the chairs lining the terminal, which were equipped with armrests that made it impossible to lie down. Luckily, Salome was small enough to fit under the armrests, so she was the only one who got any sleep.

Thanks to our all-nighter at the airport, we were in a daze the next morning when we arrived in Cuzco, a lovely, former colonial city high in the mountains. Its central square and cathedral were built on the stone foundations of an ancient Inca town. Many shops, restaurants and hostels lined the narrow, cobblestone streets leading off the square. While very touristy, Cuzco has tons of atmosphere and the prices were reasonable when we visited. Large bottles of Cusqueña beer went for about $1.50; and the non-alcoholic choice was Inca Cola, which was yellow and tasted something like Mountain Dew.

Although many of the hostels were already booked, we were fortunate to get a tidy – although unheated – room in a hillside place arranged around a flower garden and courtyard. Many of the rooms had views of the city, breakfast was included for about $30 a night. The breakfast was good, if monotonous – the only choice given to us each morning was "fried or scrambled." Everything we needed was within walking distance, another plus. One of our first tasks was finalizing the details of our two-day hike on the Inca Trail, which we had booked in advance online.

On the day of our hike, a van picked us up at our hotel before dawn and sped around Cuzco's deserted back streets gathering the rest of the passengers. The van dropped us at the train station for the four-hour ride to the trailhead.

Just outside of town, the train had to negotiate a series of switchbacks as it climbed to a higher elevation in the foothills. To do this, the train stopped, backed up for a short distance, pulled forward, and repeated the exercise as it worked its way slowly up the incline. Unaware of what was going on, at first we thought the train was heading back into Cuzco.

The weather put a damper on our excitement – drizzle alternated with light rain tapping against the train windows as we chugged into the mountains.

The train stopped at a tiny station, where we jumped out with our daypacks. A gentle rain pattered against our plastic ponchos as we started hiking up the trail. Eight of us were hiking together: Ava, Salome and I, a family of four from Portland, Ore., and our guide, Henry. Marta, the Oregon family's daughter, was stationed in Peru with the Peace Corps, and her brother, Chris, was planning to study in Italy in the fall. We got along fine and began our soggy, uphill trek in good spirits. As we wound our way up the side of the canyon, the views kept getting better. All around us were green, jungle-covered hills dotted with purple wild orchids and draped in mist. In the valley far below ran a river with train tracks alongside. Occasional trains rolled by, their horns echoing forlornly in the distance.

We passed a waterfall and in the late morning reached a 600-year-old Inca village built high on a hillside. Agricultural terraces laddered up the hillside, mixed with stone houses, temples and a sophisticated irrigation system of interconnecting stone channels. The site was deserted and quiet except for our party and three other hikers. Although we spent only spent a short time there, on that misty morning we were able to imagine what it must have been like for the Incas who lived and farmed there centuries ago.

The rain continued as we climbed all afternoon, up to and over the "Inca elevator," a series of 50 steep stone steps cut into the side of the mountain. Finally, we arrived at the "Sun Gate," where Henry had promised our first glimpse of Machu Picchu, the mysterious Inca citadel built in the cloud forest. Instead, as we passed through the stone gate, all we saw was whiteness. The entire valley was blanketed in dense fog. From what we could see, we might have been at the end of the world, peering down into an infinite abyss. Machu Zero.

Tired, wet, chilly and disappointed, we hiked downhill to the citadel, and as darkness crept around us, we glimpsed the ruins through gaps in the fog. We were bussed down the steep set of switchbacks to the small town of Agua Caliente, where we had hot showers dinner and sleep, before being roused at 5 a.m. for our trip back up to Machu Picchu. All morning we walked among the ancient stone structures, climbing up to the "hut of the caretaker of the funerary rock," where we took the classic photos of the citadel and surrounding peaks, and sat quietly for a while watching puffy clouds float above the ruins. By 11 a.m. when we left, a steady stream of tourists poured in through the main gate. We headed back to the town for soak in its natural hot springs pools nestled amid a jungle canyon and then caught our train back to Cuzco.

Salome's Journal

7/21/05 Cuzco, Peru

Our 6th day in Peru has been wonderful. First I woke up (early) went to breakfast and went back to sleep after we walked to the bus station. Then my mom and I went shopping. Now we are just about to go to dinner. On my hike to Machu Picchu the first thing we did was took a train for 4 hours which I did not like. Finally we started walking. We walked for 4 hours also. We walked to a lunch place and they had a cute little dog. Then we walked 4 more hours. We finally came to an ancient city. The next day we walked for not that long and to another huge city. That was the hardest hike I have ever walked. It was also raining both days which I liked but my dad did not. We walked through forests and I hoped we would see a bear. The guide said "there was bears and snakes!" But he said not to worry because he had a gun. Walking was tiring but so so so so so so worth it. I loved it so so so so so so much!

Before leaving Cuzco, we decided to try a local delicacy, called cuy, which is popular in Peru and Ecuador. Americans might be familiar with this dish by another name – guinea pig.

We set out to find a restaurant where cuy was served, and it didn't take long – a lively place with rough-hewn wooden tables about two blocks from the Plaza de Armas, Cuzco's main square. The restaurant was crowded with an equal mix of locals and foreigners.

Cuy was one of the more expensive items on the menu, costing about $14 U.S. We ordered one portion of the roasted rodent, along with a couple of other dishes. The food took a while to arrive at our table, and I envisioned the cook chasing a squealing guinea pig around the kitchen with a cleaver.

When the plate arrived, we were immediately put off. The guinea pig lay on its side, little paws curled up under its protruding front teeth. Ava and I each tried a bite of the meat, which to me seemed like dark chicken meat, only slightly gamier. It wasn't bad, but it made us queasy to look at the little beast, so we asked the waiter to take it away. Because I didn't see anyone else eating cuy that night, I'm not sure how popular it really is with Peruvians. But I'm pretty sure that if I ever encounter a guinea pig in the future, it will be live and cuddly rather than dead and roasted.

Our next destination was Puno, a dusty, ramshackle town on the edge of Lake Titicaca (at 12,580 feet the world's highest navigable body of water). We could never say the name of the lake with a straight face. The bus ride from Cuzco featured views of the snow-covered Andes in the background, and many farms and villages along the road. The houses and walls were built with mud bricks, which we often saw drying in the sun.

As our bus neared Puno, Salome and I started arguing about something I've long since forgotten. Soon, Salome had shifted into full tantrum mode, which spilled over into the taxi ride and the hotel lobby. We were all shaken by this major blowup, and Ava and I struggled to figure out a better way of dealing with Salome's hair-trigger temper.

Like most kids, she'd always had occasional tantrums, but her moods were much more volatile since we'd been in South America. This was completely out of character for her, and at that point we had no idea what was causing it.

Punishments such as taking away her toys didn't seem to help, and she usually didn't snap out of her mood until she'd vented – with lots of yelling and crying, saying she "hated" us, and sometimes even hitting or spitting at us, which she had never done before. We racked our brains trying to figure out what was going on, whether it was a reaction to the trip itself, or a sign that she was growing up and asserting her independence.

In any event, the emotional storm had passed by the next day, and we wandered around the town square, checking email, shopping and eating. As we walked back to our hotel in the afternoon, I heard guitar music; and we followed the melody into a tiny courtyard cantina, where a group of Peruvian businessmen laughed and drank beer.

We joined them for a brew and were serenaded by two wandering minstrels who played for tips. We toasted, "Viva, Peru," which went over well with the men at the next table.

In the morning, we got up early for a boat trip out on the lake. Instead of taking one of the fancy tourist boats, we opted for a small boat owned by a cooperative of the indigenous people of the region. The tickets were cheaper, and, according to our guidebook, the profits stayed with the locals. That decision was definitely not the smartest of our trip.

Our first stop was the floating islands of the Uros tribe. The islands are made of reeds that grow in the lake, and as they rot from the bottom, more reeds are piled on top. The islanders also use the reeds to build their houses and canoes. Our boat stopped on a small island set up for tourists. We could see the real islands, where the Uros people live, several hundred yards away on the lake. The ground on the floating island was spongy, giving way as we walked.

After a short visit, we climbed back onto the boat for the $2^1/_2$-hour ride to Taquile Island, which towered above the dark blue water of Lake Titicaca. We sat on the top of the boat, and although the day was bright and sunny, the air was frigid and our teeth chattered by the time we reached the island. There, we climbed up a long, steep set of stairs to a ridge and ate lunch at one of the small restaurants scattered around the village. Some of the passengers were staying with villagers for the night, but we climbed down to the harbor for the boat ride back to Puno after lunch.

That's when things got interesting. Those of us who rode on the top of the boat for the trip out to Taquile Island chose seats inside the crowded cabin for the way back. There were about 40 passengers on a boat that seemed built for half that number. We watched as the crew tried to start the engines, with no luck. After a lot of talking back in forth in Quechua, the local language, and poking around in the engine compartment, the crew figured out the battery was dead. Another battery was lowered into place. A crewman secured the battery connectors by stomping on them with his foot. The engine sputtered to life, and we were off.

The middle of the lake was very deep and the wind raised small whitecaps. We plowed through the water uneventfully. Periodically, the engine coughed and sputtered, and a crewman decked out in traditional clothing of a white shirt, calf-length trousers and a knitted cap with earflaps would quickly lift the engine cover, reach inside and make an adjustment, and the engine would settle back into a steady thrum. Once when the engine acted up, he pulled out a plastic tube and sucked on it, spitting the fuel over the side. My heart jumped each time the engine skipped a beat, but the crewman seemed able to coax the finicky, rattletrap engine along.

That is, until we had crossed the open stretches of the lake and were trolling through the still waters of the reed-lined canals about 30 minutes from shore. The engine coughed a few times and died. At first, the same crewman fiddled around with the engine as the boat driver tried to start it again. Soon, the rest of the crew came back for a conference, talking and scratching their heads as they eyed the uncooperative machine.

They rolled up their sleeves and leaned deep inside the engine compartment, which was at the back of the boat under the makeshift ladder that led to the top deck. After an hour, they still hadn't managed to get the engine started, and the late afternoon sun was quickly dropping to the horizon. We were hopeful when we saw a line of tourist boats heading toward us in the distance, figuring one of them would give us a tow. Wrong. They just maneuvered around us, and sometimes their passengers smiled and waved.

As the light faded, it started to get cold. When a German tourist looked down into blackness of the engine compartment and said, "I think we are taking on water,"

Salome started to cry. Adding to the drama, the boat had no lights or radio. Just as dusk descended on the lake, the crew's tinkering proved successful and the engine roared to life, prompting cheers from the passengers. The boat chugged through the canal picking up speed, and we docked in Puno about a half-hour later, tired, hungry and cold, but otherwise fine – and with a story to tell.

Our next stop was La Paz, Bolivia. We planned to ride a bus from Puno to the Bolivian border at Copacabana, on the southeast side of Lake Titicaca, and then travel on to the Bolivian capital.

Ava and I were unsure whether we should visit Bolivia (especially me). A few weeks before we started our trip, peasants in the Bolivian countryside had launched a series of demonstrations that culminated in the resignation of the president. The peasants wanted the government to nationalize the country's natural gas industry, and give more power to the country's indigenous majority. Protestors claimed foreign companies were greedily sucking the profits from one of Bolivia's most lucrative and plentiful natural resources.

What all this meant to tourists was that services were interrupted during the protests, with small explosives sometimes set off for emphasis during demonstrations. Key roads had been blocked, and protestors even shut down runways at the La Paz airport.

We followed the situation via the Internet and talked to travelers who had recently been in Bolivia. From what we could tell, the volatile situation had calmed down with the appointment of an interim president and the promise of national elections. With trepidation, we decided to stick with our plans for staying three nights in La Paz and then catching a flight to Santiago, Chile.

The first half of the bus ride to Bolivia went very smoothly. A long line of tourists waited patiently at the Bolivian passport office, a small building with a dusty yard out front. After getting our passports stamped by the uniformed officers, we got back on the bus for the rest of the ride to Copacabana. Once there, we disembarked for lunch at a hotel with a dining patio that looked out on the southern shore of Lake Titicaca. After lunch we switched buses for the final leg of the ride to La Paz.

Among the passengers were three Canadian siblings – two brothers and a sister – whom we had first met during a day tour of the Sacred Valley near Cuzco. The bus began climbing into the mountains, barreling around sharp curves in the winding road. Once that harrowing segment was over, the bus pulled up to a little village, where we were told to get off. The bus was rolled onto a flat barge to haul it across a river, and we were escorted onto a small ferry with broken windows. One of the Canadians looked out at the listing barge and said, "It would be worth sacrificing my gear to see that sucker go down!"

Soon, the tour bus was back on the road. Without warning, the bus (with all of our luggage tied on the roof rack) pulled off the pavement onto a dirt road. We were bouncing along a rutted track that would have been challenging for a four-wheel drive jeep, let alone a lumbering bus. We saw almost no other traffic in the barren canyon where we were driving for nearly two hours. We came upon a tourist van that was stuck in a gulley ahead of us and waited while the passengers got out and pushed the van through the gulley. Then it was our turn. Our driver gunned the engine and attacked the gulley at full speed. Somehow, we rolled right through and up the other side.

The only thing that kept us sane during the two-hour ride on the dirt road was a running conversation about movies among the passengers. Salome somehow managed to sleep the entire time. Finally, we came to the outskirts of La Paz, a huge city that begins on a plateau and spills down the sides of a huge ravine. Our approach to downtown La Paz was like a pinball: we rolled around and around the city on a road that descended into the ravine. We expected to be let off in the central bus station; instead, the bus pulled up to the curb on a busy downtown street, and the driver and his helper began tossing luggage down from the roof. I was unsure what to do until I noticed a woman from the bus company who was assisting passengers. She pointed us toward a couple of the hotels we had circled in our guidebook, which were down the street.

La Paz was busy, with many pedestrians, carts and vehicles thronging the narrow streets between dilapidated colonial buildings. Entrepreneurship was alive and well – anyone with a few items to sell and a small patch of sidewalk was in business. The labor was done the old-fashioned way, as men with huge bundles of goods strapped to their backs grunted up and down the hilly streets. Women wore skirts, dark sweaters and round bowler hats, with their hair tied in ponytails. The only visible remnant of the recent political upheaval was the sober-looking police officers, patrolling the streets clad in black uniforms and armed with automatic rifles.

We found a cheap but clean hotel and lugged our bags up three flights of stairs to our room. The beds were saggy, and the room had no heat, so we got into bed bundled in all our clothes. But the hotel provided plenty of thick woolen blankets, there was a TV with satellite, and showers with hot water. The price was about $18 U.S., so we didn't complain too much.

Prices in Bolivia were among the cheapest we found in South America. A glass of orange juice from a street vendor cost less than 10 cents. All sorts of items were readily available from stalls set up along many of the city's thoroughfares, from electronics to toiletries to clothing. On our first night, we had excellent plates of crunchy falafel at an Israeli restaurant.

We spent our time in La Paz walking around the city, admiring the main square flanked by the presidential palace and other government buildings. We also checked out the Mercado de las Brujas, or witches' market, where you could find potions and powders, herbs, dried frogs, and even a llama fetus floating in a jar. Our guidebook warned that taking pictures was forbidden, and we confirmed that when I pointed my camera at one of the stalls. A scowling woman charged out, waggling her finger angrily. Although her reaction would probably have been different if I'd offered a few Bolivianos, I decided to put my camera away, figuring she had a cauldron and knew how to use it. We bought Salome a little jar filled with trinkets that was supposed to bring good luck. Our ramblings also took us to the city's Coca Museum.

I felt somewhat relieved as we prepared to fly out of

Bolivia. Even though the political situation had calmed down, the presence of the heavily armed police on the streets cast a pall over our sightseeing. And I didn't want to get stuck behind any road blockades. We caught a taxi for the airport on a sunny day, enjoying the sights of the city as we drove by. Our flight rocketed from the La Paz airport on time, in the peculiar, almost vertical trajectory made necessary by the city's high altitude. (At nearly 12,000 feet, La Paz is considered the world's highest capital city.) We were on our way to Santiago, Chile, to experience its reputation as a clean, modern metropolis with a European feel.

Chapter 3

Real Estate Tycoons

What to do with Your House and Your Stuff

When people in their 20s quit their jobs and take off to see the world, things are pretty simple. They pack up their most precious possessions – in my day it was usually a couple of orange crates filled with rare Pink Floyd and Led Zeppelin bootleg records – hand them off to a friend or relative, and jump on a plane, train, bus or car. Sure, they might have to find someone to take care of their houseplants. But after that it would be "Adios, amigos, see you when I see you!"

Disentanglement was more complex for our family. My wife and I were in our 40s, we had a child, and we owned two homes: one that we lived in, and the other an investment property that we rented out. Not to mention our dog, cat and bird.

During the planning stages of our trip, we faced several key decisions regarding our tiny real estate empire. Should we sell one or both of our homes, and use part of the proceeds to fund our trip? Or should we hold on to the properties and rent them both for the year we planned to be on the road? If we opted for the latter, who would keep an eye on our houses, and how would we raise the cash we needed for our global adventure?

Early on, I was in favor of selling both houses. I liked the idea of divesting ourselves of our worldly possessions, except for what we could cram into a storage unit. I felt that by selling the properties, we would be freeing ourselves of the bonds of responsibility they represented.

Another factor in favor of divestiture was more down-to-earth. I worried that if we kept the properties, we would be taking on a huge risk by traveling so far from home. Even if we hired a property manager, I reasoned, we would be thousands of miles away from our properties, unable to do a thing in case of an emergency such as a fire, burst pipes or a tree falling on the roof. Chances are, we wouldn't even learn of such a disaster until long after the fact.

But Ava, who is less of a worrier, talked me out of that plan. For one thing, she loves our house and didn't want to sell it. For another, she argued that the rental income from the two homes would help finance our travels. If we kept our homes, she argued, we would save a lot of money in real estate commissions, closing costs and other expenses related to selling our properties and buying new ones when we returned. Finally, she convinced me that our transition back to "real life" would be much smoother if we could move back into our own familiar house after we returned, weary from our long months of international travel.

For all of these reasons, we decided to keep both houses and hire a property manager to collect the rent and keep an eye on things while we were gone. That still left the problem of cash, specifically, where to get it.

We were fortunate to have bought our home in the mid-

90s, following the real estate crash earlier in that decade. The value of our home had appreciated steeply over the first seven or eight years we owned it, so a refinance that allowed us to pull out $50,000 in cash was no big deal.

Another piece of luck was that interest rates were low in the years preceding our world trip, so we were able to beef up our travel bankroll without jeopardizing our future financial well-being. The $50,000 wasn't enough to finance the trip entirely, but it put us over the top when combined with other savings.

Once we determined we would hold on to our houses, we had to figure out the best way to protect them while we were gone. I started interviewing property managers about a year before our planned departure, to make sure I had plenty of time to make the right choice. I knew that once we were traveling around the world, I would never sleep soundly unless I had complete confidence in the person who was overseeing our vast real estate empire. Well, maybe it wasn't so vast, but it meant a lot to us.

I came up with a list of questions, such as, how much would their services cost, how often would they visit the properties, how would they handle maintenance and repair issues, and how would they keep in contact with us while we were traveling? I contacted five or six companies, and soon narrowed the list to a couple of top prospects. From these, I asked for references, whom I called.

Sean O'Sullivan, the property manager we hired, ran a real estate management and sales business in Oceanside, a company originally started by his mother. Sean and I had an immediate rapport and I felt very comfortable leaving our houses in his hands. Sean took care of finding a tenant for our house who was agreeable to a one-year lease, and we got to work packing up our belongings, finding a storage garage, and sprucing up the house for its temporary inhabitants. We put a lot of effort into patching holes, painting, cleaning the floors and windows, and anything else we could think of to make the place shine. (Our house was overdue for a serious cleaning, anyway.)

We agreed Sean would collect the rent from both houses, pay bills such as utilities and homeowner association fees, and deposit the rest in our bank account each month. I arranged to have the mortgage payments automatically deducted from our checking account, and I paid our landlord's insurance premiums in advance. Our annual property tax bill came due while we were traveling, so I paid that at an Internet café on the road. I believe we were in Austria at the time.

As for storing our furniture, I investigated many different types of storage facilities, including a place that delivered empty containers to our home, which we would then fill up with furniture and belongings, and then the containers would be hauled to a central storage building. We ended up renting a garage from an apartment complex near our home because it offered the best combination of price and security. We didn't want our storage garage to be burglarized, we didn't plan to store anything that was extremely valuable, so we didn't need Fort Knox.

After much painful deliberation, I sold my beloved 12-year-old pickup truck, which had served me well over the years and had even provided a home-on-wheels to Ava and I during a four-month trip around the U.S. in the mid-90s. We rented a parking space at an outdoor storage yard for our other car, a 1999 Subaru Outback, so we would have wheels when we returned home. That decision proved to be a God-send; instead of having to go through the bother of immediately buying a car, we had instant transportation when we finished our world travels.

All went smoothly during the final months before our planned departure in June 2005. We had moved out of our house with the help of a cavernous rental truck and the strong arms and backs of our friends and relatives. The three of us moved into a spare bedroom at my in-laws' apartment, snug accommodations that gave us a taste of the cramped hotel rooms where we would spend many nights in various foreign countries during the coming months.

One month before we were set to leave, though, fate threw us a curveball. The long-time tenants in our rental house, who had always paid their rent on time (although occasionally we noticed a pungent, skunky odor when we dropped by) announced they were moving to San Francisco, and gave us their 30-day notice.

This set off a tense flurry of activity in which we tried to get them moved out as quickly as possible, clean up the place and find new tenants. I was very nervous about the prospect of leaving on our trip while the house was still vacant. Fortunately, Sean was on board as property manager by then, and led the charge to bring in new tenants. With just a few days to spare before our departure, he succeeded.

In retrospect, the arrangement worked out well, although it took a huge effort to pack up our stuff, clean, paint and otherwise spruce up two houses, all the while taking care of last-minute details before our trip, from farming out our pets to getting our final vaccinations and making sure all of Salome's independent study materials were in order.

When we got back to San Diego the next spring, after about nine months on the road (our trip had been abbreviated due to finances and other concerns, discussed later) our houses were still standing – with only a few dents and dings.

We rented an apartment near the beach in Oceanside on a month-to-month basis so we could get Salome back into her elementary school right away, and we lucked out when the people who were renting our house asked to get out of their lease a month early because they had bought a home of their own.

When we moved back home about a month after our return to the U.S., we were thrilled to be living in our comfortable, familiar house, surrounded by our own things. Sure, the hardwood floor had suffered a few scratches and gouges, and the tenants' two massive German shepherds had inflicted grave damage on our back lawn, but we shrugged off such cosmetic blemishes as a small price to pay for the life-changing adventure the three of us had been so privileged to experience.

Chapter 4

Tango, Samba and Everything in Between

Chile, Argentina, Uruguay, Brazil

"I grew up in this town, my poetry was born between the hill and the river, it took its voice from the rain, and like the timber, it steeped itself in the forests."

Pablo Neruda, Chilean Poet

After the color and chaos of La Paz, Santiago seemed sedate, with its straight, tidy streets and well-maintained buildings. We arrived in Chile at night, and after absorbing the sticker shock of a $100-per-person entry fee for U.S. citizens, we settled into a cab for the ride into town.

In spite of studying and practicing Spanish for the better part of a month, my skills remained sketchy. But I gamely tried to converse with the cab driver, and actually felt like I was holding my own. He told me Santiago is a very clean city, and that the police were very nice. I hoped that was the case, since my mental image of Chile harkened to the days of the Pinochet dictatorship, when the police tortured, imprisoned and killed thousands of Chileans.

The Hotel Forestra, a mid-rise building with a popular piano bar on the ground floor, had an old-school formality, with a uniformed bellman and a polite, but reserved front desk clerk. We were shown to our room, a mini-suite with a small front room and a bedroom with the most comfortable beds we'd had in a while. We were promised heat at night, and a little warmth did seep from the radiators, but not much.

Santiago's streets were indeed very clean, and as we wandered in search of an ATM for cash, we could have been in the central business district of any North American city.

Breakfast at the Forestra was served in the seventh-floor dining room, which had pleasant views of the large park next door. A fixed menu provided us with toast, eggs, juice and coffee.

Right away, we noticed one big difference between Santiago and most of the other places we'd visited so far – there were very few tourists, and we didn't stand out. Of course, as soon as we opened our mouths, all that changed.

But we ended up in a very walkable neighborhood on the fringe of the downtown business district, with many sights, including museums and a well-maintained linear park that ran alongside a river just a few blocks from our hotel. On morning runs in the chilly air (I still wasn't used to winter in August), I would see park workers raking and sweeping along the paths, something I hadn't seen much of in the other countries we had visited.

We were just a couple of blocks from a station of Santiago's sparkling new subway system, and across the street from one of the strangest Internet cafes I've run across. The place was open 24 hours a day and once inside, customers were led down a flight of stairs into a warren of wood-paneled cubicles, each with a desk and a new PC. I wasn't sure why the patrons needed so much privacy, but soon got an inkling. When I logged on an instant message popped up, saying "how are u?" I immediately closed the box, but it popped up again a couple more times. Each time I closed it without replying, and finally the anonymous – and annoying – messages ceased. I found the whole thing creepy, so I ended up going elsewhere for emails and online business.

One of our first stops in Santiago was the late poet and diplomat Pablo Neruda's former home, which has been turned into a museum. The house was very quirky, with its nautical design and secret passageways used by Neruda to startle dinner guests by suddenly appearing before them. Also on display were many original manuscripts and paintings by his artist friends, such as a portrait of Neruda's wife by Mexican muralist Diego Garcia. Later that day, we joined the large crowds in line at the art museum for a traveling exhibit of Rodin sculptures. The exhibit was a great bargain because it was Sunday and entrance to the museum was free. Salome didn't enjoy the exhibit very much, but it was nice to mingle with the locals, and we promised to take her to the Santiago Zoo the next day.

We were still having a lot of problems with Salome's "meltdowns." This problem reached an alarming new level one afternoon in Santiago after we had walked a couple of miles from our hotel to the city's seafood market, a covered bazaar with stalls selling fresh fish and several popular seafood restaurants. We decided on a place called Donde Diego's, which our cab driver had recommended.

We ordered drinks and food, including a savory seafood stew. About midway through the lunch in the crowded restaurant, Salome and I began to argue and it quickly escalated into a yelling match. I'd had a couple of beers, and my frustration with her behavior had reached a boiling point. I took her into a passageway that led to the street. She was crying and yelling, which made me angry. I twisted her ear, which set off even louder howls. I heard someone talking behind me, and turned to see two grim-faced policemen staring at us. I tried to explain in English and broken Spanish that Salome had been misbehaving, ("She was being bad"). At the same time, a woman was glaring at me and speaking rapidly to the cops in Spanish.

I asked them to come with me into the restaurant, where Ava was sitting. Once they confirmed she was Salome's mother, they turned to Salome.

"Are you okay?" one of the policemen asked in English. Salome nodded.

"Are you sure?" the policeman said.

"Yes," she said.

Apparently satisfied, they left. A woman at the next table, who was dining with her family, appeared to be about to speak on our behalf, but went back to eating when the cops walked away.

This encounter left me shaken and determined to find a better way to deal with Salome's behavioral issues. I felt like we were walking on eggshells to avoid saying or doing something that would set her off, whether it was asking her to do her schoolwork or anything else she simply didn't feel like doing at the moment. She got particularly incensed if we talked about her behavior.

She dug in her heels in and refused to budge, regardless of where we were, and adopt an insolent tone both Ava and I found infuriating. If we punished her by taking away a toy, or the privilege of watching TV or having desert, she went ballistic, launching into full tantrum mode. It began to dawn on us that this was something more than mere homesickness.

The next morning we set out from our hotel to visit the Santiago Zoo. We were armed with the tiny map in our guidebook and the hazy directions I'd gotten from the hotel desk clerk. We walked through some interesting residential neighborhoods on the way to the zoo, and stopped to have breakfast at a place with tables on the sidewalk. We thought we were ordering eggs, but after 30 minutes or so, the waitress brought us hot dogs dressed with some very exotic sauces. Salome wouldn't touch hers.

The zoo was set on a hill overlooking the city, with great views and lots of people and animals to check out. It was a very crowded day, and one of the highlights was watching a monkey snatch a potato chip from another monkey's hand, just as the first monkey was about to pop it in his mouth. He who hesitates is lost.

There were signs all over the place forbidding people to feed the animals, but they were routinely ignored by the zoo's visitors. Occasionally, a staff member would admonish someone for giving snacks to the animals. The person would usually pause briefly, then go right back to feeding the animals as soon as the zoo worker walked away.

As we were leaving the zoo, Salome was transformed into a giant bunny rabbit by a face painter, and she bought a clever toy made from colored paper and string. Long paper streamers were tied to a pouch filled with sand, and the whole thing was twirled around at the end of the string, creating a rainbow effect.

Our other Santiago adventure involved a ride on the city's new subway to the end of the line, where we found a huge shopping mall. From there, we caught a local bus that drove through miles of Santiago neighborhoods to reach one of the city's famed wineries. It was a cold, drizzly day, but we were warmed by the different varieties of wine we were given to taste, and we enjoyed walking around the vineyards and through the vaults where the wine casks were stacked. On the way back, we cruised through one of the department stores at the mall to buy Salome a new rain jacket, and had lunch in the crowded food court.

Back at our hotel, Ava and Salome went upstairs, and I went for a drink in the piano bar. I'd seen someone drinking a very interesting-looking concoction with a bunch of cut-up lime chunks at the bottom. I thought it was called a churrasco, and wanted to order one and take it up to Ava. I was soon involved in a deep conversation with the bartender, the barmaid and a couple of the customers. Judging by the puzzled, slightly annoyed look on the bartender's face, it didn't seem like I was getting my point across. Finally, I gave up, smiled and left the bar.

A few minutes later, there was a knock on the door. In the hallway was the bartender, holding a plate with a sliced beef sandwich on it. I later found out that a churrasco is a popular Chilean beef sandwich, not a drink.

I should have gotten a clue when the barmaid asked if I wanted tomate with my churrasco.

I will remember Santiago for its wide streets, the river park where I went for my morning runs, the museum where we soaked up culture during a very crowded exhibition of Rodin sculptures, and the gray, overcast skies – we never saw the sun during our week in the city. Regretfully, we didn't make it to the coast or further south to the tip of South America. But I am sure we will visit again.

Our next stop was Buenos Aires, the capital of Argentina, known for its sharp dressers, tango dancing, and the famous Boca Juniors soccer club. We caught an early morning flight in Santiago and crossed South America in a few hours. This stop on our journey would be notable as the first place we would meet up with someone we knew, my brother Steve, who was flying down from San Diego. At this point we had been on the road for just over a month and were all looking forward to seeing a familiar face.

Buenos Aires offered one immediate contrast to Santiago – the sun was shining brightly on the August morning when we arrived. We caught a taxi to our hotel, the Gran Hotel Oriental, which we had found in the Lonely Planet guide.

The hotel was in the city's Congresso District, only two or three blocks from the ornate, massive building that serves as the home of Argentina's national legislature. We were just a block off Avenida Callao, a busy, north-south thoroughfare where Portenos, as Buenos Aires residents are known, could be seen walking briskly at all hours of the day and night.

Most of our cab ride from the airport was along a raised highway that afforded nice views of the city's tall buildings and the neighborhoods below. As we pulled off the highway, we gazed wide-eyed at the tree-lined streets we passed, choked with vehicles and bustling with pedestrians.

We pulled up in front of our hotel, and I had to admit, it was unimpressive. The Hotel Gran Oriental was about three stories tall, with a defunct restaurant on the second floor. The guidebook had given it good marks, and it was cheap, only about $20 a night. Through the lobby window, we could see a few worn, overstuffed chairs and some exposed wiring due to renovation work.

As the cab rolled up, the driver peered through his windshield at the hotel façade. "This is where you're staying?" he asked. "Muy feo," he said in Spanish. "Malissimo." Hardly a ringing endorsement.

We weren't beginning our visit to the city of Evita Peron on a high note. After that verbal slap at our hotel, the cab driver had the nerve to rip us off for several dollars for a non-existent "highway toll" that he added to the fare.

The room was clean, although it was dark and smelled of disinfectant. Guests reached their rooms through an open-air hallway off the back of the lobby. Most of the night, conversation and laughter bounced off the tile floor and into our room as people came and went, making us wonder what type of commerce might be going on in the Hotel Gran Oriental.

The next day, as we walked around the city, we checked out hotels and we finally settled on the Apart Hotel Congresso, a high-rise next door to our hotel. It cost more, about $60-$70 per night, but included an excellent breakfast, three big, comfortable beds, a heater that left us kicking off the bedclothes at night, and even a kitchenette. It was perfect, since one bed was in a semi-private alcove, and we were awaiting the arrival of Steve, who would be staying with us.

We strolled along Buenos Aires' wide boulevards, admiring the tall buildings above us, and rubbing shoulders with the locals. The streets were chock-full of restaurants and shops and we stocked up on provisions at a supermarket a few blocks from our hotel. Grocery shopping is always a great way to get a feel for a new city, because you see locals in their element and get to find out what they like to eat, and even the types of household products they use.

Down the street was Avenida de Mayo, which runs east and west, with the Congresso building at one end and the presidential palace at the other. Jostling for space on the sidewalks were the professional dog walkers, who often were towed by a dozen or more canines at a time.

We crossed 9 de Julio Avenue, the city's central roadway, which is 140 meters wide, one of the widest streets in the world. The avenue was so wide we could only get halfway across before the light turned red, and we had to wait with dozens of other pedestrians in the broad, park-like median for the next green light.

The stately national theater, Teatro Colon, could be seen from 9 de Julio, along with the obelisk, an iconic monument that stood like a sentry in the middle of the frenetic traffic.

Buenos Aires is home to fashionable malls and numerous parrillas, or grill restaurants, where diners can feast on everything from choice steaks to less savory meats of indeterminate origin.

Wandering around was great fun. One street was considered Buenos Aires' Broadway, and it was lined with theaters boasting live performances of everything from The Producers to tango dance shows.

Calle Florida was a pedestrian-only street lined with shops. The leather and jewelry salesmen were especially pushy.

After a couple of days, we caught a cab to the airport to meet my brother's flight. We helped him get settled in the hotel, then set out for some serious sightseeing.

One sunny afternoon, we took a bike tour that almost did us in. We pedaled for hours, covering 10 miles or so. It was especially strenuous for me, as Salome was perched in a child seat on the back of my bike. We thought about letting her ride her own bike, but the guide discouraged us. It was a good thing, too, because of the distance we covered and the heavy traffic along some parts of the route.

But we did see a lot of Buenos Aires, from the waterfront along the De La Plata River, to a park where lots of locals were out playing, to La Boca, a gritty neighborhood that is being transformed into an artists' colony. The buildings have been painted bright primary colors, and visitors can browse sidewalk art stands and indoor galleries while street musicians hustle for loose change.

Soccer fans might know La Boca as the home of the Boca Juniors, one of the most popular club teams in Buenos

Aires, and the team that gave Argentinian superstar Diego Maradona his start.

We did take in a soccer game in Buenos Aires, although not Boca Juniors. We went with a group tour to see River Plate, another of the city's top teams. The afternoon was sunny but chilly, and we were ushered into a nearly empty section in the cavernous stadium, which eventually filled up about halfway.

The stadium was decked out in red and white Budweiser beer ads, which dovetailed with the team colors. In spite of all the beer ads inside and out of the stadium, there was not a drop of brew to be had. We were told that beer had been banned from the premises for nearly 10 years due to the rowdy fans who couldn't handle their alcohol. So, we made do with a half-pint of brandy I'd smuggled in just in case. A slug in our coffee kept us cozy in the cold August air.

The River Plate fans were boisterous, chanting and waving banners through most of the match. Luckily, the home team prevailed, keeping the faithful from becoming surly.

As the end of the match neared, we watched police escort the opposing team's fans from the stadium. They had all been seated together in one section surrounded by a fence and a line of security guards. We started to leave, but noticed that all the exits had been locked to give the opposing fans a head start! After 10 minutes or so, they unlocked the gates and we were allowed to leave.

The next day, a car picked us up at our hotel for the hour-long ride out to an estancia, or horse ranch.

There are several estancias on the outskirts of the city,

offering tourists a chance to ride horses and enjoy the countryside. We picked one that got high marks from past visitors who commented in an online forum. I called the owner, Anna, and made reservations.

We pulled up to the estancia's dirt lot just as a van full of Air France flight attendants arrived. According to Anna, Air France has a standing contract allowing its employees to relax at the estancia on their layovers in Bueno Aires.

Steve perked up when he learned we would be spending the day with these slim young things, with their French accents and designer shades.

We were welcomed with coffee and pastries in the ranch house, which had a fire crackling in the fireplace. Anna and her staff, which included her daughter, began fitting us with leather leggings and riding helmets.

Soon, we were out in the corral, meeting our mounts and getting a quick course on horsemanship. Anna promised us that if we were game, she would teach us to gallop.

We took off in a group, about a dozen or so guests on horseback, with Anna, her daughter and a ranch hand keeping an eye on us greenhorns. Some of the Air France people looked pretty comfortable in the saddle. The sky was blue, with a few puffy white clouds, and the air had a bite of winter chill even in the sun. The horse path cut a muddy line through the green grass as we rode along past other ranches and pastures.

We stopped to admire a foal born a couple of days earlier. It stayed close to its mother on the other side of a fence, and our horses seemed mesmerized by the sight.

After a while, Anna asked us who wanted to gallop and who wanted to ride at a slower pace. The four of us decided to try it, and most of the French people were game.

"Does he want to gallop?" Anna asked one of the French women, referring to her boyfriend.

"Yes, he wants to gallop," the woman said.

The man didn't speak much English, but he caught the gist of the conversation.

"No, I don't want to gallop," he said.

"Yes, he does," said his girlfriend.

Anna shrugged and spurred the horses with shouts and smacks on the rump with her riding crop. The boyfriend went along for the bumpy ride, although he didn't look happy.

I gritted my teeth, gripped the horse's body with all the strength in my knees, and whacked her flank with the loose end of the reins. Galloping was exhilarating and terrifying; I had never gone past a trot in the handful of times I had ever ridden a horse before. I took Anna's advice and held the reins tightly to keep my mount from picking up too much speed. Salome loved it and couldn't get enough.

After three hours, we came back to the ranch house, where a wonderful barbecue lunch was laid out on a picnic table. The ranch hands brought small charcoal grills to the table, where steaks and sausages sizzled. Cold bottles of beer were uncapped and passed around. After lunch, I was ready for a nap, not another ride. The hammocks swayed in the breeze, inviting me to skip the afternoon session in favor of a snooze. Steve and I both wavered, but in the end we strapped on our riding helmets. Maybe we were afraid we'd miss something.

The afternoon was more of the same, with a good bit of galloping and watching for wildlife, such as the tiny owls Salome spotted perched on a row of fence posts.

As the afternoon light waned, it was time to pile back into the station wagon for the ride back to the city. We were tired in that pleasing, physical way you feel after a day of outdoor activity. It was only in the car that the stiffness and soreness brought on by six hours in the saddle – for those of us unaccustomed to horseback riding – began to make themselves known. Steve seemed particularly affected. By the time we got back to our hotel, it was all he could do to drag himself to our room, where he curled up in a fetal position on his bed, moaning in pain. We all took plenty of ibuprofen, and our muscles gradually healed over the next couple of days.

While we were enjoying our time in Buenos Aires and spending time with my brother, it was against a backdrop of continuing problems with Salome. I e-mailed the psychiatrist we had been seeing back home, and she responded that Salome's angry outbursts could in fact be related to her medication.

I lost my temper one night when Salome lashed out and tried to hit Ava. I had been holding one of her stuffed animals, and I swung it at Salome, hitting her on the side of the head. She became hysterical, and I felt so bad about my own loss of control that I had to go out for walk through the late-night streets of Buenos Aires to calm down. I resolved to do a better job of keeping my own emotions in check, and we decided it was time to take Salome off the medication even though it had helped with the eyelash pulling.

The drug's effects gradually wore off and Salome's moods returned to normal, but not before some additional rough times that made us consider ending the trip.

From Buenos Aires, we were bound for Punta del Este, Uruguay, a beach resort where we had booked a week at a timeshare resort.

We rode the Buquebus, a massive hydrofoil ferry, to Montevideo, Uruguay's capital, where we boarded a bus for the two-hour trip to the coast. The ferry ride was so smooth we might have been rolling on a train or bus as we jetted across the mouth of the De La Plata River, covering the distance in just over an hour.

We weren't sure what to expect of Uruguay; our guidebook had noted that Punta del Este was a favorite of the pretty young things from Buenos Aires who wanted to party their buns off at the beach. What we found was a nearly deserted beachside town full of high-rise hotels and luxurious mansions set on rolling lawns. The weather was blustery, sometimes rainy, which made for nice walks around the town, if not ideal for sunning on the beach. Many of the restaurants and shops were closed for the winter season and even the stop lights downtown were turned off.

We rented a compact car and stocked up on groceries for the condo at a modern supermarket, and fired up the charcoal grill on our balcony. It was the first time I had driven since we left San Diego nearly two months earlier, and it was a rare chance to enjoy home-cooked meals on our round-the-world trip. The supermarket was in the middle of a mall, which could be found in almost every South American city we visited.

Salome made friends with a playful yellow lab who lived near our condo complex, and spent hours throwing a stick or ball for him to retrieve. He was such a pest that we couldn't even get in a game of tennis without Dennis, the dog, stealing the ball. At night he would camp out on the landing outside our door, barking and refusing to go home. Although he was a pain, we put up with it because he cheered up Salome when she was feeling homesick and blue. Salome also met a little girl from Argentina, Josefina, who came over to our condo for dinner one night.

Salome's Journal

8/17/05 Punta del Este, Uruguay

Sorry it's been so long but I have some things to say. I met two really nice friends. One's a dog but he counts. Right ooooh by the way I'm in Uruguy Punta del este. Oops got to go dog's at the door biii!

One morning we set off for a hike around the neighborhood with the resort's recreation leader. Dennis the dog decided to join us as we walked along the quiet roads through fields, past large homes and manicured lawns and a golf course. The day was gray and damp, but it was very enjoyable to stretch our legs and gawk at the opulent homes. Several horses galloped past us as we walked, and we were afraid Dennis would spook them when he charged off behind them, barking like crazy.

We passed our days enjoyably in Punta del Este, relaxing in the condo and watching movies, swimming in the indoor pool and sampling a few of the local restaurants. One stood out in particular, a Basque-style seafood restaurant a few miles from our timeshare, which was recommended by our guidebook.

We also used the time to make arrangements for the next leg of our journey, to Iguazu Falls, on the border between Argentina and Brazil. Since it was a 24-hour bus ride from Punta del Este to Puerto Iguazu, on the Argentinian side of the falls, we opted to fly. This required a short bus trip to Montevideo, a flight back to Buenos Aires and a connecting flight to Puerto Iguazu. Our plan was to spend a couple of days seeing the falls from the Argentine side, then get our Brazilian visas from the consulate in Puerto Iguazu, before crossing overland into Brazil via Foz de Iguazu, the small city on the Brazilian side of the falls.

We lucked out by arriving in Puerto Iguazu on the night of full moon, the only time during the month when night hikes to the falls are offered. By silver moonlight, we cautiously traversed catwalks over the Rio Iguazu, which led us out to the edge of the falls. As we approached the falls in the darkness, we first felt, then heard, the low rumble of hundreds of thousands of gallons of water per minute pouring over a horseshoe-shaped cliff called La Garganta del Diablo, or The Devil's Throat. All we could see in the dim light was the mist churning up from what appeared to be a bottomless abyss, and we could feel the powerful surging water through the vibration of the catwalk beneath our feet. We had to shout to each other to be heard over the roaring falls.

Our taxi driver had trouble finding our hotel in Puerto Iguazu, a family run place called Residencial Noelia. The four of us were in one room with a bunk bed and a twin bed, close quarters. While the hotel was very pleasant and offered a breakfast of bread, fruit and coffee on the flower-filled patio, the tight quarters made us all a bit edgy.

By day, we hiked around Iguazu Falls national park and took an adrenaline-charged powerboat ride right up to the base of Garganta del Diablo, getting completely soaked. Salome tried to see how many butterflies she could get to land on her hands at one time; I think her record was 14. One morning on a forest path we encountered a gang of wild coatamundis, raccoon-like creatures with pointy faces and long tails. A tourist had reached into her backpack, and was suddenly surrounded by the little brutes. They were very aggressive, but luckily, a park employee happened by and shooed them away before things got nasty.

While visiting the Argentinian side of the falls, we took a tip from our guidebook and splurged on the brunch at the Sheraton Iguazu, which is inside the park. The price had doubled from $10 to $20 per person since the guidebook had been published, but it was still worth the price to dine on fancy treats with linen napkins and tablecloths and feast on the spectacular view of the falls through the huge picture windows.

The weather was quite warm at the falls, and in the evenings, we strolled around Puerto Iguazu and ate at the town's outdoor restaurants.

Our next destination was Brazil, but before we could cross the border, we had to get our Brazilian visas at the consulate in Puerto Iguazu. On the morning of our departure, we lined up outside the consulate and chatted with a medical student who was traveling around South

America on her own during a break in her studies. She was Asian, and I think she lived in London.

We handed over our passports, photos, completed applications and about $100 apiece in cash, and nervously went off for coffee while our visas were being processed. I say nervously because I wasn't crazy about surrendering my passport – it made me feel vulnerable, almost naked. But after 90 minutes or so, we went back to the counter and our passports were ready, newly adorned with Brazilian visa stickers.

We hired a taxi to take us across the border to the bus station in Foz de Iquazu, Brazil.

The taxi stopped at the border checkpoint, where we went through the slightly unnerving process of being fingerprinted and photographed, the only time that happened in our entire round-the-world trip. We had heard somewhere that the photographing and fingerprinting and the steep visa fee were all paybacks to U.S. citizens for our government's similar treatment of Brazilian visitors.

The Argentinian side of the falls is a laid-back, charming town, but the Brazilian side is a small city with a population of 200,000 or so. The downtown was very crowded with traffic and pedestrians, and the streets were lined with mid-rise buildings of 5 or 10 stories.

The bus station was our first stop because Steve had decided to head straight to Rio and try to move up his flight home; we were going to take a bus to a city called Curitiba, where we would take a one-day round-trip train ride to a colonial mountain town, billed as Brazil's most scenic rail route.

Steve had confided to me as we walked around Puerto Iquazu's quiet, tree-lined streets that he was getting homesick, and wanted to cut his trip short.

"I won't feel at ease until I'm back in the U.S.," he'd said. Rather than spend most of the month of August with us, flying back on Salome's birthday, the 29th, he would head to the airport in Rio and fly home a week or so early. I figured it was a combination of jitters from the unfamiliar surroundings and the heightened tensions from our ongoing family strife. The mix of Salome's short fuse and Steve's hardline attitude toward it ("She just needs to be told 'no,'" he would say), proved volatile and sometimes escalated a small spat into a larger blowup. Not that it was his fault, but his reaction didn't help.

Anyway, we arrived at the bus station, withdrew some Brazilian reales from an ATM and checked our bags into the luggage room. We investigated the bus schedules, and Steve bought a ticket for a 25-hour ride to Rio de Janeiro; we bought seats on an overnight coach to Curitiba.

As I look back on that day, I recall it as being one of the saddest of our trip. I felt it was a shame that Steve would be in Rio de Janeiro, one of the most visually stunning and lively cities in the world, but not get to see any of it, save the view from the window of a bus, and later, an airplane. I tried a few times to talk him into staying, but he was determined to head straight to Rio and grab an earlier flight home.

We all had lunch together at the diner in the bus station, where the beers were kept near freezing in a cooler that advertised the temperature in a bright red digital display, and then it was time for us to part company. Steve's bus was leaving in mid-afternoon, while ours was not scheduled to go until evening. We decided to use the time to visit the Brazilian side of Iguazu Falls, which was said to offer a close-up counterpart to the panoramic views of the Argentinian side.

We got directions from the woman at the tourist kiosk inside the bus station. The trip to the falls would take about 90 minutes by local bus, and involve a transfer at the bus station in downtown Foz de Iguazu.

The four of us walked outside together to wait for our bus, subdued by the thought that we would be splitting up. Almost immediately, our bus pulled up and we had to hustle to get on board. We hurriedly said out good-byes, waving to Steve as we drove off.

As our bus pulled away, a feeling of deep sadness washed over me. I fought back an almost overwhelming urge to cry that took me by surprise. I'm not sure why our separation hit me so hard; maybe because of the tensions of the past couple of weeks in dealing with Salome, or that a connection to our familiar lives was receding in the distance as we continued our journey, three travelers far from home.

After changing buses, we continued through the city to the outskirts, passing small farms and pastures. The park entrance was crowded with groups of Brazilian schoolchildren, and we boarded a bus that took us to the lookout points. Soon after we arrived, we got into a small argument with Salome, which was very common at that time. I forget what it was about – I think something she wanted us to buy from a vendor. We followed the path, which descended until we were nearly level with the bottom of the falls. We were so close that mist blew across the catwalk, soaking us and the hundreds of other tourists ogling the massive falls.

A short elevator ride took us back up to the rim of the canyon, to the shuttle bus stop, café and gift shop. As the argument wore on, finally Ava and I told Salome she could not get the ice cream we has promised her earlier.

That set off one of Salome's worst outbursts of the entire trip. She screamed, turned red in the face, and started slapping, hitting and spitting on us. All we could do was try to hold her and tell her we loved her, while she screamed that she hated us. After a while, she calmed down and, as usual after these tantrums, apologized and said she didn't mean the things she'd said. I bought her a can of juice, and we got back on the shuttle bus for the ride back to the park entrance, shaken and wondering what we could possibly do to make things right.

That evening, we were walking around the neighborhood near the bus station, looking for someplace to eat dinner as we waited for our night bus, when the feeling of despair hit me again, even harder than before. I had to sit down on a bench, and this time I didn't hold back the tears. I cried for me, and for my family. Ava and Salome tried to console me, and after this cloudburst had passed, I felt better. Looking back, I think I needed an emotional release after all the stress that had been building over the past several weeks.

We went back to the bus station, where we had dinner in the cafeteria. Then we got on the bus and rode off into the Brazilian night.

We arrived in Curitiba about 5:30 a.m. after the all-night bus ride from Foz de Iguazu, groggy, disheveled and disoriented. It was still dark when we stumbled off the bus, which parked inside a covered terminal at Curitiba's huge main bus station.

The three of us were hungry, so we hauled our bags up the stairs to second floor, where we found a brightly lit, warm and welcoming café. Our plan was to have breakfast while we waited for the ticket counter in the rail office to open. We wanted to ride the tourist train that traveled through jungle and mountains to the colonial town of Morretes, touted as the most scenic and spectacular train ride in Brazil. The train ride took four hours each way, chugging determinedly across high bridges and through tunnels.

But first, we'd have to manage to get ourselves fed, which turned out to be more of a challenge than we'd anticipated, since the menu was in Portuguese, and even our rudimentary Spanish-language skills weren't much use. We wanted to avoid a similar debacle as the night in Santiago when I thought I was ordering a rum-and-lime juice cocktail and ended up with a sandwich.

"I'd like eggs," Ava offered hopefully to the waitress, who looked at her blankly. "Dos huevos, por favor."

The waitress asked a question, which we didn't understand. We continued to scan the menu, looking for anything that remotely resembled "egg," or "huevos," with no luck. Finally, Ava sketched out a fried egg on her napkin. The waitress's eyes lit up, and she said, "ah," and scribbled on her pad, then yelled back to the cook, who was watching from behind the counter. (We finally figured out that the Portuguese word for "egg" is ovo.)

We had a fine, hearty breakfast, which made us feel much better as we headed to buy our train tickets. A couple of hours later, we were sitting in our train seats, a bit tired but enjoying the scenery rolling past. An English-speaking guide would come through our car occasionally and talk about the surrounding countryside.

The day passed enjoyably, riding and dozing in the train and walking around sleepy Morretes. We had lunch in a shady outdoor restaurant overlooking a river, and took a catnap on benches in the park before catching our train back to Curitiba.

We really lucked out when it came time to buy our bus tickets for Rio. The bus company was having a special promotion on its leitos-class buses, which are known as the "Lear jets" of highway transportation. After spending the night snoozing in those wide, cushy seats the size of Lazyboy recliners, we would ask for leitos seats every time we traveled on a night bus during the rest of our trip in Brazil, only to get a shake of the head from the ticket agent. Before boarding the bus, we showered in a clean, spacious bathhouse at the rear of a beauty salon on the second floor of the bus station, so we were well-rested and refreshed when we finally made it to Rio de Janeiro the next morning.

We hadn't booked a hotel in Rio, so our first couple of hours in the city were spent at a pay phone in the sprawling bus station, lining up a place to stay. We settled on a family-run hotel on a side street a mile or so from Copacabana Beach, which seemed like a good base of operations.

The place wasn't bad, but the windowless, ground-floor room felt claustrophobic to me. It also cost about $60 a night, which was on the high side, considering we were a brisk 20-minute walk from the beach. So our first order of business was to prospect for another hotel. We came up with the Hotel Gran Canada, a high-rise just two blocks from the beach. It was the same price as our other hotel, but much nicer, with its tiny but spiffy lobby, uniformed bellmen and free buffet breakfast.

Our hotel change coincided with a rare rainstorm, so we were a little soggy when we arrived at our new digs.

The hotel was perfectly located. Within a few blocks was anything we could possibly need, including a laundry, supermarket, Internet cafés, post office and a huge, well-stocked record store featuring live music in the evenings. Salome was happy because there was McDonald's on the same block.

Copacabana is a long, wide, sandy beach where visitors can rent beach chairs and umbrellas for a buck or two for the entire day, and a steady stream of vendors offered ice cold sodas and beer, snacks and souvenirs.

Rio seemed almost obsessively fit; at any hour of the day, women in leotards could be seen stretching, high-stepping and jazzercising in the multi-story gym directly across the street from our hotel. In the mornings, there were lots of joggers, walkers and bicyclists taking advantage of the path along the beach, which stretched for several miles. Each Sunday, half of Avenida Atlantica, the frantically busy road paralleling the beach, was closed to vehicular traffic and was instead filled with Rio residents and tourists on foot, bicycle and roller skates. People of all ages turned out on

Sunday, from grandmothers and grandfathers, to entire families, to teens in skimpy bathing suits.

After a couple of days spent wandering around and acclimating, we decided to take a city tour, which highlighted some of Rio's famous sights. Among the stops on the tour were Maracana Stadium, a holy place to the futbol faithful, also known as the house that Pele built, and the Metropolitan Cathedral, a vast place where the stained glass seemed to rise up to the heavens. We were taken to the street where the elite sit on bleachers to watch the city's Carneval parade, and a workshop where, for a small fee, Ava and Salome got to wear Carneval costumes. The only disappointment was our trip to the top of Corcovado Mountain, the peak where the famous Christo Redentor statue looms over the city. Unfortunately, the fog was so thick that not only was Rio lost, but the 98-foot-tall statue was just faint shadow of its glorious self, even when we stood right at its base.

During the tour, our guide mentioned that a restaurant down the street from our hotel served the best banana split in town, which turned out to be a great tip. She was right, the banana splits were huge, with scoops of ice cream, gobs of sauce and mounds of whipped cream. We became regulars, gorging ourselves on beef stroganoff and ice cream. We got to know one of the waiters who, each time we came in for dinner, chatted about his family and asked about our travels.

We spent our days wandering around the city or just lounging at the beach. Salome caught up on her schoolwork and we adjusted our itinerary. Although we had planned to fly from Rio to London and immediately catch a connecting flight to Morocco, we decided to try to get an earlier flight and use the time to visit Ava's aunt and uncle in London. Unfortunately, flights were full and we couldn't change our outbound flight. Instead, we opted to skip Marrakesh and Casablanca and lay over in London.

For the rest of our time in Brazil, we explored the northern coast as far as the country's third-largest city, Salvador de Bahia.

We planned to celebrate Salome's ninth birthday in Rio, and in the days before the big event, we shopped for presents and worked up a full schedule of birthday activities, including a visit to a fancy salon near Ipanema Beach.

Her behavior problems continued, though, including meltdowns in our hotel, and a major tantrum during an excursion to Pan de Azucar, or Sugar Loaf, one of the city's fabled lookout spots. This fight occurred on the neighborhood streets near the Sugar Loaf tram station, with the usual yelling, hitting, spitting, etc. So, we took what felt like the drastic step of postponing her birthday celebration for one day, which seemed to get her attention.

The next day, Aug. 30th, the party went forward as planned. We played catch at a neighborhood park in the morning, then went to the salon, which featured a snow-white cockatoo in large gilded cage next to the entrance. The bird chattered with passersby, but occasionally let out some ear-splitting squawks.

Salome got the full treatment, with a shampoo, cut and blow-dry, and a manicure, while Ava and I sipped espressos. Then, Salome chose to go on a bungy jump ride in the park, and we ended the day with dinner and banana splits at Cirandinha, our favorite restaurant.

Apart from the gloomy weather when we first arrived, Rio sizzled – and I'm not talking about the nightlife. Most days the temperature was in the 90s, and the mercury sometimes topped 100.

One sweltering afternoon, I was walking over to an Internet café when I got hungry and stopped for a hot dog at a sidewalk stand. The vendor, an older man with white hair and a big smile, reached into the back of the mini-van that doubled as his mobile kitchen, and pulled out a couple of plastic stools. He placed the stools under the patch of shade cast by the rear hatchback, and we chatted about the weather in a mix of Portugese and Spanish as I ate my hot dog, chased with an icy cold Coke. I particularly remember how he heaped the dog with onions, peppers and sauces with a flourish, as if he were a chef at a five-star restaurant. People streamed past us on their way to and from a nearby Metro station.

Rio was also where I got my first haircut of our journey, at a barbershop up the street from the beach. A helpful customer who spoke English helped translate – "over the ears, a little off the top" – to the barber. I asked the barber if he spoke Spanish; he shrugged and replied that he spoke "Portañol."

As pleasant as Copacabana Beach was for sunbathing, sandcastle building and people-watching, it had a wicked shore break that could be perilous to all but the strongest swimmers. We learned this firsthand on a windy morning when the offshore breeze whipped the whitecaps into a fine mist. I was off doing errands and Ava and Salome went to the beach. Salome was in the shallow water right off the beach when a wave decked her, and left her gasping for breath as she tumbled in the surf. Ava ran in to the rescue, but also was swept off her feet by the powerful waves. They finally battled their way back to shore, and from that point on during our trip, Salome was always fearful of swimming in the ocean whenever there was more than the slightest swell.

The days in Rio rolled by pleasantly, spent sightseeing, with daily jogs or bike rides along the beach. We even attended a beach volleyball tournament that had a definite MTV feel, with the blaring music and enthusiastic cheerleader types who doused the crowd with water and tossed out free T-shirts.

Then it was time to pack up and move on from this city of thong bikinis and bossa nova. Our plan was to take the bus north and stop off at a couple of small beach towns, Arrial d' Ajuda and Trancoso, which were described in glowing terms by travelers we met in Rio. Then we would venture on to Salvador de Bahia, considered the cultural capital of Brazil thanks to the African influences on its dance, music and food. In the 1800s, Salvador had been the main port of entry for South America's booming slave trade.

We caught an overnight bus from Rio, which dropped us off in early afternoon in Puerto Seguro, a sleepy port town on Brazil's north Atlantic coast. As soon as we stepped off the bus, in a daze from lack of sleep, hotel touts surrounded us, offering postcards and brochures for hotels in the area. The bus station was a collection of thatched-roof, palapa-style buildings, that made it feel like a tropical outpost. We gathered our huge mound of luggage and consulted our guidebook, trying to figure out which direction to take.

"Taxi, where you going?" was the constant refrain from the drivers parked alongside the bus terminal.

We eventually settled on Arial d'Ajuda, which required a crosstown taxi ride through Puerto Seguro, then a short ferry trip across the river, followed by another taxi into town.

Arrial d'Ajuda was a pretty town perched on a bluff over the beach. There was a town square where many of the locals congregated, and an upscale tourist section with boutique hotels, restaurants, souvenir shops and travel agencies. We picked a hotel a couple of blocks off the town square, which was more like an apartment building. Our unit was two stories, with a large living area and kitchen downstairs, and two bedrooms and a bathroom upstairs. The front bedroom upstairs had a tiny balcony with a hammock that looked out over the lush green neighborhood. Everything was clean, if well-worn, and there was a small pool in the central courtyard.

When we first got there, we had to rouse the proprietor from a nap. He was big, bespectacled, bearded and bore a strong resemblance to Tommy Chong of the Cheech and Chong comedy team. He spoke little English, but we managed to strike a deal for 55 reales a day, or $22.

Arrial d'Ajuda had earned the nickname of "Israel d'Ajuda," due to the many Israeli tourists who visited. In fact, the tourist we met in Rio who told us about the town had been Israeli. The Israeli backpacking set is legendary for hard partying and favoring idyllic destinations where sand is warm, the beers are cold, and money goes a long way. All three were true of Arrial d'Ajuda; it was the kind of place where you could imagine hanging out for a while, sleeping in, walking around the town, maybe riding a bike, and not doing much else.

On our first afternoon, we were walking from our hotel to the town square when we heard the beat of Afro-Brazilian music filtering into the street. It was coming from a studio advertising "capoeira," a hybrid of martial arts and dance said to have originated with African slaves in Salvador's early days.

With the music pulsing in the background, two men or woman circle each other, making rapid arm thrusts and sweeping leg kicks, not making physical contact with each other, but almost becoming intertwined during their fluid movements. We found the combination of the music and dance hypnotic and it was hard to tear ourselves away from the window of the school, where we peeked in on the class along with several neighborhood children.

As I walked through the town square one evening, I noticed an impromptu book stand selling English-language paperbacks. We had been on the road in South America for more than a month, and books in English were hard to find. So, I eagerly browsed through the books stacked on a rickety table while chatting with the proprietor, a man with long, gray dreadlocks, a gray scraggly beard, and stained, broken teeth.

When I mentioned where I was from, the bookseller, whose name was Darck, said he was very familiar with California.

"I spent 10 years working at the Del Mar Fair," he said. "Every summer I was there. I also worked at other fairs up and down the West Coast."

"What did you do?" I asked.

"Sold things."

"What kind of things?"

"All kinds of things. I worked in one of the big tents, with all the booths. I was one of those guys who gave the demos and tried to sell stuff to the tourists."

I knew those guys well from countless summertime visits to the fair. They demonstrated miracle vegetable choppers, knives that could cut through a tin can and mops that shined floors with a few effortless swipes.

He said he was originally from Rio. I asked if he was planning to move back to the U.S.

"No," he said. "I really like it here. I have everything I need."

I had a couple of books that Ava and I had already read, and offered to trade. He looked doubtful, but agreed to trade my two books and a small amount of cash for a couple of his books. I picked up well-used copies of Somerset Maughm's Razor's Edge, and Isabel Allende's Eva Luna. They were both slim volumes, which is great for round-the-world travelers.

He hadn't heard of the book I traded him, called Bel Canto. It was a recent best seller, a psychological thriller about a group of idealists who took top government officials hostage in an unnamed Latin American country in an effort to win the release of political prisoners.

"You should be able to get a good price for this," I said.

He was unimpressed. "Isabel Allende always sells very well."

We rented bikes and pedaled around town, bumping over cobblestones and rutted dirt roads. We rode to a scenic beach north of town, where we chained our bikes and walked along the shore to a restaurant with padded chaise longues and hammocks. We dozed and swam while our lunch – a whole grilled fish – was prepared. It was a good thing we weren't starving, because it took more than an hour before our food was ready. After lunch, we lazed around some more while Salome played with some dogs that were hanging around to scrounge the leftovers.

The next leg of our journey would be an overnight bus ride from Puerto Seguro to Salvador, where we would spend about a week before flying back to Rio for the exclamation point on our South American adventure. From Rio, we would catch a trans-Atlantic flight to London.

In Arrial d'Ajuda, we bought our bus and plane tickets and booked rooms in Salvador. We also arranged, by phone, to spend our last two nights in Brazil at the now-familiar Hotel Gran Canada at Copacabana Beach, and we called Ava's aunt in London, where we would stay during our first week in Europe. With all the details set, we boarded the overnight bus for Salvador, where we met a young American who was in Brazil fulfilling his missionary service for the Mormon Church, and watched Russell Crowe in Cindarella Man on Salome's portable DVD player. Salome amused herself by listening to the latest installment of A Series of Unfortunate Events, by Lemony Snickett, on my MP3 player.

The bus ride was comfortable until about midnight, when a man took the seat next to me, squeezing me against the side of the bus and putting me in the path of the frigid blast from the air-conditioning vent. By the time we arrived in Salvador, I was tired and grumpy.

From our vantage point inside the bus, the city looked sunny, green and busy, with plenty of traffic flowing on the highways. The bus station was modern and tidy, more welcoming than Rio's, and we hailed a cab for the ride to the Pelourinho, Salvador's historic district, where we would be staying for the first three nights.

The taxi stopped at the bottom end of a steep, triangular, cobblestone plaza, known as the Largo de Pelourinho, where slave auctions were held before slavery was abolished in Brazil in 1835. Three- and four-story, weather-stained Victorian buildings lined the plaza, which was closed to vehicles. Our first challenge was toting our luggage uphill over the bumpy cobblestones. The front desk of the Hotel Pelourinho was in a breezeway off the plaza.

We checked in and were shown our room, which left me deeply depressed. Maybe it was the fatigue or the stress of arriving in a new city with a slightly scary reputation, but the sight of the rickety, scratched furniture and the dreary, windowless bathroom, gave me a bad case of the blues. We were paying $65 a night for this place, and it didn't seem worth half that amount. I cheered up slightly when we went for breakfast in hotel's bright, airy dining room, with its stellar view of the cathedral and the sparkling blue Baia de Todos os Santos beyond. ("The breakfast will cost extra, since you are arriving this morning," the desk clerk said curtly.) But it was well worth the cost; we filled up on fruit, pastry, and a special Brazilian hot cereal with the consistency of Cream of Wheat.

That morning, we heard for the first time about the devastation caused by Hurricane Katrina, via a CNN broadcast on a TV in the hotel dining room. Over the coming days and weeks, we followed from afar the revelations of the federal government's monumental ineptitude in dealing with the crisis. From overseas, the view of the situation was, according to locals we talked to: "America doesn't care about poor people." Whether or not that was true, the handling of the storm's aftermath sure didn't give anyone outside the U.S. any reason to raise their opinion of the Land of the Free and the Home of the Brave.

Wandering around the streets of the Pelourinho was quite pleasant. The weather was warm and sunny, and we lunched at an open-air cafe on the central plaza. We checked out various museums, including a stunning church filled with wooden sculptures that had been covered in gold leaf. One night we saw a show featuring Afro-Brazilian dance and drumming at a theater across from our hotel and next, we checked out the grooves at an outdoor concert in the central plaza. Ava and Salome shopped and I bought a small box of aromatic Salvadoran cigars.

Central Salvador is divided into the alta, or upper, city and the baja, or lower city. Linking the two is El Laderador, an oversized elevator that moves hundreds of people up and down each hour. One afternoon we walked through the historic district and rode the elevator to the market at the bottom. We had lunch at a café in the back of the market, where teenagers performed capoiera for tips on a wooden platform. As happened all too often, our ordering eyes were bigger than our eating stomachs, and we had a lot of food left over when we finished our meal.

It seemed a little odd when several waitresses came over and began clearing the table, because they combined all of the leftover food onto one or two plates. The next thing we knew, they had put the food on the table next to us, and the restaurant staff closed in, devouring what would have made a fine doggie bag. The hostess, who seemed to be in charge, casually munched on a chicken wing that had come from our table as she sat arriving customers.

After three nights in the historic district, we moved to a hotel near the beach. The hotel had been recommended by the travel agent in Arrial d'Ajuda, and it was a fine choice. The hotel catered primarily to business travelers; the rooms were modern and clean, if small, and a hearty free breakfast was offered each morning in the cheerful dining room.

We were able to walk or take a short bus ride to the beach, which Salome loved because the water was absolutely calm.

Our only sightseeing excursion in Salvador was a day tour to a turtle preservation center and several pristine beaches. Our guide, Wilson, was a genial Brazilian with dreadlocks and a "Don't worry, be happy" attitude. He made a point of playing some of his favorite music as we rolled along, and at one point serenaded the group. Wilson made a point of repeating all of his commentary in Portugese, English and Spanish, which was appreciated by the multilingual group members. Wilson confided that he had studied numerous languages to improve communication with the various groups of foreign tourists he shepherded, including Japanese. He jumped off the bus just before the end of the tour, planning to head home, change clothes and prepare to greet a tour group from Poland that evening.

We laid low during our final days in Salvador, lounging at the beach, helping Salome catch up on her schoolwork, walking around the leafy neighborhood near our hotel and watching DVD movies on the TV in our room. One day we got caught in a sudden downpour and holed up in a café near the beach. Another day turned out to be a national holiday, and the celebration included a parade right down our street. Hundreds of families packed the nearby park. We wandered around and Salome played at the playground with some local kids.

On the day we left Salvador, we called a friendly cab driver who had driven us around several times. He picked us up at our hotel in the late afternoon for the 45-minute drive to the airport. It was near dusk as we drove through the warm evening, getting a final glimpse of Salvador's lovely beaches. The setting sun cast a soft, orange glow over everything as we neared the end of our stay in Brazil. We chatted with the cab driver about his 30-year career with the power company in Salvador. He said he still needed to work to make ends meet because his pension wasn't very big.

We spent two more nights in Rio de Janeiro at the now-familiar Gran Hotel Canada before our three-month sojourn in South America ended and we boarded a British Air Boeing 747 bound for London. We met many kind people and absorbed beautiful sights, sounds and tastes in South America. But we were full of anticipation for Europe and the next chapter in our global adventure.

Chapter 5

Book Smarts

Homeschooling on the road

Enhancing Salome's education was a crucial part of our game plan from the start. All through elementary school, she excelled in both academics and citizenship. I was determined that nothing about our trip would set back her future studies in any way.

Ava and I knew she would absorb incredible lessons from the trip itself, whether it was meeting people from different cultures and learning about their lives, gaining confidence by confronting new and strange experiences, or grappling with the realities of life on the road, from language to foods to exotic toilets.

Of course, she would also see some of the most famous historic and natural sites in the world, from the Galapagos Islands and Machu Picchu to the Taj Mahal and Angkor Wat. Such life experiences could never be duplicated in a classroom.

But I also knew that at the end of our travels, she would have to walk back into a classroom, sit down at a desk and resume her "traditional" education.

To make that transition easier, I wanted her to keep up with the fourth-grade curriculum followed by all California public schools.

My idealized version of her "school on the road" had us sitting in a library somewhere, with Salome's nose in a book as she conscientiously completed her studies.

The reality was much different. And like most things, it turned out to be harder than expected.

First off, I had naively assumed that our school district in Oceanside, California would be willing and eager to help us set up a homeschooling program that we could use on our journey. Salome's teachers encouraged our plan, assuring us she was in no danger of falling behind her peers and that she would benefit greatly from spending fourth-grade in far-flung locations around the world.

So we were flying high when we placed a call to Oceanside School District headquarters which our school principal had suggested. Our jubilation turned to frustration as our messages went unanswered and we were bounced from one unresponsive staff person to the next. When we finally reached a helpful individual – the district's assistant superintendent of instruction – he told us the local district did not have a program to meet our needs and advised us to contact another agency, the San Diego County Office of Education.

By this point, I was getting a bit nervous about whether we had hit a serious bump on the road to our global adventure, but all that evaporated when we met Franya Sidoroff, a teacher with the county education office. On the bulletin board above her desk were numerous photos and postcards from her wandering students, whose parents were either living temporarily abroad, sailing around the world or pursuing other endeavors outside the country that required a creative educational approach.

Franya didn't miss a beat when we explained our plan; she immediately bustled around the office pulling out documents for us to read and sign, which resulted in Salome's withdrawal from her home school district and enrollment with the County Office of Education. (Unfortunately, I found out during the writing of this book that the county's wonderful independent study program was later shut down, the victim of budget cuts.)

Franya explained how we would be responsible for guiding Salome through the key learning points of the state's fourth-grade lesson plans, in all of her topics, which included language arts, social studies, science and math.

Only one topic from the curriculum – California history – posed any challenge to our planned mobile schoolhouse, because it required a visit to one of the state's historic missions. Since our house is only about a mile from the Mission San Luis Rey in Oceanside, we got Salome to work on that part of her studies during spring break, about three months before our planned departure.

The rest of the educational agenda, Franya assured us, could be easily handled from the road. She gave us detailed curriculum guides, textbooks, worksheets and the forms we needed for submitting progress reports.

Since I was handling a lot of the trip logistics, Ava agreed to be education czar. One key concern was our need to travel light. Franya had loaded us up with a stack of textbooks and papers, and we needed to boil it down to make it portable. Ava copied pages from the textbooks and created a set of folders, one for each topic.

My fond hope – which was never fully realized – was that each of us would take a single carry-on bag, so we wouldn't have to check our luggage on airplanes, and they would be easy to handle as we hopped from train to bus to boat to auto-rickshaw during the overland portions of our trip.

Right off the bat, we realized that Salome's schoolwork and supplies would require its own bag; ours were already too full with clothing and other personal items.

We agreed to send dispatches from the road with samples of Salome's work in each of her subjects. Franya made it very easy for us, only requiring us to send packets every other month.

During our trip, the world literally became Salome's classroom. She would study whenever and wherever the opportunity presented itself, from neighborhood cafes, to hotel rooms, trains, planes and buses.

For the first few weeks, we tried to maintain a very relaxed attitude toward her studies, working them in around whatever activities we were engaged in on any particular day. We soon realized, however, that a different, more structured approach was needed.

Most of the arguments that erupted among our traveling family – and they were numerous – centered around getting Salome to do her schoolwork. We found it was a chore to get her to settle down to work, and the exercise often ended in shouting, tears and Salome temporarily "losing" a favored toy, or the privilege of eating sweets or watching movies on her portable DVD player.

After suffering for the first couple of months, we decided Salome would respond better to a set routine. From that point on, we would set aside the first hour or two of the day, immediately following breakfast, for schoolwork. The only exception was when we were traveling from one place to another, or doing something very early in the morning, such as hiking the Inca Trail or riding in a jeep to catch the sunrise over the Himalayas.

This worked much better, and the stress level dropped considerably.

Salome filled out math worksheets, wrote in a daily journal and researched reports about the animals and plants we saw on our trip. She wrote a book report about Harry Potter and the Half-Blood Prince, which we read aloud each night at bedtime.

Ava helped her conduct science experiments in our hotel rooms, such as observing the effects of evaporation on glasses of water under varied conditions. Whenever possible, we tried to incorporate our travel experiences into her schoolwork. Salome became a whiz at converting foreign currencies into U.S. dollars, and in spite of her antipathy toward museums, she picked up many fascinating tidbits of history and culture from their exhibits.

During a lengthy stay at a hotel in Goa, India, Salome became a regular morning fixture next to the pool, where she did her schoolwork on a table shaded by a large umbrella, dressed in her bathing suit.

As another enticement, we built in "recess" time into her study sessions, when she could go for a quick swim, or we would step outside to kick a ball around or play on a playground if there was one nearby.

Ava collected Salome's work in her file folders and tracked her progress on the forms Franya had provided. Every two months, she assembled a packet of work, containing samples from all the subjects (and drawings) that Salome had worked on over the past few weeks. No matter where we happened to be at the time, we found a post office and sent the packet back to San Diego for Franya's review.

Each time, within a few days, we received an email from Franya reporting that she had received our latest packet.

The post office visits were an adventure in themselves as we learned to negotiate the various lines, postal rates and regulations in each country. From a traveler's perspective, a post office provides a fascinating glimpse into the everyday lives of locals, from mothers juggling small children along with their packages, to businessmen with cartloads of cargo.

We returned to San Diego County in the spring of 2006, happy to be back on our home turf and dazed from our long absence. Speaking for myself, I felt a strange sense of detachment, as if I was looking at familiar places and people from a distance. One of our first tasks was getting Salome enrolled in school, preferably at the elementary school she had attended since kindergarten.

We had to fudge just a bit in filling out the paperwork, since we were renting a condo for a month while we waited to move back into our own house. The school officials obliged us by not digging too deeply into the details of our temporary living arrangements.

Salome entered fourth grade in the beginning of March, having missed roughly seven months of the school year. Thankfully, she picked up right where she left off – and even made the honor roll for the second semester. Of course, we had many stories to share with her classmates and teachers, and we were invited to give a slide show about the trip to Salome's class.

Salome's grades and test scores remained excellent after our trip, so from all indications, she suffered no harm from missing nearly a year of formal schooling. And I know the amazing sights, sounds, smells and tastes of our journey were indelibly etched on her mind.

I was gratified recently when she was asked by her eighth-grade language arts teacher to write an essay about a "life-changing event." Salome chose to write about our trip and when she read her essay out loud before turning it in, our family had a chance to relive some of our favorite adventures. Time and the press of our daily lives have rounded the corners and sharp edges of our memories, softening and blurring them at the same time. Unfortunately, some of the details have faded, but the best of our experiences remain firmly rooted, where we can pull them out once in a while and savor them.

Chapter 6

Mind the Gap

London, Western Europe

London calling to the faraway towns
Now that war is declared-and battle come down
London calling to the underworld
Come out of the cupboard, all you boys and girl

"London Calling," The Clash

We stared out at Rio through the back windows of our taxi as we drove through the sunny morning on the way to the airport, and the longest flight of our journey so far – Rio to São Paulo, then on to London. The water was bright blue, the hills were green, and everyone looked like they had somewhere important to go.

I was looking forward to London because it seemed the small, everyday things would be easier in a place where people spoke English. I had enjoyed learning Spanish, and even struggling with Portugese, but after nearly three months of immersion in foreign languages, I was more than ready for a few days of speaking good old English.

As for the flight, I thought about it as something to get through. I've always been a nervous flyer, and for me, there is little to love about air travel. Some people say the journey is at least as important as the destination, but traveling on a commercial airliner is more a trial of endurance than something to savor. So far on our trip, we'd mostly traveled by air, with a few overnight bus trips thrown in. During all that moving from place to place, nothing remarkable had happened. There'd been exceptions – our boat trips through the Galapagos and on Lake Titicaca, and the wild bus ride from Puno, Peru, to La Paz, Bolivia. Not that uneventful is a bad thing, especially when it concerns transportation. To me, air travel is all about the boredom of waiting in lines, the mild claustrophobia of sitting strapped inside a metal tube as it hurtles through space, and electric surges of fear during turbulance.

The air is stale, the seats are cramped and there is little opportunity to mingle with fellow travelers.

That would change as we rambled around Europe and later, India, by train, my favorite way to travel. On a train, the journey really is fascinating, enjoyable, relaxing and educational; all the things that travel is meant to be. Although train travel often begins with a mad dash onto a crowded coach while heaving bags up the stairs and into overhead racks, once the train gives a jolt and starts off down the track, I settle back and contentedly gaze out the window at whatever panorama unfolds before me.

Our flight to London, including the brief stopover in São Paulo, would last approximately nine hours. Even though the flight left Rio in the late morning, by the time we lifted off from São Paulo, the three of us were tired and ready for a nap. We pushed back our seats and settled in for a bit of shut-eye.

Until the flight attendant tapped me on the shoulder.

"Sir, the passenger behind you requests that you put

your seat upright."

I gazed at her with my eyes only partially open. I couldn't tell if her somber expression meant disapproval for my rash decision to recline my seat or her embarrassment at having to relay such a stupid request from the jerk sitting behind me. I decided it was the latter. I twisted around in my seat to see the offended party, a thin man with a ponytail, who was fussily arranging various items on his tray table.

"What's the problem? I'm trying to sleep," I said.

"It's not time for sleeping, it's time for drinks," said the guy, who looked like an uptight hippie throwback.

"Excuse me, but I think I'll decide for myself when to sleep and when to drink, thank you. Besides, the guy in front of me has his seat back, so if I put mine up, I'll be cramped. I tell you what, if you get everyone up the aisle to put up their seats, I'll put mine up, too."

He grumbled and continued fiddling around with his tray, which of course was annoying. For the rest of the flight, I imagined him glaring at the back of my head. After a while, he made his wife switch seats with him, so she was sitting behind me.

The way I see it, when I'm flying coach on a commercial flight, I'm entitled to two things – putting my seat up or down when I feel like it, and putting my feet in the small amount of space below the seat in front of me. Nothing gets my goat more than someone shoving their stuff under their own seat and taking up my tiny allocation of leg room. Commercial air travel is like putting too many rats in a cage that's way too small – the rats get testy.

We landed at London's Heathrow Airport expecting nothing more than a wave-through at passport control and customs before we were on our way into the city. Unfortunately, things didn't go quite so smoothly. About six weeks before we arrived in London, the city had been shaken by a series of terrorist bombings on buses and the subway, or, as it is known to locals, "the Tube." Since then, security had been tightened up to an almost impenetrable level – that is, for average travelers like us.

After being stuck in our uncomfortable airplane seats for hours, we were dismayed to see the line at passport control snaking through a series of switchbacks and far down the connecting hallway. We settled in for what appeared to be at least a two-hour wait.

When we finally made it to the passport desk, the woman threw us what turned out to be a sharp curve.

"Where are you staying in London?" she asked, looking at us as if we were hiding something, and she knew it.

At that moment, Ava and I realized that not only did we not remember where her aunt lived (the address and phone number were safely stowed in our checked luggage), but we didn't even know her aunt's last name. This particular aunt was the sister of my wife's father, Tayeb, and her Bengali name didn't exactly trip off the tongue.

"With my aunt," Ava said.

"Her name and address?" the woman asked.

"Auntie Nurie," Ava said, a bit sheepishly.

"What's her LAST name?" the woman said, now showing her exasperation.

We looked at each other, feeling both sheepish and

frustrated. She would have to ask that.

"Look," I said, "all of the information is in my suitcase. If you need it, I'll have to get it from my bag."

"We have new rules. We're not supposed to let anyone enter the country unless they can provide the address of where they're staying."

We scrounged up a phone number for Auntie Nurie and the woman grudgingly stamped our passports and let us through. Of course, when we arrived in London about two months later on our way to Bombay, we were eagerly prepared to recite the details about the hotel where we were staying – but no one bothered to ask.

As usual, our first task upon entering a new country was to find an ATM where we could get cash, in this case, English pounds. That accomplished, we began the excruciating process of trying to figure out how to place a call from the unfamiliar pay phones. We ended up shoveling several one-pound coins into the slot, paying far more than we should have for the local call to Ava's aunt's house. We reached her cousin, who explained how to take the Tube to their neighborhood on the other side of the city.

To get there, we had to take a shuttle bus from the airport to the Tube station, then change trains twice. The whole trip took about two hours, but the price of a taxi would have been astronomical.

We were now traveling a lot heavier than at the start of the trip. As an early birthday present in Rio, I bought Ava the biggest wheeled suitcase we could find. When packed full, the thing was a gut-busting beast, a behemoth of cloth, plastic and metal. We dubbed it "Big Bertha" and it caused many a porter to break into sweats and muscle spasms. Heaving it up to the luggage shelf on a train could send you to the chiropractor. The big bag was necessary because all through South America, Ava and Salome had been ceaselessly, and remorselessly, shopping. We struck a bargain – I would buy her a big, beefy bag if she would ditch the smaller duffles and carryalls she had accumulated to tote her treasures.

Getting to the platform at the Tube station required descending a long, steep flight of stairs. Normally, we would have been able to catch the train from right inside the airport, but we had to take the shuttle because of construction at the station. While the stairs were a major inconvenience, the authorities had thoughtfully stationed two burly attendants at the top of the stairs, who helped us lug Bertha down to the platform. As most people did when they lifted Bertha, the men grunted with surprise at her sheer inert mass.

Navigating around London is easy on the Tube system because the stations are well-marked and evenly spread out across the city. The subway map, however, is daunting, with its maze of lines marked in different colors and the series of stations with unfamiliar names. It reminded me of a schematic for a microprocessor, or a very complicated flowchart.

Dazed and tired, we looked out at London's neighborhoods as we sped by, admiring the tidy streets and brick row houses. We were headed to the Leytonstone station on London's Central line, the closest stop to Ava's aunt. We found our way without getting lost or pulling any muscles as we traveled up and down stairways and escalators, as well as through long passageways connecting the different Tube platforms.

Finally, we reached our stop and hoisted our bags off the train. We went outside the station and called Ava's cousin, Tariq, who soon pulled up in a compact car to drive us to his family's home.

Tariq was a slim young man with glasses, dark hair and the deep brown complexion of his Bangladeshi heritage. He was home for the summer, relaxing a bit before starting medical school in Brighton, England, in a few weeks.

We wedged Big Bertha into the car, along with ourselves and our other bags, and set off for the short drive. The strangest thing was that Tariq sat behind a steering wheel mounted at the right front seat, while the front passenger sat on the left side. The car, of course, also traveled on the left side of the road. This made us disoriented and provided a near-death experience shortly after our arrival in London. Ava, looking to the left, narrowly missed becoming road kill from a car speeding at us from the right as she crossed the street. In hopes of avoiding such disasters in the city center, London authorities had helpfully marked the curbs with the words, "Look left!" or "Look right!"

Auntie Nurie and Uncle Syed's house was in a row of narrow, two-story homes a few blocks from the Tube station. The houses had tiny front yards and very little space between them, but they had deep, narrow backyards. Tariq's sister, Tarana, a college student, also lived at home. We would be camping out on cushions on the living room floor, which was fine with us.

Each night, Auntie Nurie prepared an assortment of aromatic and spicy – and delicious – Bengali dishes. It put me off at first to watch them pick up the food with their fingers, in the traditional style. I opted for a fork because I didn't relish the prospect of my hand being burned from the hot food, or covered in sticky curry sauce. Since Salome often picks at her food with her fingers, it was no big deal for her.

On either the first or second night in London, I bit into what I thought was a green bean in a curry dish, and nearly burst a blood vessel as the explosion of heat began in my mouth and traveled throughout my body. I mopped the sweat from my face while everyone laughed at my initiation into spicy Eastern fare. After that, Auntie Nurie would describe a dish she was preparing, and say, "I only put in three peppers, just for color." She also made a point each night of reminding me not to eat the hot peppers.

Our days were spent in a whirlwhind tour of the city, which was shockingly expensive after our soujourn in South America, where prices were much cheaper than in the U.S.

Soon after our arrival, we thought it would be nice to bring home a box of donuts for our hosts. We stopped into a donut shop off Piccadilly Square, and ordered a dozen. Our jaws dropped at the bill: $25 U.S. A fish and chips lunch for three ran more than $50 U.S. at a small pub, and a spin on the London Eye (the giant, futuristic Ferris wheel perched next to the Thames River) set us back about 75 bucks.

All that paled in comparison to a night on the town that included a stay in a two-star hotel and a live performance of Mary Poppins in the theater district. The room cost $150 for the night, which was a bargain compared to other hotels, and the show tickets cost about $200. We ate at

McDonalds before the show and determined our world trip budget wouldn't last long in London.

Although pricey, the show was great, with wonderful acting, singing, costumes and sets. We thoroughly enjoyed our evening at the theater, and rode contentedly back to our hotel on the red double-decker bus afterward. As a souvenir, we bought Salome a black "Supercalifragilisticexpialidocious" T-shirt that became a staple of her wardrobe for the rest of our trip.

London and Rome turned out to be the most expensive cities on our itinerary, but we did find one bargain in the U.K. – the public transit system. For about eight pounds ($15 U.S.) we could buy a family ticket that gave us unlimited access to the Tube and buses for a full day. We got our money's worth from those transit passes on our daily sightseeing excursions.

Riding the Tube added a new phrase to our travel lexicon: "Mind the gap." This admonition to be careful when stepping from the train to the platform, or vice versa, was made by a pre-recorded voice over the PA system every few minutes. It was also featured on signs inside the stations, and I bought a T-shirt with the phrase before we left the city. The shirt drew stares in India – maybe people thought it carried some deep metaphysical message.

Our stay with Ava's relatives in London was marred only by our ongoing battles with Salome, which often degenerated into screaming matches, spankings and howls of protest.

These were triggered by innocuous events, such as Ava trying to figure out what Salome would wear that day or, more often, getting Salome to do her schoolwork. She often protested the idea of doing her work and took offense at any instruction from Ava or I. We would have our fight in the living room but we knew our shouts and cries could be heard throughout the small house.

My frustration level was rising to the point that I was strongly considering whether it would be best for our own sanity, and Salome's well-being, if we headed home. During a call Ava's parents, her father even suggested we send Salome home to stay with them. I felt that we began the trip as a family and – if necessary – should end it that way.

I think it would have helped if there had been more children for Salome to play with on our trip. Most of her time was spent in the company of adults, and we had underestimated how hard that would be for her.

Ava favored pressing on. While Salome missed her friends, Ava reasoned, she was getting to see and do amazing things every day and would have plenty of time to play with her friends when we returned home. Her bottom line to Salome (and me) was "Tough it out. We put too much effort into planning and preparing for this trip to back out now. We quit our jobs and put all of our stuff in storage, and all that would be for nothing." She felt, and rightly so, that if we ended the trip, we would come to regret it as we settled back into our "normal" lives.

Ava agreed, though, that by Sept. 30 (a couple of weeks away) we would evaluate how things were going and decide then whether to pull the plug on our trip.

It didn't help matters, from my perspective, that Ava's mom took Salome's side in all this, and called us an impolite word (think lower rear anatomy) when she learned we had spanked our daughter.

Tantrums aside, we were having a great time in London. We took a day trip to Bath and Stonehenge, the latter a place that had always fascinated me. The mystery of how the ancient Druids had transported those massive slabs of stone hundreds of kilometers endures to this day.

Our first stop was Bath, a pleasant village perched along a scenic river. We toured the ancient Roman baths that gave the town its name, which was interesting, but did become long-drawn. We wandered around, stopping to watch a street performer who stripped off his shirt and enlisted an audience member to help him wind plastic wrap around his body from waist to neck. I found it painful to watch his contortions as he labored to free himself, but Salome seemed to enjoy it.

Our next stop was Stonehenge, which I found disappointing. Although these huge stone slabs have survived for thousands of years, the authorities have apparently determined that allowing tourists too close would cause irreparable harm. So, rope barriers kept us to a path at least 50 yards away from the circular grouping of stone forms, which dates back as early as 3100 BC. Scientists have long debated whether the monument was used primarily for religious or scientific purposes, such as predicting astronomic events.

We did, however, find Stonehenge a nice backdrop as we relaxed on the large surrounding lawn, and Salome got out her "wiggles" by turning cartwheels.

We arrived back in the city about dusk and, based on a tip from the tour guide, decided to stay in town to watch a parade scheduled for later in the evening. The parade was a sight to behold, as hundreds of adults and kids, many on elaborate, multi-colored floats, crossed one of the large bridges that span the Thames River. The floats featured dragons, robots and monsters, accompanied by loud music and flashing lights. Beer flowed freely at the pubs along the riverwalk, so the audience was enthusiastic and cheerful.

We played the tourist role to the hilt in London, visiting Buckingham Palace for the changing of the guard and later touring the Queen's sumptuous digs. Although we had felt very safe walking around London at all hours of the day and night, we got a reality check when horse-mounted police officers rode past us, shouting, "Mind your valuables, there are pickpockets in the crowd!"

Also on our itinerary were the torture implements and gallows at the Tower of London, and Ava and Salome ogled the crown jewels as the moving sidewalk took us past the glittering displays of gold, diamonds, emeralds and rubies.

While we were in London, the a new Harry Potter movie came out, and a premiere was held at Leicester Square, which included an appearance by Daniel Radcliffe, the star of the film.

As we rode the Tube one morning to central London, where we planned to visit Madame Tussaud's Wax Museum, we had our second contact with law enforcement stemming from an argument with Salome. (The first had been in Santiago, Chile).

We were changing trains, and had just stepped onto the platform, when Salome, who was mad at us for some reason, refused to go with us. We tried every means of persuasion, including begging and threats, but she wouldn't budge from the train platform.

We finally walked away and she reluctantly followed. As we walked through the station to catch our connecting train, I heard a voice from behind.

"Excuse me, sir, could we have a word?" said the voice, in its proper English accent.

I turned to see a pair of police officers, one man and one woman, in starched white shirts.

"Is there a problem?" I asked.

"It appears the young lady is upset," said the woman officer, a blonde in her 40s with close-cropped hair as she gestured toward Salome. "We just want to make sure everything's all right."

"We've been having an argument, but now things are settling down," I said. Although I was alarmed to be questioned by the police, at least we would be able to communicate, unlike the incident in Chile.

"Is this your daughter?"

"Yes."

"Do you have any ID that shows she is your daughter?"

"No," I said. We had left Salome's passport back at home.

The woman cop took Salome off to the side to talk to her while her partner talked to Ava and I. We explained that we were on a world trip and that Salome seemed to be acting out because she missed her friends and her familiar surroundings.

After a bit, the woman officer came back and talked with us for a few more minutes. London commuters streamed past us with barely a glance. The cop appeared satisfied that Salome was, in fact, our daughter, and was not in mortal danger. Before letting us go, she pulled Salome aside and told her a secret and made her promise not to tell.

Later, Salome spilled the beans: the cop whispered that she should look closely at the figure of Sleeping Beauty in Madame Tussaud's, and Salome would see her chest move as if she were breathing.

In spite of our encounter with London's finest, we pressed on with our plans, and we were glad we did. We loved the wax museum, hobnobbing with the rich, famous and infamous, from George Clooney to Prince Andrew to Adolf Hitler. Some of the wax figures were very lifelike and uncannily accurate, while others, such as the figure of George W. Bush, missed the mark.

Like everyone else, we snapped photos like crazy. And to Salome's delight, we confirmed the cop's tip about Sleeping Beauty.

On our last night in London, we took Ava's relatives out to dinner to thank them for their hospitality. We settled on a modest eatery in Chinatown near Picadilly Circus, where we sat at a huge round table and feasted on roast duck and other delicacies for the reasonable price – by London standards – of about 75 pounds, or $150.

Then it was time to fly on to our next destination, Bilbao, Spain. Bilbao hadn't been on our original itinerary, but Ava had always wanted to visit there to see the world-famous Guggenheim Musuem. We spent an agonizing afternoon in the British Air ticket office in London while a befuddled clerk reissued our round-the-world air tickets with several changes we had requested. We would arrive in Bilbao in time to celebrate Ava's 47th birthday on Sept. 21 and then fly on to Madrid and Rome.

The evening flight to Bilbao started normally enough, but then degenerated into a big fight with Salome. Ava and I took turns sitting next to her, trying to calm her. By the time we landed, we were getting dirty looks from the flight attendants and other passengers, and I half expected the authorities to meet us at the gate and arrest us for child abuse.

But the bored-looking passport officer barely glanced at us as he stamped our documents and waved us through.

Exhausted after the epic battle on the plane, we sat down to contemplate our next move. It was near midnight, and we hadn't even booked a room.

"I don't know about you," I said to no one in particular, "but I've about had it. I think we should just stay here at the airport, get a flight back to London, and fly home. I can't do this anymore."

It was Sept. 20, 2005, and we had been on the road for just under three months. At that moment, it felt like a lot longer.

Ava didn't say anything for a long time. Then she dropped a bombshell.

"You two go home. I'll go on myself for a while."

Salome started to cry.

"What?" I said, not sure I had heard her correctly.

"I'm not ready to go home. I'll travel for a while longer, then meet you back in San Diego."

"I don't think that's such a good idea. I thought we were all in this together."

We were sitting on the hard tile floor of the large air

terminal, leaning against our pile of bags.

"I'm not ready to go home. I want to go on for a while, by myself."

The reality of our situation began to sink in. We were sitting in the middle of a nearly deserted airport, late at night, in a strange city in Spain we'd never seen before. Our nerves were frazzled from exhaustion and the stress of our most recent battle.

I couldn't imagine going on and dealing with more blowups in planes, trains, buses, taxis, hotel rooms and restaurants. But somehow, we agreed to get a hotel for the night and sleep on it. I got coins for the pay phone and started calling hotels, eventually finding a room for about a hundred euros on the fringe of the city's historic district. We grabbed a cab, checked in and then took off on foot to find some food since we were all starving. The only place we could find open at that late hour was a small kabob shop on a narrow side street. The sandwiches were hot and delicious, and Ava and I washed them down with cold beers. We sat and looked at each other. What had we gotten ourselves into?

As often happens, though, a situation that appears hopeless in the dark of night feels much less daunting by the morning light. In our case, a gorgeous sunny day gave us a better look at the charming city of Bilbao, a modest metropolis of about 350,000 people, in Spain's northern Basque country.

We went out for breakfast, and then began hunting for another hotel; ours was fully booked that night. We wound up at a pension on a cobblestone street in the historic district. We had to lug our bags up a couple of flights of stairs and pound on a heavy wooden door until the proprietor, looking sleepy, let us in. The price was right, only 60 euros, and it was clean and centrally located. Just a couple of doors down was a post office and across the street was a tiny pet shop where we often stopped so Ava and Salome could make faces at the puppies and kittens.

The reason we came to Bilbao was to see the Guggenheim Museum, which was designed by architect Frank Gehry, who also created Disney Symphony Hall in Los Angeles.

The Guggenheim is located next to the Nervion River, which runs through the center of town. Each morning during our stay in Bilbao, I ran along the riverfront path that led past the famous museum.

We found during our visit to the Guggenheim that the building itself was much more impressive than the actual art collection inside. The exterior is a conglomeration of metallic surfaces, lines and curves, awe-inspiring when juxtaposed against Bilbao's brilliant blue sky. A giant topiary dog greeted us at the entrance, its colorful leaves and flowers a stark contrast with the harsh titanium surface of the building behind it.

The interior of the museum was equally stunning, with large, light, airy spaces lined with warm beige limestone as high as the eye could see. We read that the machines used to cut the limestone blocks into such unusual curved and linear shapes – which fit together seamlessly – had been guided by computers rather than the hands of stonemasons.

Beyond the museum entrance, also overlooking the river, was what Salome called "the coolest playground in the world." This fanciful play space included huge climbing nets, bridges, and spinning, sliding and swinging rides. Everything was decorated in bright red, blue, green and yellow. The playground was surrounded by green lawns, a perfect place for parents to snooze in the sun while their children played.

For Ava's birthday dinner, we went to a local eatery that featured a complete dinner special, including appetizer, tasty steaks, red wine, and cake for desert. We lingered over our food, and after dinner, Ava and Salome went up to the room while I wandered around the neighborhood, stopping in for beers at a few local watering holes. I was pleased to hear one of my favorite Los Lobos CDs, The Neighborhood, blasting from the speakers of one café.

I drank a bit too much, and tipsily called my brother from a pay phone at a hip bar decorated with lots of candles, contemporary art and aquariums near our hotel.

The next morning, on my run, I noticed what appeared to be several bicycle rental stands set up along the river walk. They turned out to be part of a family festival taking place in Bilbao that day, and the bikes were free for anyone who wanted to pedal along the river for an hour. So, I rousted Ava and Salome and we went for a bike ride under a cloudless blue sky.

The central square had been turned into a children's wonderland, with a soccer game, drawing contest, stilt walking and other activities. People in period costumes demonstrated antique bicycles and posed for pictures, and a miniature raceway was set up for pedal-powered go-carts. Everything was free, and Salome got to play games with other kids, even if she was too shy to interact much.

In the afternoon, busloads of schoolchildren rolled up and the festival quickly got very crowded.

Although we had arrived in Bilbao in disarray a few days earlier, our family on the verge of splitting up, by the time we left our mood was much improved and we looked forward to our next stop, Madrid.

Our itinerary called for only three days in the Spanish capital, before flying on to Rome. Because we were traveling through Western Europe without a guidebook, we had to arrange for hotels at each destination, usually from the airport. After finding a hotel in central Madrid, we took a taxi into town. It was a warm, muggy afternoon, and we got stuck in rush hour traffic. Our driver was friendly and talkative, and when we told him our next stop was Rome, he remarked that, "Spanish people are much nicer."

Our hotel was on the top floor of an office building, and we had to ring a bell at the front door to be buzzed in. Our room was large and generally clean, although the furnishings were well-worn and the beds were creaky and not very comfortable. With the windows open, the traffic from the busy roads below drifted up, as did the conversations of the people heading into and out of swanky hotels and restaurants across the street. The nights were warm enough that we asked the front desk clerk to give us a fan for our room, which he did.

The hotel was around the corner from a wide boulevard with a children's park in the middle; down the street was the world-famous Prado art museum. Over Salome's protests, we spent an afternoon in the museum and enjoyed viewing paintings by masters such as El Greco, Goya, Reubens and Rembrandt.

We also walked over to Retiro park and rented a row boat to paddle around a man-made lake.

We sat at outdoor cafes and tasted the city's famed tapas and wine. I took Salome to the playground, but it only made her homesick when she watched the other children playing together and chattering happily in Spanish. I tried to get her to play with the kids, but her heart wasn't in it. We had a talk, and she told me that even though she was missing her friends, she was determined that if we cut the trip short, it would be a mutual decision, and not because of her behavior. I took it to mean that she was going to try hard to make things work, and I felt optimistic as we walked back to our hotel.

We were strolling along the street that night when I heard a commotion behind me. A young man came up and said, "You'd better be careful, that boy was going to steal your wallet."

Salome said she, too, had seen the boy sizing up my back pocket for a shoplifting opportunity. I hadn't noticed anything, but wasn't too worried because I kept my wallet in my front pants pocket, secured with a zipper and a Velcro flap. My most important documents, such as my passport and credit cards, were kept in a money belt under my clothes. While we had heard many stories of tourists being victimized by pickpockets, I was determined not to be one of them.

We covered as much ground as we could in the couple of days we had in Madrid, and all too soon it was time to move on again. This time our destination was Rome, where we planned to spend about five days. After this flight we would be earthbound for a while, traveling by train through Germany, Austria, the Czech Republic and Poland. We had thought about visiting other parts of Italy, such as Venice, but it didn't really fit in with our plans, which included meeting friends in Munich for Oktoberfest.

Our flight to Rome from Madrid was early on a Sunday morning, so it was still dark outside when the telephone in our room rang with a wakeup call. As the dawn suffused the city with a grayish light and our taxi rolled through the streets on our way to the airport, hundreds of young Madrilenos could be seen in every direction, making their way home after dancing and partying all night. The looks on their faces said they were tired, but contented. I envied them slightly as we drove toward the airport.

The bad thing about an early flight is having to rise before the sun; the good thing is arriving at your destination early in the day, which is especially helpful if, a) you've never been there before; b) you haven't booked a hotel room; and c) you didn't even have a guidebook to help you find a room or get oriented to the city.

As far as airports go, Rome's wasn't much different than most of the others we had passed through so far on our trip.

Passport control and customs were perfunctory; my pre-trip fears of being grilled at each new country about my diabetes and blood-pressure medications turned out to be groundless. In fact, in nearly every country we had visited, we were waved through customs. If the customs section was manned – many times it was not – the officers usually seemed bored and never asked to look inside our bags, which always came as a big relief, even though I wasn't smuggling anything. About the most that happened at any customs station was that our bags were passed through an X-ray machine, as they had been before we boarded the plane.

Once we cleared passport control and customs in Rome, we grabbed a bite and headed for the tourist information booth to find out about hotels.

As often happened at airport tourist booths, Rome's wasn't very helpful. The girl who sat behind the counter stared straight ahead with a glazed look in her eyes. When I asked about a room, she reached under the counter and handed me a booklet without even looking at me. Okay, I thought, we'll have to do this on our own.

"Do you have a map of the city?" I asked.

She handed me a one-page map of the city center with highlights such as the Coliseum and Vatican City well-marked.

"Can you suggest a good place for us to stay?" I asked, still hopeful.

She pointed at the booklet she had handed me earlier.

A dapper, silver-haired man in a dark blue blazer approached. Apparently, he was also connected with the tourist bureau. He explained that most of the reasonably priced hotels and hostels were booked up. He gave me a quick crash course on the layout of the city and told me that some of the best hotel deals hotels could be found near the central train station. If we got stuck, he said, he knew of a place about 20 minutes by metro or bus from the city center, for about 100 euros a night, or about $120 U.S. I thanked him and decided to try my luck at the hotel bureau counter. These agencies can be found in most airports; they offer rooms at select hotels and require a steep deposit for a reservation. Getting a deal at one of those places was next to impossible, but I was nearing desperation, so I got in line.

When I came up to the counter, I got a taste of the Italian flair for the dramatic.

"It's a tragedy!" said the woman behind the counter, placing the back of her hand against her forehead. "Everything is booked. But I can get you something for 150 euros."

Ava and I decided to regroup at this point. We took turns sitting with Salome in the cafeteria and – armed with the hotel list and a prepaid phone card – worked the nearby bank of payphones to find reasonably priced accommodations. We came up with a couple of possibilities; the best price was for a hotel near the train station, but I was nervous because the man at the tourist booth said that area was rough.

So, we settled on a place close to the famed Spanish Steps and a metro station. The cost was almost enough to make us gasp: 130 euros per night, or over $150 U.S., for a room in a pension with a shared bath. The place did have an elevator, though, and offered a decent free breakfast, so we snapped it up.

The hotel turned out to be a bit old-fashioned in a pleasing way, with fixtures and furnishings dating back several decades. The elevator was tiny, with hand-operated inner and outer gates. When Ava brought Big Bertha on board, the elevator groaned and lurched before starting up. I took the stairs.

The staff was also long in the tooth. The maid assigned to our floor was a gray-haired woman who wore a long skirt covered by an apron and kept her hair in a bun. She was also apparently the backup electrician – when I called the front desk to report a broken reading light, she showed up, screwdriver in hand. She made us very nervous when she dismantled the light fixture and poked around in the wiring without turning off the power. After a while, when she couldn't get it to work, she began muttering in Italian, and then left. The next day, the hotel sent the real electrician to fix the light.

The best thing about our hotel was that it was right next to a gelato shop. Say what you will about Rome – its noisy traffic, snooty locals and high prices can be enough to send you packing. But Romans make the best ice cream I've ever tasted. A gelato shop in Rome is a sensory experience, with overflowing pans of the creamy stuff lined up in all hues of the rainbow, making it very difficult to choose a flavor. The gelato is served in linebacker-sized portions, in cones or bowls.

The pizza was also delicious and relatively cheap. Rome had an abundance of corner pizza shops, where customers selected slices from different varieties displayed in glass cases. The counterman then popped the slice into an oven to crisp it, and served it on a paper plate with an ice cold soft drink. The shops offered a fast, tasty lunch usually eaten standing up.

In fact, pizza was one of the few foods that we came across in nearly every country we visited on our trip, along with Chinese food and McDonald's.

In Rome, we planned to hit the highlights, such as the Coliseum and the Vatican, wander around the ruins of the Forum, and feel the spray from some of the Eternal

City's famous fountains. We ogled at the buildings, many of which looked like they came right out of history books with their ornate facades and bay windows. Even the traffic was worth watching: at every intersection in central Rome, a phalanx of motorbikes occupied the front rows of vehicles before the light changed from red to green. Their small engines created a humming chorus that revved up several decibels when the light turned green. Their riders wore all manner of clothes, from snappy business suits and designer dresses to leather jackets. Safety trumped fashion in one regard: nearly all the riders wore helmets. After the motorbikes roared past in a pack, the cars, buses, trucks and bicycles followed.

During our first evening in Rome, we strolled to the Spanish Steps, made famous by several movies and popular songs. We found the steps packed with teenage couples, either making out or drinking from bottles in brown paper bags. At the bottom of the steps was a boat-shaped fountain, where many tourists were having their picture taken while drinking from cupped palms. We didn't know what was behind the tradition, but we followed suit. As they say, when in Rome... We found out the next day that although the local police may turn the other way when it comes to drinking wine, they strictly enforce the rules against eating. An officer approached with wagging finger as we tried to down a couple of slices of pizza while perched on the famous steps.

The hotel desk staff was friendly and warned us that if we planned to see the Vatican, we should get there early because the line quickly builds up to an hours-long proposition. So, early the next morning, we hauled ourselves out of bed and caught the Metro over to the Vatican stop. When we arrived, about an hour before opening, the line stretched back 50 yards or so. We took turns holding our spot and having pastries and coffee at the café across the street. By 9 a.m., when the gates opened, the line stretched back around the corner, at least a quarter-mile away.

Not only did we get inside the entrance to the Vatican Musuem in a matter of minutes, but we rushed through the closed ticket booths. It was International Museum Day, a holiday we had never heard of, and entrance was free!

Our goal was to see the Sistine Chapel, which is considered by some art experts to contain the greatest masterpiece ever painted, Michelangelo's The Last Judgment. This monumental painting covers the back wall of the chapel, above the altar. The figures of Jesus and his saints, elevating some people to heaven and sending others to the nether regions, were so lifelike and full of passion, nearly 500 years after they were painted. Michelangelo even painted himself into the one of the scenes, as a human skin without flesh and bones, drooping from a saint's hand.

Even more famous are Michelangelo's paintings on the ceiling of the chapel, depicting some 300 biblical characters and scenes such as the Garden of Eden and the Great Flood.

As we toured through the lavishly decorated halls and exhibits, Salome kept asking, "Is this the Sistine Chapel?" We said no, it was coming, and that she should enjoy all the treasures we were seeing (including jewelry, clothing, sculptures and paintings). Through the windows, we caught glimpses of Vatican City, most of which was off-limits to tourists.

Finally, we made our way into the Sistine Chapel, which was packed with visitors. We tried to find a spot where we could relax a bit and gaze up at the ceiling, tapestries and The Last Judgment while listening to the commentary on the audio players provided by the museum.

Salome was impressed, but her captivation was short-lived.

"Can we leave now?" she asked just a few minutes after we arrived.

Reluctantly, after spending a half-hour or so in the dim chapel, warmed by the proximity of so many bodies, we made our way back outside and continued our tour. When we finished with the Vatican Museum, we walked outside and followed the line around the corner and down the street to St. Peter's Square. We were shocked to see the line to enter the Vatican Museum had grown to literally a mile long. We felt especially sorry for the last person in line, a dark-haired, middle-aged woman, who probably didn't make it in before closing.

The line to see the inside of St. Peter's Basilica was almost as long, and none of us had much appetite for waiting. So, we hung out in the square for a bit, people-watched and snapped a few photos, and headed back to our hotel.

The next morning, we set out on a quest: to wash our laundry. Throughout our trip to this point, we had relied on a variety of means to clean our clothes, from hand-washing in the hotel sink to using a hotel laundry service, to finding the odd self-serve laundry.

After short ride on the Metro, we emerged from underground just around the corner from a Laundromat suggested by our hotel. We found out that washing clothes – even in a self-service laundry – is no cheaper than anything else in Rome: including soap flakes, wash and dry, it cost us about $30 U.S. for two loads of laundry.

While the clothes were washing, we took Salome around the corner to a café, where we sat down to do some schoolwork. The night before, we had finished The Lion, the Witch and the Wardrobe, and she was writing a book report about it.

We were also trying to keep up with popular culture, Hollywood style, as we traveled. We would see ads for the newest movies, even if they were in foreign languages, so we knew which films were current. That summer, Tim Burton's take on Charlie and the Chocolate Factory starring Johnny Depp was all the rage. We found a theater where the film was playing in English and settled down with popcorn and soft drinks. It was a weekday afternoon, and the huge theater, which even had stadium-style seats, was empty except for us and two men who sat in the row in front of us. One of them leaned back and said, "You are sitting in our seats, but don't worry, it's not a problem."

I looked at the tickets, and sure enough, there were row and seat numbers stamped on them. We had never been to a movie theater with reserved seats before, but it seemed nitpicky to make an issue of this when the auditorium was almost empty. We just smiled and acted like clueless tourists, which we were, and waited for the lights to dim. Although I had always been a huge Gene Wilder fan, and couldn't see how his performance as Willie Wonka could be improved upon, I had to admit that Johnny Depp put his own stamp of zaniness on the role. We all enjoyed the movie a lot, and headed out afterward smiling into the streets of Rome.

We did enjoy a taste of Rome's finer cuisine as well, at a cozy little restaurant around the corner from our hotel. We ordered different salads and pasta dishes, along with a carafe of house wine, and shared them. The waiters were so friendly and accommodating, we ended up eating there both of our last two nights in the city. We especially liked the outdoor tables, which were perfect for people-watching on the warm September evenings.

We would be traveling next to Munich, and I wanted to avoid the problem we had faced the last time we visited there in 2002. On the earlier trip, we had arrived in Munich on a Friday night, the final weekend of Oktoberfest, without a hotel reservation. A shady character in front of the station offered us a room in a private house nearby, but we passed, imagining what it would be like to bring a small child to stay in a house full of drunken Oktoberfest revelers.

Instead, we had pulled out our guidebook and called every hotel in it from a pay phone in the train station. Each time we were told "sorry, all the rooms are booked." Finally, I dialed the last hotel on the list, and bingo, they had a cancellation and one room was available. It cost twice the usual rate, but at least we had a place to stay.

This time, we would once again arrive during the final weekend of the annual beer and music festival. So, I wore out my fingers on a pay phone in Rome shopping for rooms. I had to patch together reservations at three different hotels to cover our eight-day stay. We also went to Rome's modern, sprawling train station to book a compartment on an overnight sleeper to Munich. The price tag for the three tickets? A whopping 395 euros, or nearly $500 U.S.

On our last day in Rome, we took a taxi to the train station and checked our luggage, since our train didn't leave until evening. The stuffy, windowless luggage room was in the basement of the train station. Two workers on duty methodically X-rayed each bag before tagging it and tossing it on the pile to be stored, making no effort to speed up in spite of the long line of passengers waiting somewhat irritably. We made it up to the counter in about an hour and then gladly escaped the dungeon-like basement.

Even though it was our last day in Rome and we had already seen most of the major tourist attractions, we were feeling lazy, so we bought tickets for a city tour on a double-decker bus. Passengers were allowed hop off and on the bus at pre-determined stops, but mostly we just stayed on board as the bus looped around central Rome. The day was warm and muggy, but it was pleasant to sit on top of the bus and watch the city roll by.

After a couple of hours, our tour bus completed its rounds and dropped us back at the train station. We went across the road to a market, where we stocked up on munchies and drinks for the trip to Munich, which would take about 12 hours. We retrieved our luggage, which thankfully took only a few minutes, and called home from a pay phone before it was time to board the train.

Our sleeping accommodations on the train were first-class. We had a private compartment with a locking door and three bunks along one wall. Each bunk was made up with blankets and pillows and had its own reading light. Over the door was a luggage rack, which held only a couple of our bags. There was a small sink and the train staff had provided toiletries for our use. The window actually opened and was equipped with a blackout shade.

Salome was beside herself with excitement about her first overnight sleeper train. She immediately claimed the top bunk and clambered up the ladder with her favorite stuffed animal. Later she came down and we played cards while Ava and I sipped wine from plastic cups.

The bunks were very comfortable, and we all slept well, rocked by the gentle swaying of the train as it rolled through northern Italy during the night.

In the morning, the conductor knocked on the door and gave us a tray with cappuccinos and warm pastries.

We reached Munich about 8:30 a.m., which meant we didn't have to get up from our bunks too early. The train station was familiar; the last time we'd seen it, there'd been plenty of happy Germans traipsing around in lederhosen and singing at the top of their lungs. This time, it was crowded, but a bit more subdued. Munich's central station, like the station in Rome, is a self-contained city with rows of shops, ATMs and food counters, with their mouth-watering wares laid out in glass cases. There were pastries, sausages, pastas and salads, not to mention candy stores and even a Burger King on the second floor.

We called our hotel from the station, using the same pay phone we had used on our last trip, and were pleasantly surprised that the hotel was only a five-minute walk from the station. Even with Big Bertha, we didn't have any problem walking there once we located the correct street.

We checked in, and while they were getting our room ready, we went to a bakery café across the street to eat breakfast and help Salome with her schoolwork. Ava and I were relieved that – by the time we reached Munich – Salome had been off the medication for a month and seemed to have regained control over her emotions. Although we still argued over schoolwork and other issues, she didn't get as angry, and she calmed down much more quickly. The worst of the emotional storms affecting our family had definitely passed.

We were looking forward to Munich because we had really enjoyed it the last time around; the city is friendly, with good food and beer, and plenty of interesting sights and neighborhoods to check out. Oktoberfest has carnival rides, games, entertainment and all manner of tasty junk food, and the added attraction of 7 or 8 massive beer tents that hold as many as 3,000 to 4,000 revelers apiece.

We were also looking forward to meeting our friends Michael J. and O and their friends from Munich, Andy and Inge. We planned to visit Neuchwanstein, the famous castle built by "Mad" King Ludwig in the late 1800s, which served as the inspiration for Disneyland's fairy castle. If time permitted, we wanted to take visit Schliersee, the picture-book village next to a lake about an hour outside of Munich, where we had stayed during our last visit.

Unfortunately, the weather in Munich during Oktoberfest is often overcast, rainy and cold. The fall of 2005 was no exception. On our second day in town, we joined up with our friends at the famed festival grounds. A steady rain fell and the beer tents – mammoth structures that accommodate a sea of picnic tables inside, with a bandstand on a platform in the middle – were packed full. Even though one of our friends supposedly had connections inside the Lowenbrau tent, we were shut out, unable to get inside the tents or get a table.

So we opted for the next best thing: a restaurant across the street from the fairgrounds that featured – who would have thought? – liters of beer in large glass mugs. Close enough for us.

The next morning, slightly hungover, we changed hotels for the second time in our Munich stay, to a family-run place called Pension Westfalia, a bed and breakfast directly across from the Oktoberfest grounds. The pension was up on the third and fourth floors of a large old building that looked a bit like the Addams Family house. It sat in an overgrown yard surrounded by a wrought-iron fence. To get up to the pension, we had to load our bags onto the tiny, boxlike elevator, push the button and hope for the best.

At night, it was creepy entering the place, because the yard and downstairs foyer were completely dark.

But we found the pension room itself to be bright, airy and clean, with a newly remodeled bathroom and comfy beds. Breakfast was croissants, cereal, fruit and coffee, served by the proprietor, a friendly man in his 50s who spent his free time hiking in the countryside. His wife, also very friendly, told us not to miss an attraction called the "Devil's Wheel" when we visited Oktoberfest on the last day of the festival.

We got settled into the hotel, then called Andy and Inge on their cell phone.

"Come over to the Lowenbrau tent," they said. "We've got a table."

The final day of Oktoberfest fell on a Monday, and Andy had told us it was the best day to go because most tourists – many from Italy and other parts of Europe – would have taken off for home, leaving the party to the locals.

When we got inside the Lowenbrau tent around noon, we found Andy, Inge, Michael J. and O crowded into one of the long picnic tables that filled up the floor area. We squeezed in, without too much complaint from the people sitting next to us. Thanks to the efficient barmaid, we soon had hefty mugs of beer sitting on the table in front of us. (Salome had a one-liter Sprite.)

Andy was lean with a shaved head. He worked with computers and had a cheerful, upbeat demeanor. He told me the day before, over beers, that he absolutely loved visiting America and felt like kissing the ground each time he arrived in the U.S. He said he had been spending his vacations in the U.S. so often that his co-workers teased him. However, he said his ties to Germany were strong and he had no desire to emigrate. He just loved the culture of the U.S., along with the food, music and the vast open spaces.

Inge was small, with brownish-blonde hair and a pretty smile. She worked as a child psychologist and had roomed with Michael J. in San Diego during college.

Michael J. Williams is a buddy from my newspapering days. He can come across as very serious, but his sense of humor often breaks through, especially after a beer or two. An accomplished guitarist, trumpeter and songwriter,

Michael is musically adventurous and has even taught himself to play the can, a flutelike Thai instrument. His first loves, musically, are jazz and blues.

His wife, Marinnee, or O (her Thai nickname), is a native of Bangkok. Her cooking skills are legendary among our friends, and anyone who gets a dinner invitation when she is preparing her native cuisine is loathe to turn it down. She works as an R.N., and she and Ava, who also is an R.N., often compare notes.

We planned to meet Michael J. and O once again in Bangkok after the first of the year, but our troubles with Salome's behavior and my own homesickness had caused me to question whether our trip would last that long.

But as we sat at the table in the Oktoberfest tent on that cool, drizzly fall day in 2005, the beer flowing like water (at 6 euros per one-liter mug), all was well with the world. The oompah band cranked out traditional German beer hall ditties and we got chummy with everyone sitting nearby. Ava and I took turns escorting Salome out to the carnival zone to play games, go on rides and sample the sausages, candy-coated pecans and other delicacies.

The plan was to spend a few hours in the Lowenbrau tent, then strike out to see the sights of Munich. At least, that's what we Americans thought. The Germans, however, had other ideas.

Michael J. suggested finishing our beers and taking off.

Andy would look at him earnestly.

"We can do whatever you want," Andy said. "But I need to tell you, if we leave, we probably won't be able to get our spot back."

Then somebody would order another round, and Michael J.'s plan would be put on hold for just a bit.

At one point, we had drained our glasses and were about to take off when some new friends sitting next to us announced they were leaving, and gave us several free beer coupons.

Andy looked truly apologetic.

"Now we cannot leave. We must use these tickets," he said, which seemed very logical and perfectly obvious. Duh.

As the afternoon wore on, the band heated up. It turned out that the best way to enjoy the music, and celebrate Oktoberfest, was to climb up on the wooden tables and lose your inhibitions. Dance, baby.

You really haven't lived until you have stood on a wooden table with a giant glass of beer in one hand, swaying and singing "Roll Out the Barrel," and "New York, New York," with thousands of happy Germans. Musically, the highlights for me were John Denver's "Take Me Home, Country Roads" and Johnny Cash's "Ring of Fire." I was surprised the crowd knew all the words to these American standards. Ava, Salome and I left at 8 p.m., after eight hours in the beer tent. We learned the next day that our friends had gone the distance, remaining at the table until midnight, when the last beer was served and the massive tent went quiet, signaling the end of the Oktoberfest. I was sorry to hear we had missed the finale of "Hey Jude."

But we didn't leave before checking out the "Devil's Wheel," one of the oddest fair attractions I have come across.

The "Devil's Wheel" was housed in a large tent. It consisted of a large circular wooden platform surrounded by bleachers that rose to the top of the tent, which were packed with hooting spectators.

The idea was that as many people as possible would cram onto the polished wooden platform, which began to spin fast enough to make the players' faces blur. Soon, these players would begin sliding off the spinning circle, to the delight of the crowd. The only people left on the wheel would be a ring of stubborn survivors, who sat with their backs together, arms linked.

Then the next level of torture began. A large, round weight bag was lowered on a rope, aimed at the people in the center of the wheel, and let fly, as the wheel continued spinning. Some of the surviving players managed to duck, but each time the game was played, the big bag found its mark a couple of times, sending players careening off the wheel.

If there were still any survivors at this point, they faced the final test, as fair workers to lasso them and pull them off the ride. The whole thing seemed to be about the enjoyment of the crowd at the expense of the hapless volunteers on the wheel. If one or two people managed to remain on the wheel for the entire ordeal, they were proclaimed winners, but from what we could see, they were awarded no prizes for their heroic efforts. Every three or four cycles, they had a special round just for kids, when the staffers wielded the big weight bag just a little more gently. Salome gamely took her turn and ended up as one of the last three or four kids on the wheel.

When we left the fairgrounds, we escorted Ava back to the pension, then Salome and I walked down the street to a

McDonald's packed with revelers. I was broke, so Salome loaned me some euros and we ordered burgers and fries.

"Daddy, you are really drunk," Salome observed helpfully.

We met our friends early the next morning at the central train station for the ride to Neuschwanstein. We were all subdued on the train, either reflecting on our journey or, more likely, in pain from the previous day's indulgence.

The castle sits high on a forested hill and has awesome views from its windows and walkways. It was well worth the trip to see how King Ludwig had run through his treasury while lavishly decorating his creation with tapestries, wood carvings and gold leaf. Tragically, he lived in the castle for just two years before his body turned up in a nearby lake under mysterious circumstances. At the time of Ludwig's death in 1886, the castle remained incomplete.

Our whole group was pretty wiped out when our train pulled into Munich that night after our tour of Neuschwanstein. We said goodbye to our old and new friends, promising to stay in touch with Michael J. and O and to let them know whether we would make it to Bangkok the following January to meet them as planned.

Ava, Salome and I took the subway the next morning to Munich Central Station, which we were getting to know like the back of our hands. There, we bought tickets for the "BOB" train, which ran every hour to a series of small villages south of the city. Our destination was Schliersee, a pretty little village next to a blue lake, surrounded by forested hills. In the fall, the foliage turned orange, yellow and red, making the town look even more like it been drawn by a German counterpart of Norman Rockwell.

Salome was excited about going back to Schliersee, mostly because of an amusement park that was built on a mountaintop overlooking the town. There were two ways up to the top – taking a sky tram, or walking up a meandering road that passed grazing cows, goats and feisty ducks. The views became increasingly spectacular as the road neared the summit. I especially enjoyed watching a train slowly chug around the distant lake, the church steeple and chimney smoke in the foreground.

At the top was a small resort that featured a hotel, a restaurant and an amusement park. The activities included a trampoline, a small coin-operated roller coaster that rode on a hilly, circular track, and a sort of luge ride that ran back to the bottom of the mountain. The luge ride consisted of a green plastic half-pipe that twisted and turned through the forest for at least a mile down the mountain. Riders sat on a flat, wheeled cart with a handle that came up through their legs. Pulling up on the handle released the brakes and made the cart go faster; and letting go activated the brakes. Salome and Ava rode together while I brought up the rear on my own cart. As soon as Salome and Ava took off, it was apparent that Salome was terrified. She screamed and cried, even though she had begged earlier to go on the ride. Somehow, they made it to the bottom without incident. I came along behind them, putting on the brakes when it seemed the little cart was likely to careen off the track at a sharp curve. Somehow, without my noticing, my pants leg had hiked up, causing my leg to rub on the side of the plastic track. By the time I reached the bottom, I had a nasty road rash.

We wandered around the town and then walked to the

lake, where Salome played on a playground, and Ava and I sat on a bench and watched, sipping pear brandy from a family-run distillery we discovered on our last trip. The lakeshore was tranquil that day, but we reminisced about our previous trip, when several horses escaped from their corral and made for the church cemetery, where they had feasted on flowers until the exasperated owner came to round them up.

For our last full day in Munich, we rented bicycles and rode through the city to the famed English Gardens. We had already been on two different walking tours of central Munich, which focused on many former Nazi sights, including Hitler's Nazi party headquarters building, the square where Hitler once led an unsuccessful coup attempt against a group of policemen, and the Hofbrau House, a famous beer hall where the Nazi dictator had given speeches during his rise to power.

So, we were up for something a little different and the English Gardens fit the bill. The map provided by the bike rental shop was more confusing than helpful, so we took off pedaling in the general direction of the gardens without a clear idea of how to get there. We found ourselves dodging buses, cars, pedestrians and bikes on the busy city streets.

After a few wrong turns, we finally made it to the gardens, which are expansive, beautifully landscaped and maze-like, with many different paths crisscrossing and winding past each other. We rode through forested areas, past green meadows, and came to a lake in the center of the park, where Salome fed the cranky geese and ducks. When we returned our bikes to the rental shop at the central train station, we bought train tickets for our next destination, the central Austrian town of Schladming, where we had booked a week in a timeshare condo. By then it was early October, and the air was crisp and a bit chilly, although we still enjoyed some sunny days in Munich and later, Austria.

The Munich station was one of the most user-friendly we encountered during our trip. An information desk was dedicated solely to answering travelers' questions and providing them with individualized itineraries for where they needed to go, including connecting trains and alternative schedules. Once you had obtained the itinerary from the information desk, you simply brought it to the ticket counter and bought your ticket. While other cities had such an information desk, Munich's was by far the most efficient and friendly.

The night before our departure from Munich, Ava and Salome went back to our hotel to pack and I went to a tiny hole-in-the-wall jazz club I had spotted earlier. The club was possibly the smallest I had ever been in, but its bar was very elegant, with a mahogany top and shiny brass fixtures. The barman – and owner – was a black man named Anthony who had moved to Munich from the Bronx, New York. After a while, the members of a jazz trio arrived and set up on a postage-stamp sized stage. Anthony had owned the club for several years and attracted a loyal clientele, many of whom traveled from across the city to soak up the vibe and the music. After a couple of beers, I headed back to finish my own packing and get ready for Eastern Europe, where we would be spending the next three weeks.

Chapter 7

Say Aaaaaahhhh!

The Blue Cross representative sounded so calm and friendly – his earnest desire to help radiated through the phone. He really seemed to want to sell us a family health insurance policy. I almost felt bad for him as we worked through his questionnaire, peeling away the layers of our checkered health history. I could almost see the smile fading from his lips a little more each time I answered a question, revealing yet another health condition that afflicted a member of our family. Me, with my litany of ailments past and present, including cancer, diabetes and high-blood pressure. Ava, who has asthma, and has dealt with various and sundry other conditions in the past.

What had started out with so much hope and promise was rapidly turning into a downer – as far as Blue Cross was concerned, I was banned for life from purchasing a policy on the open market. Ava's chances of being covered were slim to none.

My heart sank as I hung up. This, I thought, could be a deal-killer for our world trip.

In the months before we left, I sat at my desk for many hours, planning the details – searching for air tickets, booking hotels, reserving space on cruises and hiking expeditions. One of my most important tasks was to find an affordable health insurance policy that would cover us in the event of a serious illness or injury during our year of overseas travel.

I had assumed – in retrospect a naïve, even dangerous mind-set – that I would simply pick up the phone, call a few health insurance companies and pick the best, most cost-effective policy. After that initial conversation with Blue Cross, I realized we would need a "Plan B." What I took away from my research was that anyone who had ever stepped foot in a doctor's office, let alone been diagnosed with any illness or condition, faced long odds against finding a reasonably priced policy.

As is the case for most working Americans, since adulthood, I have always received health insurance through my employer. Since Ava and I intended to quit our jobs to travel the world, we would not have what I came to regard as the luxury of employer-sponsored health insurance. We were on our own, a cold and lonely place to be when it comes to health insurance in the United States.

After ruling out insurance on the open market, I called the hospital where Ava worked to find out about the COBRA plan, an option that allows employees to purchase the same policy they received from their employer for up to 18 months after leaving their job. The only catch is that once a worker leaves his or her job, the employer no longer helps pay for the policy.

In our case, a year of coverage under Ava's employer-provided health insurance would have cost $15,000, about three times what I had budgeted. And the coverage for illness and accidents occurring outside the U.S. was paltry.

I knew we had to come up with something fast or our trip was in trouble.

I hit the Internet to research our options and found a few possibilities. One was a program run by the state of California for people deemed "high risk" by the insurance industry; in other words, anyone who had ever suffered more than a common cold.

In desperation, I made an appointment with an insurance broker from our area, who turned out to be our savior. This man suggested that because I was self-employed as a freelance writer, I might be able to qualify for a small-business policy that would act like an employer sponsored plan, meaning we would not be disqualified for what the insurance industry has so politely labeled as "pre-existing conditions." He advised me to get a city business license and open a business checking account. While some insurance companies require a company to be incorporated with the state before it qualifies for a group health insurance policy, the broker found us a company that would accept my documentation.

Through this arrangement, I was able to purchase a basic policy – with a relatively high deductible – that would cover us in the event of a catastrophic illness, for around $6,000 for the year.

The next item on my health punch list was travel insurance. The plan was that our basic health insurance policy would cover us in case of a major illness or injury, after we paid a steep deductible. I figured that we could pay out of pocket for any doctor visit or minor medical issue that came up during our travels. But I wanted to make sure we could get back home for treatment in case we got seriously sick, which is where the travel policy came in. I searched for a policy that would cover the costs of medical evacuation, meaning transportation from wherever we got sick or injured to a place where we could get good care, including, if needed, a medical flight back to the U.S.

After researching a number of different travel insurance companies, I settled on a policy with World Nomads, an online company based in Australia. For $1,000, our family was covered for a year; the policy included several features designed to soothe the nerves of anxious travelers like me. The World Nomads policy included access to a 24-hour, 365-day-a-year emergency center that we could contact if we had an illness or injury. The center was set up with a list of international phone numbers, so theoretically, we could call for help wherever we happened to be, whenever we needed help. The center was tasked with arranging transportation and other services for its policyholders.

We were also able, through World Nomads, to register our itinerary and receive emergency bulletins by email in case of a natural or manmade disaster in a place where we were headed. We were also able to submit questions to the security service as we traveled, and file claims online.

Before embarking on our trip, we all had physicals and dental checkups while we were still covered by our insurance. We made an appointment at a travel clinic, where each of us rolled up our sleeves and got vaccinations against such dreaded diseases as typhoid, hepatitis A and B, yellow fever and tetanus. It took a lot of tears, cajoling, bribery and armlocks by us and the nurse, but we even managed to make sure Salome got her shots.

Because there is no vaccine for malaria, we analyzed our itinerary with the help of the travel clinic and determined that that only place we needed to take preventive anti-malarial drugs was India, a destination we wouldn't reach until several months into our trip. The clinic wrote us prescriptions for anti-malarial drugs, but we didn't fill them before we left, which was probably a mistake. Later, as time grew short before our arrival in India, we scrambled to find the drugs in the Czech Republic and Poland, countries where the occurrence of malaria is nearly non-existent, meaning the drugs were almost impossible to find. In London, our last stop before Mumbai, we managed to find the drugs we needed in the nick of time. We would have been much better off if we had bought our drugs before leaving home – it would have saved us a lot of stress and anxiety.

We tried to stock up on the drugs we needed for our chronic conditions, such as diabetes and high blood pressure for me, and asthma for Ava. But it would have been too cumbersome to carry a year's worth of medications in our small suitcases, so we planned on restocking our medications as we traveled. We each obtained a stack of prescriptions for our needed drugs, which I carried with my important travel documents. As is turned out, we had no problem getting our drugs on the road and were rarely asked to produce a prescription. Throughout South America, India and other parts of Asia, pharmacies were readily available and our meds were nearly always in stock at very reasonable prices, at or below what our co-pay would have been under our health plan's prescription drug coverage. In most of the places we traveled, we were even able to find Ava's nicotine gum, which she used to quit smoking.

I got pretty good at walking up to a pharmacy counter in whatever country we were visiting at the time and either writing down the medications I needed or giving my order to the clerk verbally. In India, the pharmacies were found along the streets of most commercial districts, wedged between shops selling every type of goods, from groceries to clothing. The counter of the narrow, deep shop was usually set up right at the edge of the sidewalk under the shade of an awning, and the clerk would duck back between shelves stacked with boxes of drugs to find the needed item. Getting our medications was certainly easier in India or Brazil than it would have been in the U.S.

Over all, we were very fortunate to enjoy excellent health during our trip. The occasions when we needed medical attention were few and far between. At various times, all three of us suffered from minor stomach irritations, but they never lasted long or knocked us off our feet. As much as possible, I tried to follow the advice given to me by an Indian doctor I met, who said to stick to hot foods, and to avoid salads and fruit that could not be peeled. (Of course, occasionally I did eat a fresh salad, but luckily, did not suffer any ill effects.)

Once, in Thailand, Salome caught a bug and ran a moderate temperature. The hotel sent a nurse to check on her. My biggest health problem was a toothache that started in India. Foolishly, I tried to ignore it, figuring I could get it taken care of when we returned home. Within a few weeks, though, we were in Thailand and the pain became unbearable. My tooth ached and throbbed all the time, and electric bolts of pain shot into my jaw with even the slightest pressure. I had no choice but to go to a dentist. I needed a root canal, and the dentist was able to drill out the abscess and put in a temporary filling, relieving my pain, for a very small fee. I realized it would have been much smarter to have had it looked at and fixed by a dentist in India before it became so bad.

One of the countless anxieties I suffered before leaving on our trip was that we would be grilled about our prescription drugs every time we entered a new country. I made sure to carry prescriptions for all our medications and whenever possible, to keep the drugs in their original, labeled containers. That proved to be a non-issue, however. Very rarely did customs officials even look into our luggage, and when they did, our bags were given only a very cursory glance. We were never asked about our medications. Of course, our bags were always X-rayed before we boarded a flight, but that went very smoothly as well. The most rigorous airport security checks we encountered were in the U.S., although I'm not sure they made us any safer.

I have to admit a feeling of relief when our flight from Tokyo touched down in San Jose, California, the better part of a year after our first flight carried us east from San Diego. We had circled the globe and returned unscathed to tell the tale. But in retrospect, our few dealings with doctors, dentists, nurses and pharmacists were marked with courtesy, friendliness and professionalism, and it's likely we would have been fine if one of us had gotten sick on the road. I'm glad, however, that we never had to find out.

Chapter 8

Life after the Iron Curtain

Austria and Eastern Europe

"Hope is not the conviction that something will turn out well but the certainty that something makes sense, regardless of how it turns out."

Vaclav Havel
Playwright & Former President of the Czech Republic

We boarded the train for Austria on the morning of Saturday, Oct. 8, 2005, and soon were rolling past sun-drenched green fields and villages. The houses were neat and tidy with fresh paint and trimmed lawns. We had to change trains twice to reach Schladming, a ski resort that attracts visitors year-round for such activities as hiking, paragliding, horseback riding and mountain biking. Since it was early fall, we didn't expect to see any snow on the ground and hoped the weather would be warm enough to spend time outdoors.

We were paying our second visit to Austria – the first had been a couple of years earlier, when we had also cruised the Rhine in Germany and stayed in Munich. On that trip, we made a day trip to Salzburg, the birthplace of Wolfgang Amadeus Mozart. Salzburg is a delightful city with scenic pathways along the river and an imposing castle on a hill overlooking the cobblestone central square.

On our world trip, we would be crossing the entire length of the country and heading east to the Czech Republic, our first foray into Eastern Europe, and behind the lines of the former Iron Curtain.

The final leg of our train trip to Schladming was the most scenic. The train wound its way high among hilly terrain, offering panoramic views of the valleys below. We passed stone houses built close to the train tracks. In the corridor, we chatted with a retired train engineer. He was spending the day with his wife just riding this stretch of the Austrian railway, which he told us was famous for its beautiful views.

Somehow, we managed to make it to Schladming without missing a connection. The station was small and sleepy. We called our timeshare resort from a pay phone and they sent a taxi to pick us up.

We are fortunate enough to own two timeshare weeks, which were given to us by my parents. The good thing about timeshares is the sheer variety; you can trade your week in your "home resort" – in our case the Lawrence Welk Resort in northern San Diego County – for resorts all over the world. We have used timeshares in Mexico, Hawaii, France, Turkey, Germany, Uruguay, Austria and Thailand.

We got to the Alpine Club in the early afternoon. With our mound of luggage and our casual dress, we stuck out a bit from the other guests, who were mostly well-heeled Europeans who had driven to the resort in shiny rental cars. We were excited about staying in a place with its own kitchen and cooking our own meals for the first time in weeks. The hotel had a dining room and served breakfast, lunch and dinner. But to us, dining in would be a luxury and we planned to take maximum advantage of the kitchenette in our apartment.

Our condo wasn't quite ready when we arrived, and we found out that the only nearby grocery store closed at 5 p.m. on Saturday and would also be closed on Sunday. So we left our luggage with the front desk and walked down the hill to go grocery shopping. Along the way, we tried to pet the cows and goats in the field next to the road, but they were pretty standoffish.

The market was medium-sized, not a supermarket, but big enough to have anything we would need to stock the larders of our condo. It had sections for produce, bakery goods, meats and plenty of canned and dry goods to choose from. It also had a respectable selection of beer, including local varieties from the brewery across the road. While most of the labels were written in German, we didn't have too much trouble figuring out what we were buying, although the origin of some of the meats and sausages was a mystery.

It's always an adventure to prowl the aisles of a foreign grocery store, something I've enjoyed in many of the places we've traveled over the years. It can be fun to try to figure out what the different foods are, whether animal, vegetable or mineral. It can also be bewildering, as we found at a small market in Bodrum, Turkey. Ava, Salome and I were traveling with my brother, Steve, in 2001, and all of us were starving. We went into the market hoping to find some food that would be quick and easy to prepare. When we stepped inside, however, we found ourselves literally in another world. There were all sorts of tubs and packages on the shelves, but we had absolutely no idea what anythingwas because all of the labels were in Turkish. One tub held a reddish-brown blob with the consistency of tofu, which didn't look remotely appetizing. Fortunately, we were able to find a loaf of bread and something we were pretty sure was cheese, and a couple of apples, so we didn't starve.

The Austrian store was much easier to navigate than the market in Turkey. Our cart bulging with all manner of food, plenty of munchies and a couple of six-packs of Austrian beer, we checked out and looked for a taxi to take us and our booty up the hill.

By the time we got back to the Alpine Club, our condo was ready, so we began shuttling groceries and luggage down the hall and up the elevator, making a spectacle of ourselves.

Salome was so excited that she ran from room to room in a frenzy, ending up in the smaller bedroom. "This is my room!" she shouted.

Our bedroom had a balcony and beyond we could see the mountain peaks across the valley. We had a living room with a TV and DVD player, a tiny kitchen and dining area, and a bathroom. We were in heaven.

The resort consisted of two buildings, each four or five stories tall, connected by a passageway that led from each building to an indoor swimming pool. There was a Jacuzzi, but the finicky nature of the Austrian management required that it be refilled each time a different guest or family used it, at a cost of five euros per soak. It didn't look all that inviting and besides, the sauna was free.

We were hoping there would be some kids Salome's age she could play with. Although we saw a family with a girl and a boy who looked to be roughly her age, for some reason they never hit it off. They probably didn't speak English, and Salome was reluctant to approach children she didn't know.

The resort also had a small playground and a tennis court. A few times we borrowed rackets and swatted a tennis ball back and forth.

On our first morning in Schladming, armed with a map showing our preferred route marked in ballpoint pen by the smiling girl at the front desk, we set off to explore the town and find the tram that would carry us to the top of one of the two local mountain peaks. The town was very cute (one Web site calls it gemutlichkeit, which means "cozy") with narrow streets, houses with window boxes sprouting geraniums, and a river that leads to a picture-book perfect waterfall just a short walk from the center of town on a wooded path.

We walked along for about a mile until we came to the tram station, which was deserted except for a couple of workers and an occasional mountain biker in muddy clothes. Because we were too early for the ski season and there was no snow on the slopes, on this sunny Sunday in mid-October the mountain was populated by families and seniors out for a hike, mountain bikers who took the tram to the top and then hurtled down the ski slopes, and paragliders who launched themselves into the sky by running down a steep, rocky slope.

Inside the tram station, we bought tickets and climbed

into an empty car for the ride up the mountain. The views became increasingly spectacular as we gained altitude. As we reached the summit, it seemed like we were on top of the world, looking down at the green valley, the tiny village and the craggy peaks in the distance.

I had read that Austrians greet each other with the phrase Grüß Gott, which means "God bless you" or literally, "Greet God." Sure enough, the first couple we encountered on the mountaintop path used this greeting, which I tried to return casually, although I'm sure I mangled it. Up on a hill above us, we noticed some people poking around through the scrub brush. We learned later, talking to one of the staff at our timeshare, that they were probably gathering mushrooms, a local delicacy.

The path began in an open, rocky meadow, but soon descended into a forest. Along the way we came across some very unusual wood sculptures of animals, elves and other woodland creatures, carved in trees and stumps. They were interesting, but just a little creepy in the cool, shady and nearly deserted woods.

We found plenty to keep us busy during our stay in Austria. We hiked up the path past the waterfall, rented mountain bikes and rode them all over town, and checked email at the local Internet café, which was very expensive (even compared to other European cities).

Our favorite excursion was a hike into the hills outside town, with Christine, the cheerful, outgoing recreation director from our condo resort, as our guide. A hearty, trim woman in her 50s with a gruff, smoker's voice, Christine led us uphill along on the path, pointing out edible cranberries and other animal and plant life, which made Salome's day. Along the way, we fed apples and sugar to a group of donkeys that brayed loudly when we ran out of snacks.

We hiked to what the Austrians call a "hut," a hillside restaurant with great views of the valley. We sat at wooden picnic tables on an outdoor patio and lunched on sausage sandwiches. An older couple from our resort, who had walked with us up to the hut, treated us to shots of a local liqueur, and then it was time for the entertainment. The owner of the hut pulled out an accordion, and Christine and some of the other guests began dancing. Salome and several children she met at the hut played with the bunnies and guinea pigs that were kept in outdoor pens.

Salome's Journal

10/12/05 Schladming, Austria

Hi it has been so long before I talked to you but I have missed 2 months. Not too much to right about now. But I will work on it. I am now in Schladming, Germany. We are in a timeshare just where I was when I stopped writing in my journal. The place is called Alpine Club. They have a bunch of activities. The activities are too many to remember but all's I know is that there is a lot! 2 days ago I was on a hike through the forest and we went up with a tour guide from here and two other people that did not speak English. But most of the people do they are from England or the U.S. where I'm from. So anyway about the hike. We saw a huge ant hill as big as a half of a tall wall the biggest any of us had ever seen. We walked on and we were hiking to a little hut between two tall mountains. It was a restraint the owner had a huge box with guienea pigs and rabbits. I was shy at first to hold or pet them

but after I was queen of them. There was a baby guienea pig
and he got out and got in a hold and we couldn't get him out
but finally we did. After I was so sad of leaving we went and
fed some donkies and ponies. One donkey got made at my dad
and brayed at my dad for more sugar cubes and (I) was so
scared but had so much fun that day! Tomorrow we are going
horseback riding and I am going rock climbing. I filled you in
as much as I can!

Between these small excursions around Schladming, we
enjoyed cooking our meals and watching DVD movies in
our condo, calling our friends and families, and working
with Salome on her lessons. During the entire week in
Schladming, we ate only one meal in a restaurant. Salome
became an expert at cooking her favorite meal, macaroni
and cheese, for herself each night.

We also tried to sort out the various feelings, both good
and bad, each of us had about our trip so far. In light of the
struggles with Salome's mood swings, I felt we needed to
evaluate how things were going and whether continuing
our travels made sense. Each of us wrote down a list of
what we considered to be the pros and cons of traveling
on vs. going home. We compared lists during a family
meeting.

Our lists were pretty similar, a good thing. Salome and
I put more emphasis on such negatives as homesickness
and missing our friends and family, while Ava's list
highlighted the positives of the adventures that still lay
ahead and the experiences that would last a lifetime if we
continued. I also suspected, although she didn't say it, that
Ava would resent it later if we quit.

The exercise helped us acknowledge and give voice to our feelings, and by the end of our meeting, we agreed to keep going for the time being. To me, the big decision point would come in a few weeks, when we prepared to board a flight from London to Bombay. That flight would put us literally on the other side of the world from our home, and into what promised to be the most culturally "foreign" and challenging of our planned destinations.

As a result of our family meeting, we vowed to ease Salome's homesickness by letting her call and email her friends as much as possible. Ava agreed to help lessen my stress by taking a more active role in planning our trip, such as booking hotels and buying train tickets.

Although Salome could still be a handful, especially when it was time for her schoolwork, her moods were evening out. She was much less likely to lose her temper and if she did, she calmed down much more quickly. As a whole, our outlook was positive as we prepared for our next destination, Prague, the capital of the Czech Republic.

We got to the little train station in Schladming early on the morning of our departure to find the platform and waiting room deserted, as they had been when we arrived in town the week before. Thanks to Austrian efficiency, a signboard showed a diagram of our train, with the correct order of the numbered cars. That helped us find our reserved seats and make sure we weren't on a car that would ultimately be heading off in a different direction from our destination. We had two or three train changes before reaching Prague, including a stop in Vienna, the Austrian capital. Although it would have been nice to spend a little time in Vienna and see the sights, our connections didn't allow us time to leave the station. Instead, all we saw during our brief stop was grimy rows of industrial buildings and walls marked with graffiti.

I had no real qualms about going to the Czech Republic or Poland, even though both countries had once been under Soviet domination. But I felt a twinge of apprehension as the train rolled across the Czech frontier that afternoon, entering a place formerly hidden behind the dreaded "Iron Curtain" of Communism.

Times had certainly changed; when we visited the Czech Republic in the fall of 2005, the curtain had been pulled open for more than 15 years and the border guards who methodically worked their way through our train car barely glanced at us as they examined and stamped our passports.

Late-afternoon sun gave the city's mid-rise apartment buildings a warm orange glow as we clicked and clacked through the outskirts of Prague. Movies such as The Unbearable Lightness of Being, and stories of expat writers and artists haunting the city's cafes had left me with a romantic sense of Prague, and I had always wanted to go there. Now, I was on a train arriving in the city and of course, the view I saw from the windows bore little resemblance to the ideal of Prague that lived in my mind's eye. Not that it was bad; it contained real buildings, cars and people with all their flaws and gritty details, instead of 20-somethings sitting around café tables and arguing about the true nature of art.

Our hotel had arranged for a taxi to meet us at the station and we found the driver easily once we had hoisted our bags off the train and gotten our bearings. We piled into his well-worn sedan for the 20-minute trip to the outlying district where we would be staying for the next week or so. The ride took us along an elevated expressway that gave us views of the Saturday night traffic in central Prague, which included plenty of billboards, neon signs and tall, modern buildings. Capitalism was thriving in this former Communist bastion just over a decade since the "Velvet Revolution" put poet and activist Vaclav Havel in power as the country's first post-Soviet president.

On the way to our hotel, a limo full of young women partiers passed us on the highway.

"Many people from the U.K., they come to Prague to celebrate before they get married," the driver told us in broken English.

Apparently, both bachelors and bachelorettes have turned Prague into something of a destination for pre-nuptial flings because of the relatively cheap prices and Prague's reputation for having the best beer in Europe.

"They love to party here," the driver said with a wink.

The taxi delivered us to the front door of the Hotel Excellent, an upscale property on an austere, working-class street. We were definitely off the beaten tourist path, which suited me fine. Although the hotel was some distance from the historic city center, the subway station was a block away, and we could zip into town in just a few minutes on Prague's efficient underground train.

Once we were settled into our hotel, I tried to get in touch with Roy, our friend from Orange County who was planning to be in Prague at the same time as us. After several tries, we reached his cell phone and agreed to meet at Prague's Old Town Square.

The square is dominated by a baroque tower housing the Astronomical Clock, one of Prague's most famous attractions. The oldest part of the clock dates back to 1410 and includes an astronomical dial that shows the positions of the moon and sun. The clock also features animated figures that parade around its face every hour. We saw none of this, however, because the entire tower was covered in scaffolding due to a renovation project.

We saw Roy shortly after we emerged from the subway into the chilly Prague night; Salome ran over and tagged him, shouting, "You're it!" This was a continuation of a game of tag they'd started the last time we'd seen each other, back home in Southern California.

We walked around the cobblestone square a bit and then took a short stroll on the famous Charles Bridge. We had dinner in one of the touristy restaurants on the square, which have plenty of atmosphere with their outdoor tables and colorful umbrellas, but offer bland food at high prices.

Roy was traveling with Sherry, a friend of his from Orange County, and Shane and Sue, also his long-time friends who had recently moved to Ireland. All of his companions, tired from a day of sightseeing, had opted to stay at their hotel that night.

The next morning, I took off for a jog around the neighborhood. I headed uphill, past a number of drab, high-rise apartment buildings, until I came to a large wooded area crisscrossed with dirt paths. My main objective was to get some fresh air and exercise without getting lost. I decided to run through the woods, keeping to one central path so I wouldn't lose my bearings. Since people generally didn't speak English in Prague, especially outside the tourist areas, it could have been a problem getting directions back to the hotel. Other than the strange looks from the people I passed – who appeared to be headed to work – I completed my run without incident.

We had arranged to meet Roy and his friends at Wenceslas Square, a long, narrow plaza flanked on both sides and at each end by tall buildings. This square was where Soviet tanks rolled in to crush the Prague Spring uprising in 1969, some 20 years before Mikhail Gorbachov's perestroika and glasnost led to the dissolution of the Soviet Union. In those days, the only perestroika – restructuring – was related to the skulls and faces of unlucky student protestors who confronted soldiers and police.

By 2005, the tanks and guns had been replaced with Big Macs and tacky souvenirs. The square is lined with hotels, restaurants – including three McDonald's – and tourist shops selling everything from T-shirts to paperweights in the shape of the Charles Bridge.

Shane took over as tour guide and we set off to see the Jewish Quarter and Prague Castle – which sits on a hill overlooking the city center – the Vltava River and the historic Charles Bridge. We enjoyed strolling the wide span, admiring the city views from its stone railing, checking out the sculptures along the bridge and listening to the street musicians who serenaded us.

Like much of Eastern Europe, Prague's Jewish population was decimated by the Nazis during World War II, so what remains of the historic Jewish Quarter – called "Josefov" – is a collection of museums and ancient synagogues, most of which have also been converted into museums. A couple of the synagogues are still used for worship by Prague's tiny postwar Jewish population.

We walked through the Jewish cemetery, trying to make out the inscriptions chiseled in Hebrew on the cracked, jumbled tombstones that jutted crazily at all angles on both sides of the cement path. The cemetery dates back to the 1400s; sadly, the letters and numbers on many of the headstones have worn away over time.

I was particularly interested in the Jewish Quarter. Although I had been brought up in a Jewish household, and had even been Bar Mitvah'ed at age 13, I had not practiced the religion since I was a teen-ager, and had only gone to temple on the major holidays such as Rosh Hashanah and Yom Kippur when my mom had put on the pressure. Since her death, though, my attendance at synagogue had pretty much dropped to zero, except for an occasional Sabbath when we went to observe the anniversary of one of my parents' deaths.

When we decided to visit Eastern Europe, however, an interest in my Jewish roots had been rekindled, as I suppose happens with many people. Both of my grandparents on my father's side had emigrated to the United States from Poland when they were children. Those who hadn't left by the 30s were wiped out by the Nazis, along with their entire villages.

Prague's Jewish Quarter includes the Old-New Synagogue, considered "new" when it was built in the 13th century, but later relegated to "old" status when newer houses of worship were built in the 16th and 17th centuries.

We eavesdropped on a guide who gave a talk about the synagogue to a tour group, and then Salome and I walked across the street to a gift shop, where we bought candles, which we lighted in the ancient temple in honor of my mom and dad.

Our next stop was Prague Castle. The afternoon was very cold, and we felt nearly frostbitten as we walked among the cobblestone paths in the castle grounds. We did make it inside St. Vitus Cathedral, whose Gothic spires can be seen looming above Prague in many famous photos of the city. But because it was getting late in the afternoon, we didn't tour the other parts of the complex, and instead walked back down the hill into the old town area after posing for pictures with the palace guards, and snapping keepsake photos of the city panorama spread below us.

That night, we regrouped at a restaurant near the hotel where Roy and his friends were staying.

The dinner was excellent, and because it was a Sunday night, we were about the only diners in the place. There were seven or eight of us, and we took up a big table in a side room. Roy's friend Shane entertained Salome with tricks, such as balancing a spoon and fork on the edge of a glass (with the aid of a toothpick). The finale to the trick involved setting the toothpick on fire, but I don't remember why that seemed so impressive at the time. He also showed how to make a group of bent toothpicks form a star when beer foam was spooned onto them.

We lingered over the meal, which cost a whopping $32 for the three of us, including appetizers, beer, main course and dessert. The reasonable prices for most things in the Czech Republic were a relief after the high cost of travel in Western Europe.

We planned to spend a couple more days in Prague before we caught the night train to Krakow, and journeyed on to Eastern Poland to visit my friend, journalist Adam Wajrak.

Our schedule the next day included changing hotels because ours – the Hotel Excellent – was fully booked. We moved to a small pension down the street, which was homey and comfortable. The chatty proprietress had a good friend who lived just a few miles from us in Southern California, and we enjoyed talking to her over breakfast in the dining room, which was nestled under the peaked roof on the third floor of the building.

After moving our stuff to the new digs, we wandered into town, where we visited an art gallery and perused the Museum of Communism, which contained dusty exhibits detailing the rise and fall of Soviet influence over the Czech Republic, and its predecessor, Czechoslovakia. The museum did have some interesting Communist-era posters and displays of how the average Czech citizen lived under Communism. Ironically, the museum was on the second floor of a building whose ground floor was occupied by that stalwart of Western capitalism, McDonald's.

Since we had been in Europe, Salome had been eyeing the elaborate horse-drawn carriages that took tourists on bumpy rides over the cobblestone streets of Rome and other cities we had visited. In Western Europe, the carriage rides were too expensive, and we had turned down her soulful pleas. But we relented in Prague, where the fare was slightly more affordable, and enjoyed the jaunt around the old town square, reclining against the red plush seats and covered by a blanket.

I had also read about Prague's famous "black light theater," which combines comedy and dance in a unique, and somewhat bizarre, performance. The shows were popular, and we were lucky to get tickets at the last minute when someone cancelled their reservation. We entered the small theater, which was already packed, and were seated in the front row. The walls, ceiling and floor of the stage were painted black, and the dancers' costumes and props were painted in fluorescent greens, reds, blues and yellows. The effect of the black light was to make the dancers appears as if they were floating and gliding through the air above the stage, although they were actually hooked up to nearly invisible wires.

Between dance numbers, a comedic story about husband-and-wife robbers pursued by a bumbling policeman was carried out in pantomime, so even us foreigners could follow the plot.

For our final day in Prague, we had promised Salome a visit to the city's highly regarded zoo. This required a trip across town on local buses, which was a great way to get a ground-level view of the city's neighborhoods.

A couple of years before our visit in 2005, the Vtlava River had risen over its banks and flooded the zoo, which is right next to the waterway. The catastrophic flood destroyed many of the buildings and even killed one of the zoo's prized elephants, a story that made international news.

After the flood, the zoo had been almost completely rebuilt,and is now one of the nicest, and best laid-out, zoos we visited on our trip. The grounds are well-landscaped and divided into areas representing different parts of the world. The animal enclosures are clean and well-maintained, and the larger animals have outdoor spaces designed to resemble their native habitats. Ava, Salome and I have been spoiled by San Diego Zoo and Wild Animal Park, but the Prague Zoo made for an enjoyable outing.

Our guidebook recommended taking the bus to our next destination, Cesky Krumlov, a medieval town about 200 kilometers south of Prague. The train to Cesky was slow, and the station was located inconveniently outside the center of town, so we opted for the three-hour bus ride.

Salome's Journal

10/20/05 Prague, Czech Republic

Today I had to wake up very early and get ready and now I am on a bus we are going for a couple of days and then to Krakow. Yesterday I went to the zoo. There was a baby goat who I fed. He was so cute. The big goats wanted some so they were butting him. My mom slapped one and he did not like it. There was also a 10 month gorilla. He was so cute. His mommy was teaching how to climb and she was always there for him if he needed help. It was so so so much fun!!!!!!!!!

Cesky boasted a castle dating back to the 13th century that was built on a rise overlooking the town. A cylindrical tower painted in pastel shades of pink and green dominates the castle grounds; it was one of the first things we saw when the bus dropped us off.

We set out with our luggage, crossing a stone bridge over the Vtlava River and ducking in through an arched gateway. We bumped our way across the cobblestones with our wheeled bags and came to the Pension Danny, which was in the heart of the action, just a half-block from the castle gate. As with many of the smaller pensions we had stayed at, there was no elevator, and our room was on the third floor. I thought the trek was worth it, though, when I saw the room, which was tucked under the eaves with the mattress in a sort of loft below the beamed ceiling. Another plus was the tray of bread, fruit, cheese and coffee brought to our room each morning.

The river winds through the medieval town center in an S-shape, with bridges linking the different sections. In the warmer months, it's possible to rent rafts and float around the town, but our visit was in October – and it wasn't warm enough for a dip. Cesky's town square is ringed with cafés, hotels and the local tourist office. There were plenty of eateries to choose from, and even a tiny grocery store right outside the castle grounds.

One of the coolest things about Cesky's castle could be found just below the stone bridge leading through a passageway to the inner courtyard: bear pits, with live brown bears. The bear pits had been part of the castle for centuries and the bears that live there today are reportedly descendents of the original animals.

Across town from where we were staying – right next to the river – was a modernistic playground with fanciful structures that children could slide, climb and spin on. On the first or second day of our stay in Cesky, Salome met some kids who spoke English, including an 8-year-old girl named Paloma. The kids played for several hours, reluctantly leaving the playground after dark. It was a rare treat for Salome and we promised to bring her back the next day.

Our bus trip back to Prague was timed to give us one more evening in the city before catching a sleeper train to Krakow, Poland, a shorter trip than the one from Rome to Munich. We boarded the train about 9 p.m. and were due to arrive in Krakow before 6 a.m. The train was very comfortable, and once again, we had a private compartment with three bunks. Fitting the three of us, and all our bags, into that tiny space proved challenging, almost like solving a Rubik's Cube puzzle.

But we got settled and the train rumbled to life. We crossed the Polish border at about 3 a.m. and soon after, we heard a sharp knock on the door of our compartment. The gruff voice of an immigration officer called, "Passports, please."

It seemed like I had just fallen back asleep when there was another knock on the door. This time, it was the conductor, who shouted, "Krakow, 30 minutes!" It was about 5 a.m., and still pitch black outside.

I woke up Ava and Salome, and we went through the drill of dressing hurriedly in the cramped compartment, trying not to hurt ourselves or each other. We hustled our bags out the door and down the passageway just as the train slowed for its arrival at Krakow station.

The platform was in the bowels of the station, several levels below ground. It was cold, dark, and as we later found out, raining. The platform was lighted with cold, blue-tinted fluorescent bulbs, and we made our way into the corridor. We needed to get some local currency and, with the help of our guidebook, find a place to stay. There were touts in the arrival hall, trying to hustle us to stay at their place. But I was always wary of those folks, figuring they would steer us to some over-priced, bug-infested dive, laughing as they pocketed their commission. Instead, we put our trust in Rick

Steves' guide to Eastern Europe, and picked a mid-priced place he described as quirky and ramshackle.

We hurried out of the train station, trying not to get soaked from the frigid rain that fell steadily in the pre-dawn darkness. I was feeling a bit blue, a mood that only intensified when we reached our hotel, whose locked entrance was next to a street-level clothing store.

The sleepy desk clerk buzzed us in, and we hauled our luggage through the entryway to the office, a hodge-podge of desks and kitchen equipment behind a small breakfast room.

The hotel clerk led us out of the office up the stairs, which stretched up above us into the gloom. We climbed past the first-floor landing, and the second, huffing and puffing as we tugged, lugged and bumped our heavy bags up the stairs. Finally, we reached the third floor and entered a series of locked doors and passageways to our room.

The guidebook's description of the "ramshackle" rooms was apt. The floor was uneven, and the carpet threadbare. The walls were stained and the flimsy curtains over the single large window were torn. The rickety furniture was scratched and scuffed, and it wobbled on the sagging, creaky floor. Combined with the crummy weather, the shabby room left me depressed.

Later that morning, after getting all our luggage (emphasis on "lug") up the stairs, I went down the street to an Internet café, where I found an email from my friend, Tim, back in San Diego, which cheered me up. Tim's message shared news of home, and ended, "Take care of yourself and your family. You are an inspiration."

The words of encouragement, along with my first

daylight view of Krakow's charming main market square, jump-started my spirits, and I was soon enthusiastic about exploring the city.

Our hotel was run-down, but it did have a few things going for it: they served a very decent free breakfast of bread, cheese, fruit and cereal, and it was relatively cheap at about $65 a night. The best thing about it was the location, inside the ring-shaped park called the Planty, which circles Krakow's Old Town and is two blocks from the Rynek, or market square, which dates back to the 13th century. The square is home to outdoor cafés, souvenir shops, trendy restaurants and atmospheric bars. Each morning, I came down the stairs of the "Bed and Breakfast" in my running clothes and ran the full circular length of the Planty, which had wide asphalt walkways in the middle of its trees and lawns.

It would have been easy to while away our days in Krakow by sitting at a table at one of the open-air cafés on the Rynek, sipping coffee or beer (depending whether it was before or after noon) and watching Salome feed some of the thousands of pigeons that coo and strut on the cobblestones or perch on the buildings. Salome was so captivated with the pigeons that she would happily feed them for hours, breaking off pieces of the large, pretzel-like pastries sold from carts stationed around the square. She even came to recognize some of the pigeons and give them names.

The square was always busy, especially on sunny days, with pedestrians, bicyclists and horse-drawn carriages moving about. A cathedral stood watch from one corner of the 10-acre plaza, one of Europe's largest, which is ringed by three- and four-story Victorian buildings. A long, low building – the 16th century cloth hall, in late 2005 undergoing renovations – stands in the center of the square.

But we had an ambitious agenda for our time in Krakow, which included visiting Auschwitz, the Nazi concentration camp; the Wieliczka salt mines; Kazimierz, the old Jewish Quarter; and the Royal Castle, which is built on a hill overlooking both the Old Town and the Vistula River. We also wanted to try the "milk bars," government-subsidized cafeterias that serve traditional hearty Polish fare at what were dirt-cheap prices. Our guidebook said the milk bars were a holdover from Poland's Communist days, but remained popular with locals, especially university students, and budget-conscious tourists like us. Finally, we needed to line up our onward train tickets and touch base with Adam, my journalist friend in Eastern Poland.

Krakow's public transit system included streetcars powered by overhead wires and a network of minibuses that shuttled people around town and to outlying areas. We found the minibus station and tracked down the one heading to the salt mine, about 10 kilometers away.

As the minibus drove through residential neighborhoods, we tried to catch the names of the stops as the driver announced them in Polish. Luckily for us, a Polish family was also heading for the salt mines, so we followed them as they got off the minibus and walked a few blocks to the mine entrance.

Salt was first mined at Wieliczka in 1290, and mining continued until 1996, when the salt deposits were exhausted. Since then, the mine has operated as a tourist attraction. We bought our tickets and joined the line for the English-language tour. An elevator took us about 200 feet underground, where we started our tour. (In all, we walked about a mile through the mine's passageways, and to a depth of about 400 feet.) The mine was worth visiting to see the fantastic sculptures carved by salt miners over the centuries. There were religious figures, chandeliers and even a bas-relief of Da Vinci's Last Supper, all carved in the brownish-gray salt.

Miners also carved figures of animals and people, including famous carvings of Jesus Christ and Polish astronomer Nikolaus Kopernikus. One of the largest spaces we saw was the Chapel of Saint Kinga, where weddings and concerts are held.

Near the end of our tour of the salt mines, we ran into a boisterous group of Israeli teenagers, who told us they were in Poland to visit the concentration camps at Auschwitz and Birkenau, which have been preserved as museums. We later learned that along with the Israeli teens, every high school student in Poland is required to visit the camps. We planned to go the next day.

Although both Ava and I thought it would be worthwhile to visit Auschwitz, we felt a certain amount of dread at the prospect. Also, we went back and forth on whether we should take Salome. I consulted the museum's Web site, where I read that visitors were discouraged from bringing children younger than 12. We opted to take turns visiting the concentration camp museum , so that one of us could stay in town with Salome.

My turn was first, and I boarded the minibus in Krakow with trepidation. The bus ride took about an hour, traversing some pleasant farms and rural areas.

Before the camp tour, visitors are ushered into an

auditorium, where they are shown a documentary
that includes footage shot by the Ukrainian troops
who liberated the camp in 1945. While those images of
emaciated men, women and children were hard to look at,
the rest of the camp was equally grim: above the entrance
was a wrought-iron sign inscribed with the infamous
slogan, "Arbeit macht frei," German for, "Work makes
you free." (In 2009, thieves stole the sign, creating an
international uproar until they were arrested and the
artifact recovered.)

Inside the camp, we saw exhibit cases with mounds
of suitcases and shoes taken from the prisoners, and
even a display of prisoners' hair after it was shorn by
the SS guards. Another display case contained hundreds
of empty canisters of Zyklon B, the poison gas used to
exterminate millions of Jews. Our tour, conducted in
English by a middle-aged, somber woman, included
rooms where Jews were tortured and subjected to medical
experiments, and the "killing wall," where thousands were
executed by firing squad.

We saw the reconstructed ovens where the bodies of
the murder victims went up in flames, and the courtyard
where Auschwitz commandant Rudolf Hoess was hanged
in 1947, following a trial for war crimes. One of the most
chilling details I remember from the tour was that Hoess,
considered one of history's worst mass murderers, had
actually brought his wife and children to live with him in a
house on the grounds of the death camp.

After touring Auschwitz, I decided I had had enough
death and misery for the day, so I skipped the second part
of the tour, a short bus ride to the Birkenau camp, known

as the "factory of death" for the hundreds of thousands of Jews murdered there. Birkenau's gas chambers and other buildings were razed after the war, but the train sidings, which were used for the "cattle cars" that brought Jews and other political prisoners to the camp, remain intact. Birkenau was used as a filming location for Steven Spielberg's Academy Award-winning movie, Schindler's List.

While in Krakow, we also satisfied our craving for movies. I consider myself a movie buff, but the opportunity to sit in a darkened theater munching popcorn was rare during our travels. Occasionally during our ramblings, we found a theater showing a current release in English. In Krakow, just off the main square, we found a multiplex cinema in a restored Victorian building. Each auditorium was unique because it had been converted from what appeared to be residential quarters. We saw two movies during our stay in Krakow, Broken Flowers, starring Bill Murray, and a new version of Oliver Twist by director Roman Polanski, which left Salome traumatized because of the cruel treatment of the children.

The day after my trip to Auschwitz, we walked down to the Kazimierz area, also known as the old Jewish Quarter. Kazimierz is anchored by a picturesque square with lots of trees and old buildings, some of them historic synagogues now converted into museums. There was also an incredible Jewish cemetery with hundreds of headstones in neat rows, shaded by large trees. The headstones date from 1551 to 1800. Although not as ancient as Prague's Jewish cemetery, the Krakow graveyard – when I visited it by myself a couple of days after our family walk to Kazimierz – was more interesting because the inscriptions on most of the headstones were legible.

Our culinary tour of Krakow included stops at a couple of "milk bars," where the food is displayed in glass cases, and dished up to customers who line up in queues that extend out the door.

Ordering at the milk bar was a challenge because the workers didn't speak English and neither did the customers, most of whom appeared to be college students. As we waited our turn to order, we tried to see what the people in front of us had on their trays so we could order the same items. Even though we could see the food behind glass panels on the steam table, we didn't know what many of the items were, and there were no signs in English or Polish to help us out.

We ordered savory little dumplings called pierogis, although we had no idea what was inside them, and Salome stuck with the chicken noodle soup. One of my favorite items was the purple yogurt drink that we later found out was made with pomegranate. The milk bars were simple places, where customers found their own Formica tables and bussed their own dishes. As a budget-conscious traveler, I loved paying the bill at the milk bar, which, thanks to the government subsidy, was usually under $10 for the three of us.

A day or two before our departure, I managed to reach Adam, my Polish journalist friend, from a pay phone on the main square. He gave me directions to his village in Eastern Poland, in the Bialowieza Forest, from Krakow, which I scribbled into a little notebook I carried. The journey involved at least two trains, including a change of trains in Warsaw, to the city of Bialystok, where we would catch a bus for the final segment. We were supposed to get off the bus at a small town, where Adam's girlfriend, Nuria, would pick us up. Adam didn't drive; he had been a passenger in a terrible car crash several years before, which had convinced him to avoid getting behind the wheel.

Before leaving Krakow, I wanted to attend a service at one of the few functioning synagogues in the city. So, on Friday afternoon, I set off for Kazimierz, leaving Ava and Salome in our hotel room (they opted to watch a movie on our portable DVD player).

I walked to Kazimierz and arrived an hour or so before sundown when the service began. I killed time by walking around the cemetery and having coffee and cake in a little Jewish café on the Kazimierz central square. The synagogue was a small, squarish building across from the café. A plaque on the front of the building noted that a synagogue had occupied the same piece of land for more than 500 years, a fact that fired my imagination.

I walked up to the door, and a man told me the temple was closed to tourists because services were about to begin. When I said I was Jewish, however, he stepped aside and let me in. I took a yarmulke from a little basket on a table near the door and stepped inside the sanctuary, which was brightly lighted with electric bulbs in an ornate, wrought-iron chandelier.

Although I had attended many Jewish worship services in my life, mostly when I was a child, this service was different from anything I had experienced before. Because it was an Orthodox service, whose adherents strictly interpret ancient Jewish rites, men and women were separated; the men sat on wooden pews in the tiny sanctuary, while the women sat in a room behind us, separated by a gauzy white curtain. Also, the entire service was in Hebrew, with a little Polish mixed in, so it was hard for me to follow. It had been more than 30 years, after all, since I had studied Hebrew in preparation for my Bar Mitzvah. The leader of the service, who I took to be the rabbi, mostly stood with his back to the congregants, chanting in a voice that rose and fell with the ancient Hebrew cadences. Both the rabbi and the people sitting in the pews seemed to know when to stand and when to dip and bow reverentially during the recitations.

Some of the prayers, and the melodies in which they were sung, stirred dim memories that had been locked away in my brain for years. Looking around, it appeared that some of the young men in the pews were tourists like me, but I had no idea where they were from. Others seemed very familiar with each other, and probably belonged to the small congregation.

I was surprised when the service ended abruptly after about 30 minutes and the congregants gathered in the tiny anteroom and wished each other "Shabbat shalom," which I'd often heard at Sabbath services I'd attended.

I found the service satisfying because, in spite of the fact that I didn't know anyone, there was an underlying sense of familiarity in the prayers and rituals that lessened my sense of isolation in the world, even though I was thousands of miles from home.

The next morning, we got up early and caught a taxi to the train station for our journey to Eastern Poland to visit my friend Adam Wajrak in the Bialowieza Forest.

Adam and his girlfriend, Nuria, a wildlife biologist,

lived in a tiny village in the midst of the last primeval, or ancient, forest on the European mainland. Poland's Bialowieza Forest is near the border with Belarus, a former Soviet satellite now ruled by a dictator.

I had met Adam a couple of years before, when I was a public information officer for the county government in San Diego. In October 2003, a devastating wildfire – started by a lost hunter's signal flare – consumed hundreds of homes across the eastern and central portion of the San Diego region. Adam, an environmental writer for Poland's largest daily newspaper, which was based in Warsaw, was assigned to travel to San Diego to write about the wildfires. Apparently, many Poles were interested in California, due to their fascination with Hollywood culture and because many of their countrymen had emigrated to the Golden State. During the wildfires, I worked 12-hour shifts for the first full week, responding to media inquiries from around the U.S. and many foreign countries. I was quoted in the New York Times and did many radio and television interviews as well. One day, while on duty at the county Emergency Operations Center, my cell phone rang.

"I am Polish journalist," said the deep voice in my ear. "I am coming to California to cover fires. Can you help me make contacts?"

Apparently, he had found my cell phone number on a press release posted on the county Web site. Over the next couple of days, Adam called me a few times to update me on his travel plans. He wanted to stay in a hotel near the County Administration Center, so I could help him with the logistics of covering the fire. I was happy to help, both because it was my job and I found it very interesting that he was traveling so far to cover a local disaster.

It was a Friday Adam called again.

"I am here in San Diego. I am in county building. Can I come up to see you?"

I gave him directions to my office, not sure what to expect. Adam turned out to be a friendly guy in his 30s. He was tall, broad-shouldered, a bit rumpled from his international flight, and he smelled of tobacco smoke. He had come to my office directly from the airport and still had his luggage, a somewhat worn rucksack. I helped him line up a hotel room nearby and called some fire department sources to take him out to the fire lines. I agreed to pick him up at his hotel the next morning for a tour of some of the more remote and rural areas that had burned.

I'd been immersed in the details of the horrendous wildfires for nearly two weeks by this point, but my Saturday tour of the fire zones with Adam was the first time I saw the devastation in person. We drove around the hilly country of east San Diego County looking at the burned hulks where homes had once stood. Adam had a small 35mm film camera and a little hard-cover book with lined paper, into which he scribbled his notes. At some of the home sites, we were lucky enough to encounter the owners, most of whom were happy to talk to Adam, whose English was pretty good. Although I spoke no Polish, I tried to help him when he got stuck during his interviews.

He seemed genuinely moved by the devastation from the fire and the plight of the newly homeless people he encountered. While many of the victims had owned their homes and were eligible for insurance money to help them rebuild, some of the people we met were uninsured renters who had lost all their possessions in the fire.

Both Adam and I were impressed with the dignity these fire victims exhibited as they rummaged through the debris in the hopes of finding treasured personal objects. Every single person we met was happy to talk to us and exhibited no ill will at our intrusion on his or her privacy.

As we drove around, Adam told me his background. He had grown up in Warsaw when Poland was still under Communist domination. As a teenager he had delivered an underground newspaper, a part-time job that led to his arrest. After the collapse of the Soviet Union, the same newspaper became the nation's premier daily, and Adam worked his way up to the position of reporter. He had been working at the paper for about a decade when I met him, and had begun to be recognized for his environmental writing. His passion for animals had also led him to write a children's book about a crow he had adopted as a boy. In addition to his reporting work, much of which was done from his base in the Bialowieza Forest, Adam had been traveling around Poland to produce videos for the Polish edition of the Animal Planet cable television network. Adam and Nuria's home was also something of a menagerie due to his penchant for taking in wounded or sick animals and nursing them to health. At the time of our visit, the couple had three dogs, two ravens and a buzzard. Adam had also nursed a baby owl that was abandoned by its mother, which had taken up residence in a tree in his yard. Adam sent away to Warsaw for frozen mice, which he left on a stump in his yard, hoping the owl would get the hint and learn to hunt for its own food.

After our tour of the fire zone, I invited Adam to our

house in Oceanside for dinner, knowing he was alone in
the city. Ava and Salome both enjoyed his stories about
the animals he had taken in, such as a mischievous river
otter that learned to turn on the faucet in the bathtub
and lay under the stream of water, splashing water in all
directions. Adam and Nuria would often come home to
find the inside of their house soaked, the unrepentant otter
basking in the tub.

Adam planned to write an article about the San
Diego wildfires for his newspaper's Sunday magazine
supplement. After he returned to Poland, he sent me a
copy of the magazine, which featured a cover story about
the wildfires. I was even quoted in the article, which was,
of course, written in Polish: "blah, blah, blah, blah, Joe
Tash, blah, blah, blah, blah." At least I didn't have to
worry about getting in trouble with my boss for saying
something stupid!

At the time of Adam's visit to San Diego in the fall of
2003, we were already talking about and beginning to plan
our world trip. We told him we wanted to visit Eastern
Europe, including Poland, and he invited us to visit him in
the forest.

We had to schedule our visit to the Bialowieza Forest
around a short trip to London Adam took in late 2005.
He'd had been selected by Time magazine's European
edition as one of 35 influential Europeans for 2005, due to
his environmental writing and activism. As one of the 35
honorees, he was in good company: others in the group
included anti-poverty activist and rock musician Bob
Geldof, Spanish film-maker Pedro Almodovar, and a man

who had heroically rescued victims of the London subway bombings of July 2005.

Before leaving Krakow for Eastern Poland, we arranged to meet Nuria in the small town of Hajnowka, a short ride from Teremeski, the tiny village of 60 people where Adam and Nuria lived.

The train ride from Krakow to Warsaw was unremarkable; we arrived in the Polish capital in early afternoon, ate at a diner inside the train station, and boarded our train to Bialystok. The second part of our journey was much less comfortable; the weekend we had chosen to travel fell just before All Saints Day, a national holiday. A college student we met on the train described the holiday as a mix of our Thanksgiving and Memorial Day holidays. Poles travel home to enjoy a feast with their families, and then visit cemeteries to pay tribute and place flowers at the graves of their loved ones.

The train from Warsaw to Bialystok was so crowded that we had no chance of getting seats. For the entire two-hour-plus trip, we stood in the passageway, crammed up against our luggage so tightly that we couldn't even make it to the bathroom. Salome at least was able to sit on our bags, but Ava and I had to remain on our feet the whole way.

At Bialystok, which, from our vantage point on the train was a less than attractive industrial city, we dragged our suitcases up and over the tracks on a pedestrian bridge, to the bus terminal next door.

Adam had given me detailed instructions on which bus to take, and even the timetable. The buses pulled up to concrete islands that were arranged in neat parallel rows. We were able to find our bus number and verify when the next bus was due from a posted schedule. We waited in the chilly air until our bus chugged up, and then bought our tickets from the driver. The bus ride from Bialystok to Hajnowka took about 90 minutes; by the time we arrived at our destination, a velvety dusk was settling on the town. There were only a couple of passengers left on the bus, and to our dismay, we found out there were actually three stops in Hajnowka – and we didn't know which one was ours. A helpful passenger advised us to wait for the final stop, which we did, and luckily, Nuria was waiting there for us in her green jeep.

Adam had arranged for us to stay in a farmhouse a couple of doors down from his house in the village. The cost was 120 Polish zlotys per night, or about $36. For that price, we got two rooms in the cozy farmhouse, which was kept heated to the point that we almost didn't need to use any covers at night.

On our first evening in the village, we went to Adam and Nuria's yellow, wood-frame house for dinner and met some of their animal co-inhabitants, including the three dogs. Nuria served homemade chicken soup and pirogis stuffed with bison meat and wild mushrooms, all of which was delicious.

Their house was a happy, jumbled mix of languages, cultures and animals. Nuria, who is Spanish, speaks fluent Polish, but in the house, she and Adam mostly speak English. They have taught the dogs to respond to Spanish commands, such as venga (come) and sienta (sit). Behind the house are walk-in cages where the ravens and buzzard share residence.

While in the Bialowieza Forest, we also hoped to see one

of the wild bison that roam the area, so after dinner, Adam took us outside, and we scanned the fields surrounding his house with a powerful searchlight. We had no luck spotting a bison, but we did catch a glimpse of the "crazy owl" he had raised since it was brought to him as a chick that had been abandoned by its mother, several months earlier.

The grayish owl was maybe eight or 10 inches tall with large, brown eyes. The three dogs refused to go outside when the owl was around; Adam had to coax them out with sausage just to get them to go to the bathroom. We soon saw why they were afraid. As soon as the dogs stepped outside, the owl swooped down at them, and then flew back up to roost in the tree. While it was a playful game for the owl, the dogs were having none of it. According to Adam, the owl also swooped at villagers walking in the lane, which had caused some of them to carry umbrellas even when the sun was shining. Adam swore the owl posed no danger to people; there had been no reports of owl-related injuries.

My favorite of their three dogs was Tropo, a white-and-brown cocker spaniel with an easy-going personality. When one of the other dogs would come up and lick Tropo's muzzle, the long hair on each side curled up like Salvador Dali's mustache.

The day after we arrived, Adam took some time off from his work and we hiked through the forest to a rustic animal preserve/zoo that housed species from the surrounding area. There were wild horses, moose, bison, boars, wolves and deer. We enjoyed the hike through the woods, as well as the warm, spiced beer we drank at a little snack stand near the zoo. It was very cold, though. I had put on practically every piece of clothing I had in my backpack and still my teeth chattered.

Although it was against the rules to feed the animals in the zoo, Adam had special dispensation, since he knew the zoo's operators from his journalistic work. We fed leaves to the deer and almost caused a stampede in the boar enclosure when we tossed in pieces of bread.

By late afternoon, when we were leaving the zoo, the air had turned even more frigid. We starting walking back to Adam's house and were overjoyed to see Nuria pull up in the green jeep. We drove for a few minutes in the late-afternoon gloom, when Nuria suddenly gestured excitedly out the window. There, in a clearing, stood a wild bison, calmly grazing. The beast, which was covered with a dense brown coat and must have weighed nearly a ton, didn't seem worried by our presence, and soon, another car had pulled over even closer, to get a better look. Adam warned us to keep our distance because annoyed bison had been known to charge unwitting tourists.

After a few minutes, the bison wandered back into the forest, out of our view, and we piled back into the jeep, happy at our good fortune.

That night, Adam made dinner reservations at a hotel in the next village. Because there were so few travelers that time of year, the hotel chef prepared only enough food for diners with reservations, and only from a menu that changed nightly. We were treated to savory beef stew with homemade whole wheat bread. After we ate, Salome started playing with some kids in another section of the dining room while Ava, Adam, Nuria and I had coffee and talked. We couldn't stay long, though, because we were

177

heading to a party thrown by some of Adam's friends.

Until 1917, the Bialowieza Forest was part of the Russian empire and used as a royal hunting park by the Russian tsars. After that, it fell into the hands of the Germans, and the forest reportedly suffered heavy damage during World War I, when soldiers slaughtered hundreds of bison. The territory later came under Polish control and was dedicated as a national park.

The party was in celebration of a theatrical production that some of Adam's friends had staged, and it was to be held in a restaurant housed in a former train station used by Russian royalty.

According to Adam, his friend, Zmicier Wajciuszkiewicz, had recently opened the restaurant after a meticulous restoration that must have cost tens of thousands of dollars. Every inch of the place was pristine, from the freshly painted woodwork, to the polished wood floors, to the period furniture. The walls were adorned with stuffed animal heads and paintings of tsars and their noblemen.

We were ushered into a private room and seated at a long wooden table big enough to accommodate two or three dozen people.

We chatted with Adam's friends, including Mikolacz, who also worked as a reporter at the Warsaw daily, covering government and politics. Mikolacz told us he had lived in Rome and covered the Vatican during the reign of Pope John Paul II, who was revered in his native Poland. His work included traveling with the press entourage on the Pope's private jet during many of John Paul's official trips. Mikolacz and his wife, a television producer, were expecting their first child.

After dinner, the group moved to the main dining room, where the lights were dimmed and the restaurant owner served frozen shots of Polish vodka. Todar, a member of the theatrical group, played mournful ballads on a baby grand piano. Because the lyrics were in Belarusian, we weren't exactly sure what he was singing about, but the haunting emotions of sadness and longing came through, and we found the performance very moving.

The singer later explained, in halting English, that the dictatorship in Minsk did not allow such traditional Belarusian folk songs to be played or sung, out of fear they would foment resistance to the regime. I was never able to verify this, but Todar also told us that the dictator, Aleksander Lukaszenko, was an avid Rollerblader, and had spent a sizeable amount of his country's scarce cash on constructing asphalt skate paths.

Happy, stomachs full and feeling a warm vodka buzz, we piled into Adam's jeep late that night, glad Nuria was serving as designated driver. We walked the few steps from Adam and Nuria's house to the farmhouse in the dark, still night, and tried not to make too much noise as we climbed the stairs to our room.

Before leaving the Bialowieza Forest region, we spent a day walking in and around the little village where Nuria worked at a scientific institute. We walked through the grounds of a large park that included a partially frozen pond amid the lawns and trees. The ground was covered with a deep carpet of fallen leaves; and we spent a couple of hours making large piles of leaves and jumping into them while laughing and screaming.

In the morning, we thanked our hosts and rolled our

bags down the lane to the only market in the tiny village, where we would catch the bus that would take us back to the train station in Bialystok. We had hoped Adam would travel back to Warsaw with us, but he received a last minute assignment and was preparing for a trip with a photographer from the paper. He insisted on writing out a request for three first-class tickets to Warsaw from Bialystok, which turned out to be very helpful when we presented it at the train station ticket window.

Nov. 1 was All Saints' Day, when Poles honor the graves of their deceased relatives. Along the way, we passed several cemeteries packed with families dressed in their finest. They carried bunches of flowers to place at the graves of their loved ones, along with picnic baskets and folded blankets. Apparently, the All Saints' Day tradition in Poland includes picnicking in the cemetery. The streets around the cemeteries were jammed with cars on this national holiday, and cops were out in force directing traffic.

Maybe because we were traveling on the actual holiday, the train back to Warsaw was much less crowded than the one a few days earlier from Warsaw to Bialystok, and we easily found seats in an empty compartment. We had plenty of room to stash Big Bertha and our other bags, and still stretch out in comfort. I spent the time gazing out the window at the passing farms and towns, reading a book and dozing.

I had a few brief moments of anxiety when I realized the train stopped at three different stations in Warsaw. But I asked around and learned the final stop was the city's central station, which was supposed to be close to the hostel where we had booked a room. I relaxed and enjoyed the final few minutes of the train ride, which passed through gritty, working-class areas of Warsaw, featuring blocks of square gray apartment buildings.

Our train pulled into Warsaw's central station in the waning light of a late afternoon. I was gun-shy about being ripped off by predatory taxi drivers and figured we could walk to the place we were staying, the Okidoki Hostel. I called from the station to get directions, and we set off on foot, pulling our bags behind us.

As we emerged from the station, a huge dark shape loomed before us. The massive building we saw was called the Palace of Culture and Science, which was built during the 50s by the Soviet Union as a gesture of "friendship" from dictator Josef Stalin to the Polish people. The squarish building was designed in a Gothic style, with a huge central tower topped by a spire. It was – and still is – the tallest building in Poland, and in Central Europe as well. The building remains controversial in Warsaw. Some see it as an unwelcome reminder of the period of Soviet domination. Others feel that, in spite of its origins, the Palace is a landmark and part of Warsaw's identity. We read that the Poles, known for their irreverent humor, made the building the butt of many jokes, including its popular nickname, "Stalin's Penis."

Later on our visit to Warsaw, we got to see the Palace at night, when it was lighted. I had to admit that it did exhibit a certain regal charm.

After taking in the Palace and the surrounding streets, we got moving – night was coming on and we needed to find our hostel.

We walked for 10 minutes or so in the direction of

the hostel and reached the intersection of two major boulevards. The hostel desk clerk had told me the hostel was very close to that intersection, but we had no idea which direction to take, and the sketchy map in our guidebook was no help. So, we picked a direction and started walking. Ava and Salome were pulling their bags, while I was wearing a backpack and pulling a second bag. We were cold, tired and hungry.

We did come across some interesting sights, such as a church with a statue of the late Pope John Paul II. Hundreds of candles in red, yellow and orange glass holders had been lighted and placed on the steps in front of the bronze statue, and as we watched, tour buses pulled up and more visitors piled out to place their own candles. At the time, we wondered if it was some sort of anniversary related to John Paul, but I later realized the display must have been in honor of All Saints' Day.

It was getting later, colder and darker, and still no sign of the Okidoki Hostel.

"Daddy, when are we going to get to our hotel? I'm tired of walking," Salome said, just a hint of a whine in her voice. Clearly, we would have to do something soon, as the natives were getting restless.

We stopped a man who was walking by, and headed in the direction he pointed, which was back toward the intersection we had passed through earlier. That proved to be the breakthrough we needed – we tried a narrow side street and came out upon a small square park surrounded on four sides by apartment buildings. On the corner of one building, about two floors up, was a small, lighted sign that read "Okidoki Hostel."

The Okidoki was one of the few hostels we stayed at during our trip. Mostly, we aimed for small, mid-priced family-owned hotels, which worked out well. We didn't have the money for five-star lodgings, and even if we had, I wouldn't have wanted to stay in such fancy digs. From what I saw on the road, top-end hotels insulated their guests from the local sights, smells and sounds in a cocoon of security guards and luxurious trappings, from satellite TV and foo-foo shampoos, to cushy comforters and in-room coffee makers. Not that those things are bad, but if that's what we wanted, we could have booked a room in the Hilton or Hyatt near the beach in San Diego and saved ourselves a lot of time, energy and money.

That said, we weren't really into staying at bargain-basement accommodations, either. Our travel budget was ample enough that we didn't have to seek out the very cheapest lodgings, or set any records for spending the least amount possible to put a roof over our heads. Our demands for lodging were pretty straightforward – we had to feel safe coming and going, day or night, and the place had to meet basic standards of cleanliness. We put a premium on hotels that were well-located with regard to public transportation and services such as shopping and dining. We wanted a private bathroom whenever we could get one (although a shared bath wasn't necessarily a deal-breaker, if the facilities were well-maintained); a working TV was also a plus.

Warsaw's Okidoki Hostel was on the third through fifth floors of what appeared to be an office building. To reach the lobby, we had to carry our bags up several flights of stairs. There didn't appear to be a bellman on duty. So, we slowly made our way upstairs, relieved to have found the place and to be out of the chilly air of a November night in Warsaw.

We found the lobby to be a cheerful hive of activity. The walls were painted bright orange, and the staff were all in their 20s, possibly college students. The guests were foreigners of varying ages, from their 20s through their 50s. We were the only family with a child, but the staff quickly made us feel at home.

We gave our names and presented our passports, and were soon hauling our bags up one more flight of stairs to our cozy room. We had a private bath, a queen-size bed and a cot for Salome, and a radiator that emanated warmth. We were set.

One floor up from our room was a space that doubled as a pub each evening, and a dining room in the morning. During happy hour, guests could buy cheap draft beer, listen to music on a CD player, and play cards or board games. Red mood lighting completed the ambiance. The basic breakfast of milk and dry cereal, yogurt, bread, butter and jam was served on the bar.

On our first morning in Warsaw, I had teacher duty while Ava went out to continue her quest to get malaria pills for our upcoming trip to India. Warsaw was our next-to-last stop before Mumbai; if we struck out here, we would have to get the meds in London or arrive in India unprepared. We had read, and been told by our travel clinic, that you needed to start taking malaria medications for a full week before arriving in a malarial area. During our stay in Warsaw, we were already within the one-week window and the days were dwindling.

Before leaving on our trip, we had been given

prescriptions for an anti-malarial drug called Larium. But fellow travelers had warned us that the drug, although one of the newer anti-malarials, sometimes caused serious psychological side effects such as insomnia, anxiety and nightmares. I did some research online and found that as many as 25 percent of those who took Larium experienced some level of side effects. Ava and I decided that Larium was not for us and instead looked into some other anti-malarial drugs.

We tried a couple of pharmacies in Warsaw without luck. Malaria is practically non-existent in Poland, and neither doctors nor pharmacists have much familiarity with anti-malarial drugs. One clinic told us that the only way we could get a prescription for anti-malarial drugs would be to contact the national health ministry. Suffering from an uncharacteristic bout of anxiety, Ava concocted a plan to "doctor" some of the extra prescriptions we have been given by the travel clinic back home to obtain the anti-malarial drugs we needed. I convinced her, however, not to worry about it, because I was pretty sure we'd be able to get the drugs in London.

Our favorite lunchtime haunt was a kebab stand around the corner from the Okidoki Hostel. Varshovians, as Warsaw residents are called, would start lining up at this stand (actually a counter set in the wall of a mid-block building) in late morning. Customers ordered and paid at the window and a few minutes later, the food would be handed out at an adjacent window. Thin strips of succulent meat were wrapped in pita bread, topped with chopped tomatoes and yogurt sauce. The sandwiches were delicious, cheap, and we would join the locals in perching on a nearby curb, or just standing on the sidewalk while wolfing down our kebabs.

Sometimes, we would take Salome to a nearby McDonald's restaurant, which was decorated with photos of other McDonald's outlets in cities around the world. By this point in our trip, it felt like we had visited most, if not all, of the restaurants shown in the photos. In reality, we still had quite a few more to go before we made it back to Southern California.

In the afternoons, we set out on foot to see Warsaw, armed with our guidebook and a small map provided by the hostel's front desk. We visited Lazienki Park near central Warsaw, which once served as the summer palace of Poland's last king, Stanislaw August Poniatowski. The park is scenic and peaceful, with many paths through lush, forested areas, ornate buildings, a lake, bridges, and peacocks roaming throughout. At one end is a famous statue of the Polish composer Frederic Chopin, set in a rose garden, where free classical concerts are held on summer evenings. In early November, the rose bushes were bare of flowers or leaves, but the surrounding trees were still cloaked in the brown, yellow and red leaves of autumn.

A man near the entrance to the park sold little clay bird whistles. When filled with water and blown just right, they produced a very respectable bird-like warble. We bought one for Salome, who had some difficulty getting the whistle to work. She kept trying as we strolled, and soon she was able to whistle a bit, although not nearly as well as the vendor, who had lots of time to practice.

We also bought Salome a bag of seed, which she used to feed the many peacocks strutting around the park.

We were lucky enough to encounter several males that treated us to shows of their magnificent tail plumage. The peacocks were not the most considerate birds; they ran roughshod over any smaller birds in an effort to get at the seed we scattered on the ground. The peacock's high-pitched cries, which sound nearly like a human baby's, echoed through the park.

Our rambles took us in all directions from our hotel, to sights that included a monument to Poland's war heroes, a tomb of an unknown soldier guarded both by an eternal flame and a platoon of stoic soldiers.

We also walked to Warsaw's historic district, which included some of the city's most ritzy hotels, where I found a cigar shop selling Cuban puros. They weren't cheap, but good stogies were hard to find in Eastern Europe, so I bought a couple.

Late in the afternoon, we reached Warsaw's Old Town, or Stare Miasto, which included the city's Royal Castle. The brick buildings and cobblestone streets had a slightly unreal feeling, making the area seem more like a movie set than a medieval city. That's because every inch of the historic district, from the castle ramparts to the picturesque square, had been painstakingly recreated over the past 50 years, following the complete destruction of the area by the Nazis in retaliation for the Warsaw Uprising of 1944.

We walked around, bought Salome magic tricks from a costumed vendor who sported a trained parrot, and headed back to our hotel as the sun dropped to the horizon and the air turned chilly.

We spent our last night in Warsaw packing and settling our bill with the hostel. We wanted to be ready to leave first thing in the morning to catch our flight to London.

During the early morning taxi ride to the airport, we got a good look at Warsaw's outlying neighborhoods, which consisted mostly of blocks of apartment buildings, stretching out as far as the eye could see. The squat, colorless buildings were a legacy of the Communist era, when ugly architecture was the least of the population's problems. We were glad to have spent time in Warsaw and gotten to know some of the locals, who had a good sense of humor and appreciated their newfound freedoms, even if they seemed a bit weary of struggling to get ahead financially. Thanks to the early hour, the streets were deserted, and we cruised to the airport, where we boarded a jetliner for the two-hour flight to London, which also passed uneventfully.

Compared to our arrival in London a couple of months earlier, when we were grilled by an overzealous immigration inspector and nearly denied entrance because we couldn't remember the last name of Ava's aunt (who was putting us up) our arrival in Great Britain on this November morning was easy as pie. There was hardly any line at customs or immigration, and soon we were riding the Tube to our hotel near Hyde Park.

We had booked a room at the Best Western Phoenix Hotel from Adam's computer in the Bialowieza Forest, and the room rate was a shock to our modest budget. Four nights at this mid-level hotel, a glorified Holiday Inn, set us back about $600, the most we paid for lodgings during our entire trip. The rooms were clean, comfortable and quiet, with soft beds and fluffy pillows, and they provided a decent hot breakfast, so we sucked it up. The best thing about the Phoenix was its location: just three blocks from sprawling Hyde Park, where I took my morning runs, and a short walk to every conceivable service, including a Tube station, Internet café, laundry, post office, shops, restaurants and even an ice-skating rink.

Our goal for the four days we would spend in London on this leg of our trip was to obtain and start taking the malaria meds that would protect us during our upcoming foray to India. We also planned to visit a few museums, see Ava's relatives and have lunch with Paul and Abbie, a couple we met over the summer in the Galapagos. Our only other task was to stock up on reading material at London's excellent, if pricey, bookstores, since we weren't sure how easy it would be to find English-language books in India, Thailand or the other Asian destinations on our itinerary. (On our first swing through London in September, we had bought Harry Potter and the Half-Blood Prince, the sixth book in the series, which came out in July while we were in South America.)

We arrived in London for the second time on Saturday, Nov. 5, 2005, which was the day the city traditionally erupts in bonfires and pyrotechnic displays in celebration of Guy Fawkes Day. This holiday bears some similarities to the American Fourth of July, but only on the surface. Britain's fiery fiesta commemorates the apprehension of a group of conspirators who planned to protest what they saw as religious persecution by blowing up the Parliament building, with practically the entire government, including the king, inside. The celebrations sometimes include the burning in effigy of the infamous Guy Fawkes, the most famous of the plotters.

What really makes the celebration interesting, though, is that in England, everyone is a pyrotechnics expert. Fireworks are readily available and people throughout the city stage backyard displays that would put to shame many professional fireworks shows in the U.S..

We checked into our hotel, napped for a while, then hit the streets in the early evening to see the fireworks. Night fell by 6 p.m. or so, and explosions could already be heard in every direction. By the height of the celebration, at 9 p.m., it was easy to imagine what the London blitzkrieg during World War II had sounded like. Colorful bursts lit up the sky everywhere we looked, and we walked through residential neighborhoods trying to find a good spot to watch the show. After wandering around for several blocks, we came to the top of a hill; directly below us, in a backyard, an amateur pyrotechnics display was underway. We were so close to the explosions of colored sparks and smoke that it felt like we were literally in the line of fire.

The next day we inquired at the local pharmacy about malaria meds. After all the frustration of trying to get the drugs in Poland, we were overjoyed to learn that the medication we needed could be purchased right off the shelf, without a prescription, and a two-month supply for the three of us would only cost about $150. We made an appointment at the British Air travel clinic on Piccadilly Square just to be sure, and the nurse there confirmed the drugs we had obtained would do the job.

So there we were, in a holding pattern in London, waiting for what the three of us knew would be the biggest leap of faith of the entire trip. Our plans called for flying into Mumbai, India, early on the morning of Nov. 10 and traveling in the subcontinent until Jan. 15, when we would fly from Mumbai to Bangkok. For more than two months, we would be on our own in a nation of more than 1 billion people, and we didn't know a soul, except for the friend of a friend whom we had met briefly in Oceanside.

We had hotel reservations for the first few nights of our stay and a vague outline of the places we wanted to visit.

India would be radically different from anyplace we had experienced before. The food, customs, religious practices and native languages were all very distant from the culture we left behind in the U.S. Mentally, we braced ourselves for India's noise, pollution and poverty, and the images we had seen of beggars and cripples in the streets. India also was the furthest from home in terms of distance – it was roughly halfway around the world from California as the crow flies (the time difference is 13.5 hours). In my mind, our flight to Mumbai served as a demarcation point for our trip: once we boarded the British Air jetliner bound for Mumbai, the shortest route home would be onward through Thailand, Hong Kong and Tokyo. There was literally no turning back.

All of these thoughts careened around in my head during those four days in London, inspiring anxiety and excitement at the same time. Part of me wanted to cash in our tickets and head back to California, while the other part was eager to begin this challenging, even risky, new phase of our adventure. We prepared ourselves as well as we could: our medications were in order, we had washed our clothes in the coin laundry, and we carried a stack of new books. All too soon, the day of our flight arrived: India beckoned.

Young men practice capoeira, which combines martial arts, dance and music, in Salvador de Bahia, Brazil.

Carved Buddha faces at Bayon Temple,
Angkor Wat, Cambodia.

Monastery in the foreground of Kanchenjunga,
Darjeeling, India.

Cow strolls on the beach in Goa, India.

Street performer in Bangkok, Thailand.

Boy on Taquile Island, Lake Titicaca,
between Peru and Bolivia.

Iguazu Falls, from the Brazilian side.

Marine iguanas, Galapagos Islands, Ecuador.

Camel fair, Pushkar, India.

Salome and Joe get a lesson in snake charming,
Jaipur, India.

Noodles in Hong Kong.

Temple on the outskirts of Tokyo.

To see more photos, log on to www.bewareofwildmonkeys.com

Chapter 9

Dollars, Reales or Rupees, It's All Money

The idea of gallivanting around the globe is exciting, even intoxicating. But taking such a trip requires more than wanderlust – it takes cash.

How much to take, and where to get it, are questions that must pop up in the mind of anyone who has ever contemplated a round-the-world journey.

The answers, of course, depend a lot on the tastes and bank account of the traveler-to-be. In our case, I started planning our budget with the general proposition of spending $100 a day, times 365 days, for a total of $36,500. That amount was intended to cover our daily living expenses, including food and a roof over our heads. I knew from the start that our trip would lean more toward Lonely Planet than Lifestyles of the Rich and Famous.

From there, I added in major expenses such as our round-the-world airfare, ground transportation, health insurance, and preparatory costs, such as storing our furniture. The grand total I came up with was about $90,000 for our trip, which was originally planned to last 11 months. The sum also included a cushion for incidentals, such as buying souvenirs, clothes and other items along the way, and a $10,000 reserve to help us get started again when we returned home.

In the end, this planning budget proved to be very close to the actual amount we spent on the road, although our money didn't last quite as long as we had anticipated.

We were in a good position financially as we started planning. We owned two properties, our home and a rental; we had zero debt other than our mortgages and a fair amount in savings. However, we didn't have enough cash to pay for a world trip, even on a tight budget, considering that we would not be working for the better part of a year. My original thought was to sell one or both of our houses, use some of the money for the trip, and bank the rest to buy another house when we returned.

Ava and I went back and forth on this point; I liked the idea of selling the houses because it would free of us of the responsibilities attached to property ownership, and we wouldn't have to worry about what was happening to the houses while we were traveling in distant lands.

But Ava argued that if we sold the houses, we would have to pay both the sales costs and the costs associated with buying a new home after the trip, depleting our nest egg by thousands of dollars.

She prevailed. With some trepidation, I agreed to hire a property manager and rent out both homes during our absence. This put us ahead in several ways: we brought in rental income during our trip, and we avoided the steep costs of buying and selling real estate. We also had a place to return to once our trip was over and our tenants had completed their lease, another cost saving.

The major downside, in my mind, was the risk of having tenants living in two properties while we were so far away. But we had insurance and a trustworthy, reliable property manager.

As mentioned earlier, since we couldn't use the proceeds of selling our house to finance the trip, we refinanced our home and pulled out $50,000 in cash. That sum, along with savings and cashing in some smaller investments, put us over the top.

Next, we had to come up with a plan to access our cash from the road, other than carrying huge wads of greenbacks in our suitcases or money belts. I'm a strong believer in plans backup plans, and backups to the backup plans, especially when we would be in exotic, unfamiliar locales many thousands of miles from home.

From previous travels, I knew that electronic banking had progressed to the point where ATMs were available in virtually every corner of the world. Thus, each time we arrived at a new destination, one of our first tasks was to find a cash machine and withdraw our daily limit in the local currency, which is generally the equivalent of $300 U.S. for each card.

Just in case, we bought a few hundred dollars' worth of travelers checks, which we split up and kept in our money belts, along with a stash of American dollars. Both Ava and I had our own ATM cards with unique PIN codes, which eased our minds a bit when unforeseen circumstances cropped up, such as a bank cash machine in Rio de Janeiro that ate Ava's cash card. We each carried a credit card in case all else failed.

I made sure to notify our credit union about our travel

plans, so that alarm bells would not sound when we used our ATM and credit cards in Ecuador, Uruguay, Cambodia or other places we visited during our trip. But in spite of best-laid plans, wrinkles did arise. Soon after we left home, due to a widespread hacking incident, the credit union decided to cancel all of its customers' ATM cards and issue new ones. My father-in-law emailed us with this potentially disastrous piece of news, and we were able to reach the credit union by phone during a shore excursion on our boat trip through the Galapagos Islands. The credit union helpfully agreed not to shut off our cards.

We also grappled with a problem that we knew was coming. Before we left, the credit union had notified us that it would be canceling all of the credit cards it had issued and sending out new ones to its customers, due to an overhaul of its financial systems. The problem was, they didn't know exactly when this would happen. I didn't want to be left without a backup credit card for most of the trip, so I kept in email contact with a woman in the credit card department, and she was able to send my new card by FedEx to our guesthouse in Jaipur, India. I was grateful for the credit union's cooperation, and also somewhat proud of myself for successfully orchestrating this bit of international high finance.

The wide availability of Internet cafes in the biggest cities and tiniest towns along our route made handling our family finances online a virtual snap.

I kept the bulk of our travel funds in an interest-bearing savings account, and periodically transferred sums to our checking account, which we could access from the worldwide ATM network. I don't know if it made sense or not, but I reasoned that even if our cash cards and PIN codes fell into enemy hands, the thieves would at most be able to clean out the checking account.

Before leaving, I had set up most of our recurring bills on automatic payments, with the rest to be handled by our property manager back home. Rent payments were deposited into our checking account, which I could monitor online. I was even able to pay our property tax bill from an Internet café in an Austrian mountain resort.

So, with a combination of our cash cards, a handy network of ATMs stretching from Chile and Argentina to Spain and Poland, Mumbai and Delhi to Bangkok and Siem Reap, we were able to pay for all of our expenses while traveling, and we never even had to resort to our emergency stash of U.S. dollars and travelers checks (except once in Peru, when the tour company for our Inca Trail hike demanded payment only in American currency.)

I felt quite comfortable withdrawing the daily limit from an ATM and carrying the bulk of our cash in our money belts. We would keep some of the bills in our pockets or wallets for convenience, and the rest stashed out of sight under our clothing. The cash generally lasted two or three days, and we would then make another withdrawal. This system seemed to work well and we never found ourselves short of cash.

For larger purchases, such as paying a hotel bill, we would make extra cash withdrawals or, when possible, pay with my debit card, which was linked to our checking account.

After we got off the plane in San Jose at the end of our trip, I pulled the wrinkled, torn envelope containing my traveler's checks from my money belt and splurged on dinner to celebrate the completion of our round-the-world journey.

Chapter 10

Hungry Monkeys and Sacred Cows

Mumbai to Delhi, India

"I believe that all of us, individual souls, living in this ocean of spirit, are the same as one another with the closest bond among ourselves. A drop that separates soon dries up and any soul that believes itself separate from others is likewise destroyed."

Mohandas K. Ghandi, Father of Modern India

"Please put on your oxygen masks! There has been a drop in cabin pressure! Please put on your oxygen masks! There has been a drop in cabin pressure!"

My eyes shot open, all remnants of sleep vanishing from my mind like smoke swept away by a powerful wind. I was instantly awake, but my mind was still unable to process what I could see and hear.

I had been dozing on a long-haul British Airways flight from London to Mumbai. The cabin lights had been turned off, and passengers huddled beneath blankets, sleeping, watching movies on the seat-back screens, or reading in small pools of light.

Suddenly, the peace and quiet shattered. Every light on the plane flashed on in full brightness, and the clipped British voice began delivering its loud, urgent message over and over without any change in inflection.

I looked next to me at Ava and Salome, who appeared as wide-eyed and shocked as I felt. All around us, as the recorded voice blared the same order again and again, I saw arms raised up, fingers grasping at the empty space where oxygen masks were supposed to be dangling.

Salome started to cry, and I tried to calm her: "It's okay, honey, everything's going to be all right." I hugged her close to me, but was far from sure I was telling her the truth.

Still, the passengers' arms reached up, groping at the consoles above them. They reminded me of sightless Zombies walking across a field in Night of the Living Dead. For some reason, even though I knew it was pointless, I too reached up and fumbled around the panel above my head. Maybe because there was nothing else to do. Flight attendants scurried up and down the aisles, their faces tight, but providing neither reassurance nor direction.

"Are you okay?" I asked Ava and Salome. "Can you breathe all right?"

They both nodded.

"Me too," I said. "It must be some kind of glitch, otherwise the masks would really come down."

We could hear the roar of the plane's engines, which seemed to be strong and steady, but terror lurked inside me as I waited to see what would happen next. Would the engines just stop, causing the plane to plummet to the earth? I felt helpless, and realized that whatever happened, there was absolutely nothing us passengers could do except sit in our seats, hearts pounding.

Then, as abruptly as the voice had started, it stopped. There was silence in the airplane, except for the drone of the engines. Then the passengers started talking excitedly; I could also hear a few muffled wails.

The lights remained on, and in a few minutes, the proper English voice of the captain came over the PA system. "Hello, folks, sorry for the disturbance. We have run a check of all vital systems, and everything seems to be in order. We surmise there must have been an electrical malfunction that triggered the warning, but we can detect no change in cabin pressure. From what we can tell, the aircraft remains quite serviceable, and we will continue on to Mumbai. Again, we apologize for this inconvenience."

The captain clicked off, and Ava and I looked at each other.

"Quite serviceable?" I said. "Not exactly the reassurance I was looking for. Maybe that's just the British way, you know, keep a stiff upper lip."

She nodded. "It would have been nice to hear him say, 'Don't worry,' or, 'Everything is just fine.'"

From my calculations, we still had about three hours remaining on the flight, and for the entire time, we sat in our seats nervously, listening for any slight change in the thrum of the engines. To compound our anxiety, the main cabin lights stayed on for the rest of the trip, and every once in a while, they would blink off and on. The flight attendants tried unsuccessfully to reset the in-flight video system, which had been knocked out by the electrical malfunction, whatever it was. And even though the cabin lights were on, the reading lights didn't work any more, so we couldn't even read. Some of the passengers pulled up their blankets and tried to go back to sleep, but I just sat in my seat, trying to push thoughts of fiery explosions out of my head.

My imagination had come up with many potential disasters that could befall us in India. The one thing I had felt complete confidence in was British Airway's ability to deliver us safely to our destination. Now, as we approached the subcontinent, I had no idea what to expect.

Eventually, the jetliner approached Mumbai, and we cruised in for a smooth landing at Chattrapathi Shivaji International Airport. We arrived in Mumbai about 12:30 a.m. local time, our nerves jangled by the airplane's electronic hijinks, and still apprehensive about our upcoming nine-week sojourn in India.

We progressed through customs and immigration without incident, and proceeded to the exit, looking for the driver of the prepaid taxi who was supposed to meet us. We had arranged for the Railway Hotel, where we had booked two nights, to send a car.

By the time we cleared customs and picked up our bags, it was after 1 a.m., but the sidewalk outside the terminal was crowded with people, and the air was hot and muggy. We found our driver, and stopped at an ATM near the airport entrance to withdraw some rupees. At the time, one U.S. dollar was worth 45 rupees.

The driver helped us out to his car, which resembled a VW minibus. He cranked up the puttering engine, and we rolled out into the Mumbai night. Ava, Salome and I huddled together in the back seat of the minivan, quietly watching the dimly lit city streets through the window.

At that time of the morning, the streets were nearly empty of vehicles. We bumped along on surface streets, as there didn't seem to be a highway leading from the airport. Soon, we noticed a shocking sight – all along the road, which was lined with market stalls, were people sleeping on the ground under thin blankets. The luckier ones slept on wooden tables or benches, which were probably used to display goods during the day. The homeless residents of Mumbai spread out before us as we drove to our hotel; there were literally miles of people sleeping shoulder-to-shoulder in the night, their bed the dirt edge of the road, their pillow a bundle of clothes, or nothing at all. We had seen homeless people; San Diego, like all cities, has its share of unfortunates bedding down in doorways and on sidewalks. But we had never before witnessed poverty of this magnitude, and it caused me to wonder just what we had gotten ourselves into. The scene of desperate poverty had an otherworldly feel, as the only lighting came from our van's headlights, a few reddish streetlights and an occasional cooking fire.

The ride to the Railway Hotel took about 45 minutes, and we were underwhelmed when we pulled up in front. The hotel was on the corner of a squalid block, where motorized rickshaws, called "tuk-tuks" parked, their blanket-wrapped drivers asleep in the back seats. The tuk-tuks were small vehicles used to ferry passengers around India's choked streets. The driver sat on a seat resembling the front half of a motorcycle, with the throttle in the handgrip. Passengers sat on a small bench seat behind the driver, and the whole thing was enclosed in a canopy that was usually open on the sides. During busy commute times, we would see entire families of 6 or 8 people, or more than a half-dozen uniformed schoolchildren, packed into a single tuk-tuk. The dreary scene outside the Railway Hotel was enlivened by strings of colored lights adorning the building, which we figured had been put up for Diwali, India's festival of lights, which had ended a few days earlier.

As we groggily climbed out of the minivan and crossed the sidewalk, a large rat scurried along the gutter and into a crack in the wall.

Welcome to India.

We had chosen the Railway Hotel because it was just down the street from the city's central train station, known as Victoria Terminus when the country was under British rule, but now renamed Chattrapathi Shivaji Terminus. Both the international airport and train station are named after the founder of the Maratha empire in western India in 1674, who is revered in the modern-day Indian state of Maharashtra, of which Mumbai (called Bombay until 1995) is the capital. The city is reportedly the most populous in the world, with 13 million residents.

One of our first orders of business in India would be buying train tickets for our trip to Pushkar, in the northern desert state of Rajasthan. We planned to spend a couple of days in Mumbai before heading up north for the Pushkar Camel Fair, a wildly popular annual festival.

But on the early morning when we arrived in Mumbai, all we had in mind was climbing into bed for a few hours' sleep. The hotel lobby was small, but well-furnished – so well-furnished that several employees were sacked out on the sofas, snoozing under light blankets. The bleary-eyed desk clerk looked like he had very recently been doing the same. He was friendly, though, and asked us where we were from, and whether we were Christians, which I found disconcerting.

Although it was nearly 3 a.m. by the time we got into our upper-floor room, we were all hungry and thirsty, so I asked the bellman if the hotel kitchen could make us some food. He came back in a few minutes with three ice-cold bottles of Pepsi on a tray, which we gratefully accepted.

The room had a TV with decent reception, although most of the channels were in Hindi. There was a good air conditioner and three soft single beds. We settled in for some shut-eye, after asking for a 7 a.m. wakeup call, so that we could be first in line for train tickets in the morning.

Before we left on our trip, and during our sojourns in South America and Europe, I had handled most of the planning for transportation and lodging, excursions, finance and health insurance. Armed with guidebooks, a fax machine, Internet connection, email and an international calling card, I spent hours each day in my home office, planning the details of our trip.

By the time we reached India, about five months into our trip, this had become a sore point between Ava and me; she didn't realize how much it was stressing me out to be responsible for all the logistics. After some "discussions" about this, she readily agreed to take on some of those duties, and her first task in India was a big one – on our first morning in Mumbai, she would walk

to the train station and book our sleeper car tickets to
Rajasthan while I stayed at the hotel with Salome.

With the help of our guidebook, we determined we
needed train tickets from Mumbai to Ajmer, a mid-sized
town in Rajasthan, some 19 hours by train from Mumbai.
From Ajmer, we would take a taxi or bus the last 15 or so
miles to Pushkar, where the camel fair is held. The trip
from Ajmer to Pushkar included traversing a mountain
pass, but was supposed to take only 30 minutes.

But we had read, and been told by Indian friends,
that the trains are prone to fill up during November
and December, the most popular time for travel on the
subcontinent. So we were a little concerned about getting
train tickets for the evening of Nov. 11, because we had
prepaid hotel reservations in Pushkar for Nov. 12, the start
of the camel fair.

Ava and I woke up early that morning to the sound
of honking car horns on the street below our hotel room
window. Salome was still sleeping soundly, and Ava,
with an apprehensive look on her face, dressed and got
ready to go.

"All right," she said, "I'm off the train station. I'll see
you in a bit."

"Do you have money and all three passports?" I asked.

"Yep," she said, patting her money belt. "All set."

"Are you sure you want to do this?" I asked. "Maybe I
should go."

"It'll be fine. I'll get the tickets and be right back," she
said, looking less sure than her words suggested, and
giving me a peck on the lips.

"OK, well, good luck. Be careful," I said.

"I will," she said.

The door closed, and I tried to go back to sleep, achieving only a light doze. After what seemed like just a few minutes, I heard the door open, and she was back.

She was keyed up, but smiling. "I got the tickets. It was an adventure though," she said breathlessly.

She told me she had arrived to find a huge line of people already standing at the ticket windows before they even opened for business. Luckily, she was able to get in a shorter line reserved for foreign tourists. She nearly triggered an international incident when she panicked at the ticket window because she couldn't find our passports in her purse. Accusingly, she asked another foreign tourist in line if he had seen the passports; then she remembered they were tucked in her money belt under her clothes, as I had insisted.

But the good news was we had three second-class sleeper tickets for Ajmer, which cost under $100 U.S. total. Ironically, our train would depart from Bandra Terminus, across town from the "conveniently" located Railway Hotel.

Salome was still asleep, so we decided to snooze for a bit more before venturing out to see Mumbai.

It felt good to sleep in after our long – and nerve-wracking – plane ride, and the next thing we wanted, after waking up about mid-morning, was a shower to wash off the road grime. In reading about India, we noticed that hotels advertised a couple of ways of delivering hot water to their guests – the geyser, and "bucket hot water." (The geyser is an electrical device in the bathroom that heats the water as needed, which we would come to know very well during our travels.)

The Railway Hotel, a modest place on the edge of Mumbai's financial district, had opted for the latter system, and we soon learned how it worked. We called down to the front desk and asked for hot water. "No problem," said the deskman.

A few minutes later, there was a knock on the door. We opened it to see a hotel bellman carrying a large, plastic water bucket. He was breathing hard from carrying the bucket up the stairs, and he gamely carried the pail of steaming water into the bathroom.

"I'll be back," he grunted, and returned a few minutes later with a second bucket.

The water was hot enough that we had to mix in cold water from a tap in the tiled shower area of the bathroom. All three of us, unsure about the whole bucket business, found that we were cleansed and refreshed by this Indian style of bathing, in which we poured warm water over our heads using the plastic containers provided in our bathroom, lathered up, and then rinsed with another dousing of warm water. All was well – as long as we didn't have to haul the water up the stairs ourselves!

Washed and rested, we headed down to the breakfast room on the ground floor of the hotel, hoping we could still grab a bite. We were pleasantly surprised to find a cheery, if windowless, room, where fruit, bread and less familiar delicacies were laid out. I helped myself to a soupy lentil dish that I thought might be daal, and a piece of flat bread. The food was tasty, but very spicy. The waiter served us coffee, and offered to bring eggs which Salome eagerly accepted. Our fellow diners appeared to be Indian businesmen, dressed in button-down shirts, neatly pressed slacks and sandals. There were no other families with children.

Finally, in the heat of early afternoon, it was time for us to check out the streets of Mumbai. The first thing I noticed were the hordes of yellow taxicabs, whose drivers seemed to feel that the horn was as important to proper driving as the steering wheel or gas pedal. The cabbies drove hunched over toward the windshield, one hand on the wheel and one pumping the horn. The sound of honking horns was so constant in Mumbai and every other Indian city we visited, that soon it just blended in with the rest of the street sounds so that you could hardly notice it.

The next thing that struck me was the cows. Bovines wandered wherever they wanted, among cars stopped at traffic lights, along the gutters and even on the sidewalks. Down the street from our hotel, in the middle of a frantically busy traffic circle, was a sort of corral, where women dressed in rags gave food and water to the animals. While it was hard to find a hamburger in Mumbai – even McDonald's served a double-decker concoction called a "Chicken Maharaja Mac" made with spiced chicken patties – it was no problem locating a head of beef roaming the city's streets.

Mumbai is known as the home of Bollywood, the Indian movie studios that crank out Hindi movies with lots of singing, dancing and colorful costumes. It's also the nation's financial hub, where the national stock exchange and many banks and insurance companies are located. As we walked the street on our first full day in the country, a hot and muggy November afternoon, we saw hordes of office workers striding purposefully on the sidewalks and in the streets, dodging cars, bicycles, carts and cows. Most wore what appeared to be the country's national uniform – neatly pressed dark slacks, button-down dress shirts, and sandals. We saw few women among the constant parade of office workers.

Our noses were assaulted with smells as we walked. The stink of cow dung and urine alternated with delicious aromas of spicy food and perfumed incense, as we passed restaurants and shops. Buildings such as the central post office and train station boasted ornate Victorian architecture, but closer inspection showed they were marred by dark water stains, peeling paint and rusted metal gates and railings.

Our first destination was the Gateway of India, which was probably a mile or so from our hotel, along major thoroughfares. We also wanted to see the Taj Mahal Hotel, across from the Gateway monument, which was said to be one of the most luxurious lodging establishments in all of India.

As we walked along the hot, crowded streets, we saw few foreigners, and we attracted stares. At one point, we passed a complex separated from the street by high gray walls – from our map, we figured out it was a Navy base. The wall and sidewalk were much cleaner and neater than the other blocks we had passed – I saw a sign on the wall with the stern warning "No Public Urination."

And that was another thing that put us off: it was very common to see men standing next to buildings, doing their business as if they were in the privacy of their own bathrooms. People cleared their throats and spit onto the ground wherever they stood, causing us to pay close attention to where we were walking.

As we neared the waterfront and the Gateway arch, we began to see street vendors selling their wares, and we got our first taste of India's legion of hawkers. One vendor sold oversized children's balloons, and he followed us for half a block, calling out, "You buy for your little girl, very good price, three for 50 rupees."

The Gateway of India is a stone arch crowned by four towers, built by the British to commemorate the visit of King George V and Queen Mary in 1911. Construction was completed in 1924. These days, the gateway is a gathering point for locals and tourists alike, and it is the place to catch excursion boats to Elephanta Island, where fantastic elephant-headed sculptures were carved inside caves centuries ago. There were plenty of vendors who regaled us to buy their goods, from ice cream to henna tattoos. Ava couldn't resist the latter offer, so Salome and I waited while a dark-brown pattern was stenciled onto her palm.

Sari-clad women holding babies also came up to us, their arms extended, palm up, with pleading looks. We gave them whatever coins we carried, saddened by their condition and knowing that even if we emptied our pockets, we still wouldn't put much of a dent in the city's poverty. One woman was more persistent than the rest, and took advantage of our Western guilt.

"Please, my baby needs milk," she said, holding up a bundled infant. I started to give her some money, and she stopped me.

"No. Come. Buy milk." She gestured, and the three of us followed warily.

She led us to a tiny market on a side street just a block or two from the Gateway monument.

"Milk," the woman said to the proprietor, who looked at me. "200 rupees," he said.

I pulled out some rupee notes and paid him. The woman smiled, took the carton of milk, and whisked away down the street. As we turned from the counter, I realized we'd been "had": a carton of milk should have cost far less than the $4 U.S. I had just paid. Once we left, the woman would probably come back to collect her share of the booty from the shopkeeper.

It was an inexpensive lesson, so we wandered along Mumbai's streets, getting better at sidestepping the hawkers whose merchandise was displayed on little sidewalk carts.

We picked out a small restaurant on a side street and ducked inside to escape the heat and grab a snack. The place was billed as a tea shop, and we ordered appetizers and cold drinks. The staff was very friendly, explaining to us what we were ordering. This was our first taste of samosas, triangular pastries stuffed with potatoes, minced vegetables, onions, or paneer, a type of cheese prevalent in India. The goodies were served with a tray of different sauces, including chutney. The tea shop adjoined a clothing store, so while I relaxed in the air-conditioning, Ava and Salome went shopping. Ava ordered an Indian pants suit, which I picked up the next morning from the shop.

By the time we left the tea shop, it was getting late in the afternoon, and the city's office workers were heading home for the day, clogging the sidewalks and even spilling into the street. Stands selling clothing, toiletries, books, music CDs, sunglasses and anything else you could think of had been set up along the major streets, and we browsed, eventually picking up a few pirate DVDs. As in South America, these illicit DVDs featured some of the latest films that had just come out in U.S. theaters, for a fraction of the price, although the quality was also spotty. We were always on the lookout for DVD movies since we'd brought a portable DVD player and were able to watch the movies in our hotel room at night.

We walked toward our hotel, admiring the classic architecture of the Prince Albert Museum and Bombay University. Red double-decker buses, reminiscent of London, moved slowly along the city's busy streets. When we got back to the Railway Hotel, I stopped by the front desk to ask where I could find a market.

"What do you need?" asked the clerk.

"Oh, just a few things, nothing special."

"Just tell me what you need, and we can get it for you," he said.

I was surprised; I wasn't used to such personal service from the moderately priced hotels where we had been staying on our trip.

"That's okay," I told the clerk. "I don't mind going myself and I would enjoy the walk."

"It's not a good idea. When they see you are a foreigner, they will charge you more," the clerk advised.

In spite of the warning, I decided to take my chances, and went for a walk through the evening streets. Most of the shops I saw were merely counters fronting on the street, rather than spaces where the customers could come inside. I passed what looked like a pharmacy, and decided to buy my diabetes and high blood pressure medications, since my supply was running low. I showed the shopkeeper my prescription and he looked at it, rummaged around the shelves, and came back with my pills, individually wrapped in perforated sheets. He punched the buttons on a calculator, and held it out to me. A month's supply of my meds cost just a few dollars, and he didn't even take the prescription form I had brought from home.

While I never came across a supermarket, most of what I needed (toothpaste, soap, etc.) was available at the street stalls, or the sundries shops lining each block. After walking around for a while, I saw the familiar red and yellow sign of a McDonald's restaurant. Even in Bombay, we were never far from the Golden Arches. I ordered takeout to bring back to the hotel, and Ava, Salome and I enjoyed the sauces and spices peculiar to the Indian versions of McDonalds' menu items, including wraps and chicken sandwiches. The Cokes and French fries were pretty much the same the world over.

The next day, we were to depart by train to the desert state of Rajasthan and the Pushkar Camel Fair. But our train didn't leave until late in the evening, so we decided to spend the day touring Mumbai. The hotel graciously arranged a minivan and driver to show us the sights and then drop us off at the Bandra train station, north of the city center. The full day's excursion for the three of us cost 800 rupees, or $18 US. Before we left, the hotel staff presented Salome with a parting gift, a box of chocolate candies wrapped with a shiny red bow.

After packing in one more buffet breakfast at the Railway Hotel, we loaded our luggage into the minivan and set off with our driver to see the city. He took us to Marine Drive, a curved six-lane road with high-rise apartment buildings on one side and the placid Arabian Sea on the other. We parked and stretched our legs, and Salome found herself in the middle of a flock of pigeons large enough to have carried her away.

The minivan then began winding up Malabar Hill to the city's famous Hanging Gardens. There, we found a tranquil setting with topiary sculptures, city and bay views, and a playground where about a dozen young women in red, yellow, blue and green saris laughed hysterically while playing on a teeter-totter. They gestured for Salome to join them, but she was too shy, and gripped our hands fiercely.

According to accounts we had read, the Malabar Hill district is one of the poshest in all of India, and its apartments are among the most expensive in the entire world.

Our other stop that morning was a behind-the-scenes peek at one of Mumbai's major industries – outdoor laundry. Dozens of men in threadbare shorts and T-shirts labored at cement basins set in long rows in the hot sun. They pummeled the clothes, sheets, towels and other items, bringing them to a level of cleanliness seldom seen. Unfortunately, this vicious treatment left many of the shirts missing buttons. Huge dryers ran nonstop in shacks surrounding the washing area, and linens also hung by the hundreds and thousands, drying in the sun.

After a full morning of sightseeing, our driver took

us to one of his favorite restaurants, a place definitely off the tourist track. The restaurant was packed with locals, and featured linen tablecloths and waiters wearing neatly pressed white coats. We enjoyed our first authentic Indian meal, of chicken tikka masala, naan, rice, and a couple of other dishes. The bill for the whole shebang was ridiculously small, about $10 for the four of us.

By this point, it was getting on in the afternoon and the driver was running out of ideas for things to show us. Suddenly, he had an "ah-ha" moment and steered the minivan purposefully through traffic. He soon pulled up to the Nehru Science Centre, a tall, cylindrical building that resembled a huge hair curler standing on end. In an adjoining dome was our target: a planetarium show. With a self-satisfied flourish, the driver ushered us up to the ticket window and inside the auditorium, which was packed with schoolchildren. The lights dimmed, and images of stars and planets were projected onto the curved darkness of the ceiling. The booming narration was in Hindi, but we enjoyed the pictures, as well as the chance to relax in the cool, dark auditorium (I was so relaxed I started to nod off during the presentation).

When the lights came back up, we filed out of the crowded auditorium, thanking the driver and letting him know we had enjoyed the show. The light outside had softened as the day morphed into evening, and we rounded a corner to see the sun, which had become a brilliant reddish-orange ball suspended above the Arabian Sea.

On the way to the train station, we asked the driver to stop so we could buy bottled water and snacks for the 19-hour train trip.

I'm not sure what I expected the railway station to be like, but whatever image I might have come up with in my mind, it would have been nothing like the reality we encountered after we had unloaded our luggage from the minivan and said goodbye to the driver. The three of us rolled our bags up a concrete ramp that led into the station.

Inside was controlled chaos. People carried bags and boxes and pushed carts piled high with goods back and forth through the high-ceilinged main building and the stark platforms beyond. Cows and mangy dogs competed for space with the human traffic. The station was a cross between a freight warehouse and a passenger terminal, with a cement floor and institutional green paint on the walls. There were few seats for waiting passengers. Instead, people squatted on their luggage or just sat on the ground.

Purposely, we arrived a couple of hours before our train's scheduled departure. I had hoped to check in at the ticket counter and verify our train, car and platform number. The only timetables I could find were in Hindi, and a long line of passengers was queued up at what appeared to be the only ticket counter in the place. Outside on the platform, passenger lists were posted on bulletin boards under dim lamps. I managed to find our train number, and made my best guess as to where we would board.

The three of us sat on a cement block that anchored a support pillar and played cards while waiting for our train.

After a while, a long passenger train rumbled into the station. As it did, a crowd quickly formed around the rear cars, and people began jumping in the doors and open windows before the train came to a full stop. Salome looked at this mob scene and her eyes widened.

"Is that our train?" she asked, fearfully.

"I don't know," I said. I walked over to the train and checked the number.

"I think this is our train, but we're not in those cars," I said, pointing to the unreserved cars at the rear, much to Salome's relief. "Let's try to find our compartment."

We moved up the train slowly, checking the car numbers, and finally found the right car about mid-train. We hoisted our bags up the steep metal stairs and rolled them through a doorway into the sleeper car. It was still an hour until departure, so we had the reserved, air-conditioned car completely to ourselves, in spite of the anarchy in the unreserved cars farther back.

Our open compartment contained two facing sets of three bunks to the right of the passageway. We would share this tight space with three other travelers. We learned during our train travels in India that, although each passenger is assigned to a specific bunk, those assignments usually change based on who most firmly or quickly lays claim to a particular sleeping spot.

Each cushioned bunk was covered with blue leatherette, which on this train was in like-new condition. Later, attendants would come down the aisles, handing out sheets, pillows and blankets.

A word about Indian trains: in Europe, we were spoiled with private, locking compartments, which usually had a sink and reading lights for each bunk.

Although private compartments do exist on Indian trains, they are not found on every route. They can cost double or triple the fare of non-private, air-conditioned sleeper cars that are clean, comfortable and offer the additional advantage of the chance to meet and talk with fellow travelers, something unlikely to happen when travelers are shut up in their own private compartments.

In all, there are eight classes of Indian trains, ranging from AC-1, which is an air-conditioned car with private compartments, to unreserved second class, which is a car with bench seats and open windows, where a passenger with slow reflexes could easily find him- or herself without any seat, especially when the train is crowded.

One more thing about Indian trains: they often are very full, especially during the more popular travel months of November through February. Reservations for a sleeper ticket are required, and the further in advance, the better. We had good luck using the railway's online booking service, through which we could reserve our tickets, pay for them with a credit card, and request the tickets be delivered to our hotel at our next destination. Failing that, tickets can be obtained at any railway station, and a small quota of tickets is set aside for foreign travelers, allowing them to travel on shorter notice. Although I bristled when we were charged a higher "foreigner" entry fee to attractions and museums, we did appreciate the foreigner train ticket quota, and special foreigner windows at train stations (which usually had shorter lines).

As our departure time neared, the other passengers began arriving in our sleeping car.

Our seatmates turned out to be an elderly woman traveling alone and a family including a mother, and her grown sons.

Although we had brought enough snacks to keep us

fed for a week, it turned out there was also plenty of food available on the train.

Almost immediately after the train rattled, shrieked and groaned to life and started up the track to begin the 19-hour ride to Ajmer, a steady parade of food and drink vendors began making their way up the passageway of our car.

"Tomato soup!" "Chai tea!" cried the vendors, who carried metal cannisters with handles on top and spigots near the bottom, and stacks of paper cups. The chai tea was delicious; it was hot, milky and laced with cloves, cinnamon, ginger, cardamom and other exotic spices. A cup sold for six rupees – or about a dime.

Other vendors carried trays of chips, crackers and cookies, and buckets of cold drinks. In the early morning and before noon, attendants came by and took orders for full meals, cooked in the train's sweltering kitchen car, which was off-limits to passengers. Our only meal choice was conveyed tersely by the attendants: "Veg or non-veg?"

And if that wasn't enough, our traveling companions were eager to share the home-cooked food they had brought for the journey.

Before bedtime, the elderly women travelers had pulled out plastic containers and foil-wrapped packages concealing cakes, rice and curry dishes and other delicacies. The woman who sat directly across from us was insistent as she offered a Tupperware dish full of food. "Try some," she said. "It's very good."

Salome, the most finicky eater in our group, smiled and shook her head. Ava and I, not wanting to offend, took the container and shared the rice and curry.

The woman told us she was visiting her daughter and grandchildren in a town about halfway between Mumbai and Ajmer. From her dress and speech, we deduced the woman was Hindu. And, while friendly to us, she was downright frosty to our other seatmates, who were Muslim.

The Muslim young men were escorting their mother home to Ajmer after her completion of the hajj, or pilgrimage, to Mecca. The young men wore white, loose-fitting suits that reached to about their knees, over white cotton pants. The mother was very proud of her accomplishment, and eagerly shared the details with just a small amount of prompting.

"It was very crowded, and very hot," said the woman, who was in her 50s, with short, reddish-brown hair, which she revealed when she took off her head scarf. Both her sons also had red hair. "Every Muslim must make the hajj sometime in their life. Now I have made mine, praise Allah."

She indicated a large plastic bottle, held in a shopping bag and hung from a clothes hook over the window between the two sets of bunks. "This is holy water from Mecca, I carried it all the way back with me."

Not to be outdone by the Hindu woman, she also offered us food from her family's stash, which we accepted to be polite, although we weren't hungry.

After a couple of hours, all of us passengers began to feel sleepy and lowered the seat backs into place as middle bunks. Salome climbed to a top bunk with her portable DVD player, and Ava and I settled into our bunks. The two older women claimed the bottom bunks.

In the morning, after a fairly restful night on the swaying, rollicking train, the Hindu woman rose early and kept shooting baleful glances at the Muslim woman's son, who remained ensconced in his middle bunk opposite from where she sat.

"He should get up now, it's late. No one can sit in those seats until he gets out of bed," she grumbled.

Finally, poking his tousled head out from his blanket, the young man awoke, climbed out of his bunk and folded it back against the wall, providing additional seats for the rest of us.

Once the sun came out in full force, the inside of the car heated up, in spite of the AC. We spent the day reading, dozing, snacking and looking out the window at low brown hills, scrubby bushes and sandy plains, and the occasional somnolent train station. The Muslim woman's son (the late sleeper) was fascinated by Salome's portable DVD player, and asked to look at it. Later, he explained that his father was a well-known mullah in Ajmer, who oversaw a mosque and a school. He offered me a business card-sized color photo of his father, and invited us to stay with his family if we visited Ajmer during our travels.

After breakfast, nature called, and I made my way to the bathroom, located in the corridor between cars. I was about to become initiated in the use of the Asian-style squat toilet, under the most extreme conditions – while riding a moving train.

The bathrooms were Spartan and relatively clean, although far from spotless. There was a sink, a scratched, metallic mirror and the toilet itself, which consisted of a hole in the floor of the car, with footpads on either side. The train tracks, visible through the hole, rushed by below.

Bars were mounted low on the walls on either side of

the toilet to provide handholds for those who successfully reached the squatting position without pitching into the hole, which yawned cavernously beneath me.

As I worked my way into position, careful to keep my clothing out of harm's way, the train seemed to lurch more violently than at any other time on our journey, although that might have been my imagination. In spite of the unfamiliar and uncomfortable position, I accomplished my mission and made it back to my seat.

We pulled into Ajmer station in the late afternoon, where a frenzy of porters, arriving and departing passengers, hotel touts and taxi drivers awaited.

We said goodbye to the Muslim family, and watched as the mother was surrounded on the platform by relatives who showered her with hugs, kisses and flower garlands, loudly chattering and laughing all the while.

We were used to carrying our own bags, but an insistent porter met us as we stepped off the train. He grabbed Big Bertha, Ava's suitcase, in spite of our protests. We watched in amazement as he hoisted the huge, heavy bag onto his head, staggering with the weight. His turban slipped off as he grappled the bag into position, and we handed it to him. Then he took my bag, which wasn't light either, and slung it over his shoulder!

We followed as he scurried along the platform, up the stairs to the bridge leading to the main station, and back down the stairs. By the time we reached the station entrance, he was sweating heavily.

Ava tipped him 400 rupees (about $10 US, much more than Indian train porters are used to receiving) and he hailed us a taxi.

The taxi was an Ambassador, an Indian-made vehicle with a rounded roof and fenders, resembling a smaller version of a 1950s American sedan. This car had seen better days, and the driver huffed and puffed while loading our luggage into its spacious trunk and fastening the rickety trunk lid with a piece of rope. He still had to put a couple of bags in the back seat, which was roomy enough for Ava and Salome. I rode shotgun.

In front of the station was Ajmer's main road, a sight the three of us couldn't stop gawking at. A furious torrent of traffic flowed past the train station in both directions. This included cars, trucks, buses, motorcycle rickshaws, bullock carts and bicycles. Mixed in with the people walking alongside and through the traffic were cows, camels, pigs, goats and monkeys. The noise from this mass of machines and living things was incredible: a blend of revving engines, bleating horns, tinny music and voices, all pouring forth from the most frenetic city scene we had ever witnessed.

Our destination, Pushkar, was only 11 kilometers from Ajmer, but the trip took about 30 minutes, because the two-lane road wound up and over Nag Pahar, or Snake Mountain.

Along the way, we saw entire families of monkeys scampering around tree branches and peering down at us, to our delight, especially Salome's.

The taxi stopped at a makeshift roadblock at the edge of Pushkar; the driver told us he could go no further and unloaded our bags. We stood scratching our heads, but we needn't have worried: a man pushing a flat wooden cart materialized and offered to take us and our luggage to our hotel. As we were finding out in India, there is no shortage of people who make their living by lifting, carrying or delivering things for foreign visitors or well-heeled Indian travelers.

Once our bags were loaded on the cart – along with Salome – we began the mile walk to our hotel through the densely crowded streets of Pushkar.

We had arrived in time for the annual Camel Fair, which is a spectacle to behold. Pushkar is an idyllic town chock-full of temples, shops, restaurants and hotels, built around a circular sacred lake. According to Hindu tradition, the lake was formed when Lord Brahma, the creator, dropped a lotus leaf. Around the lake are ghats, or cement steps, which pilgrims use when they come to bathe as part of their religious rituals. Reportedly, Ghandi's ashes were scattered at the lake following his assassination in 1948 and subsequent cremation on a marble slab in Delhi.

At this time of the year, Pushkar's population swells from a few thousand to more than 200,000 souls, including pilgrims, tourists, camel traders and visitors from throughout Rajasthan. The town's dirt streets, as we followed the luggage cart in the warm dusk, were full of women in saris, many of whom wore gold nose-rings and earrings linked with gold chains; sadhus, or solitary men in search of enlightenment, in bare feet and colorful turbans, who wore tunics wrapped around their waists, and large handlebar mustaches; Indian visitors carrying their belongings in dusty duffel bags; and a few Western tourists.

Motorbikes mingled with the foot traffic, the drivers impatiently tooting their horns to clear a path. To either side were food and tea stalls, shops selling tourist trinkets, clothing, books and music CDs, and archways, through which we caught glimpses of the sacred lake and the ghats across the water. Sewage ran in an open channel along the side of the narrow dirt street.

We took in the scene, which had the unreal quality of a movie set, as we walked along, finally reaching the entrance to our hotel, which was at the top of a steep, crooked set of cement stairs. The hotel, although basic, offered great views of the city from its hilltop balconies and rooftop patio.

As we entered the open-air lobby of the Hotel Paramount Palace, a man rushed forward to greet us.

"Ah, the Tash family. We were worried about you!" said the man, who turned out to be one of the two brothers who ran the place for their father, who owned the hotel.

"You should have called us from Ajmer, we would have picked you up," he said, offering us tea, and inviting us to sit down on a sofa.

Salome's Journal

11/14/05 Pushkar, India

Hi I am in India a much different place then Londen and we have been here for about a week. First Mumbai. In the Mumbai streets there were only men hardly no women or children. We went to the gate of India and my mom got a hena. I did not get one but I regret it now. While my mom was getting her henna I got a bubble that stayed a bubble for a long time. They were hard to blow but they did work. After we went to our first Indian restraunt. It was good but spicey! Next door was an Indian clothing store so my mom and I could not miss that and we ended up buying 2 things for my mom and 1 beautiful shirt for me. The next day it

*was time to leave but not until 9:00 at night so a taxi took
us sightseeing and we saw so many things. We went to the
laundry place where mostly everybody brings their laundry
and they sometimes broke buttons and heres why. They stand
in soapy water dunk the clothing and thrash it on the rock
about 3 times. It gets it the cleanest you can get but as I said
they sometimes broke buttons. We saw so much more and
now we are on a train to a little town called Pushcar where
the camel festival is. It was such a good thing we had reserved
seats because (we) would be trying to fight with 3,000 people
at least. We would have ended up sitting on the ground for 19
hours or not getting on at all. We met some people including
a Muslim family and 1 older lady whom was pretty cranky.
Proubly a religious thing and kind of kranked the whole way.
So we are sleeping right now and off to Pushcar. We have
just arrived in Pushcar. A small olderly porter insisted on
carrying big birtha (my mom's bag on his head) and had a
ruff time getting it up there but he managed. Then he grabbed
my dad's bag (which is pretty heavy itself) and put it on his
shoulder. He carried it up and down stairs with it and we got
into a taxi. We drove through town and saw cows, monkeys,
dogs and the city's poverty. The taxi could not drive so a
young porter no younger than 25 put all our laguge including
me. He was yelling move move to anyone who got in his way.
The motorcycles our crazy. The way to describe this town is
noisy, poor, animals running everywhere, crowded but fun.
We went to the camel festival and rode a camel. It was so
crazy. There was thousands of camels. This is where I will
stop for now. Catch you up soon!*

Our room was plain, but clean, with a large bed covered
by a canopy of mosquito netting, a private bathroom and

a tiny balcony, which we had requested when making our reservation. Some of the windows had been replaced with bright red, blue and green stained glass. From the balcony, we could see across the town, including its many temple spires, and the brown, spare hills beyond.

As we would quickly learn, due to our hilltop perch, the multitude of sounds from the wild festival spread out below us rose into a crazy sonic stew that carried on all night long.

The sounds included Hindi music and prayers blared from loudspeakers mounted on temple rooftops; crowd noises from people packed in the dirt streets; and above everything, from the fairgrounds, we could hear the voices of carnival touts, amplified to the point of screeching distortion.

Without a doubt, it was the noisiest place I'd ever been, and the sound continued to swell and grow until it reached a frenzied crescendo on the night of the full moon, two days after our arrival.

Satisfied with our accommodations, for which we had paid the stiff price of 3,500 rupees per night, or about $78 US, we decided to walk down to the fairgrounds, a half-mile or so from the Paramount Palace. The price of accommodations in Pushkar skyrocketed during the Camel Fair. The hotels ranged from dingy and basic to very luxurious, including lavishly furnished tents near the fairgrounds that rented for hundreds of dollars per night. Outside of the festival period, rooms cost as little as a tenth of what we paid.

We got directions to the fairgrounds from the brother on duty at the hotel's front desk, and walked into Pushkar's crowded streets.

Along the way, we passed every kind of stall imaginable and immediately became the target of hawkers, who easily picked us out from the people who thronged the streets around us.

That first night, wide-eyed, we strolled up and down the fair "midway," a broad dirt avenue with carnival rides, circus tents and stalls set up along either side. As we walked, a group of laughing young men pulled me into an impromptu, joyful street dance. Salome went on a couple of carnival rides, and we cringed as the loudspeakers blasted us from both sides.

Our senses were assailed with the sights and smells of many different unfamiliar foods. We were leery of eating anything that was sitting out, unwrapped and uncovered, because of the flies that swarmed around. But we did go for some pineapple, which had been carved and sliced thin to create delicate henna-like patterns.

We also sampled pakoras, chunks of deep-fried, spiced dough that resembled fritters, and chapattis, small rounds of bread that can be dipped in a variety of sauces.

To wash down the food, we had to settle for bottled water or soda. Although an ice cold beer would have been wonderful, I was out of luck: Pushkar was a completely dry town, thanks to its religious bent. The same went for beef, chicken or even eggs – the city was vegetarian from top to bottom.

The next morning, we straggled up the stairs to the rooftop deck, where other guests were already eating breakfast. We took one of the photocopied menus and ordered a breakfast of toast, fruit and coffee. One of the staples of Indian breakfasts, at least for Westerners, was porridge, which was basically hot oatmeal. Many a morning over the next couple of months would find us stirring milk and sugar into our bowls of porridge.

The staff, including the main cook, a young man who suffered from a severe limp, had to climb three flights of stairs from the kitchen, which was next to the lobby, to the rooftop deck where guests ate their meals.

From the deck, we could survey Pushkar, from its round, sacred lake, to its whitewashed buildings, and the baked desert that surrounded it. The entire vision shimmered in the bright, clear, hot day.

After breakfast we went back to the fair. Our mission was to take a camel ride around the fairgrounds and we had no problem finding mounts. The camels were kept in an outdoor arena at one end of the fairgrounds. The arena was where some of the main competitions, such as camel races, were normally held. In 2005, to our disappointment, most of the events were cancelled out of respect for an Indian leader who had recently died.

The beasts had been decorated with tapestries, clanking brass ornaments and brightly painted designs. Getting on the camels was easy. The guides ordered the animals to rest on their knees, and we clambered up to sit on a padded seat, like a saddle, mounted behind their humps.

The guides took us up the main avenue of the fair, and then to the outlying areas, where camels and their owners spread out for what seemed like miles on the dusty, hot desert ground.

The ride was smooth and, although we were pretty high up off the ground, I felt safe. This, in spite of the fact that leading my camel was a boy who looked to be 8 or 9 years old.

Getting down from the camels was trickier: first, the camel bends its front legs, causing passengers to nearly pitch forward. Then, the animal bends its back legs, lowering the passenger to the ground, where it is easy to disembark.

After our ride, the driver invited us back to his encampment on the edge of the fairgrounds for tea. We accepted the offer, and sat on stools as we sipped our tea, which was served in small glasses. Salome posed for a picture with two younger girls.

"If you want to take a long camel tour, out to the desert, I can arrange it," said the guide, a turbaned, slender man with a large black mustache.

The guide glanced around, then lowered his voice. "You want steak, or beer? I can get it for you," he said.

I had a sudden vision of cops swooping down on me as I stood in a back alley, raising a forbidden bottle of beer to my lips.

"Hmm, that's tempting," I said, thinking I would wait to quench my thirst until we had moved on to wetter pastures.

Before leaving the fair, we gave in to the barkers' calls and watched a magic show and a circus. The circus was held in a tent without chairs or bleachers; we sat with the rest of the sparse crowd on the dusty ground. The highlights of the show were a girl who danced with hula hoops, and a father-daughter act in which a young girl performed acrobatics on a tall pole balanced on her father's forehead.

Pushkar's strict food and alcohol rules weren't too onerous for us to follow, especially because the restaurants offered a wide variety of tasty vegetarian fare, from pizza, pasta and Indian curry dishes, to a fantastic spinach and mushroom enchilada.

For dinner, we decided to try the hotel's rooftop restaurant. The hobbled cook, whose name I can't recall, came up to take our order, offering suggestions from the menu based on what ingredients he had been able to round up that morning. We chatted, and he revealed that his disability stemmed from a motorcycle crash he'd been in a few years back. In spite of his limp, he nimbly climbed up and down the stairs carrying trays full of food, and we also saw him riding his rusty bicycle to the market.

Each time we ate at the hotel, the cook would take our order, then say, "I'm not going to rush, it will take a while because I want to make it right." Invariably, it would take an hour or more for our food to be prepared, but it was always good. After a few days, I got wise, and put in our breakfast order as soon as I woke up. By the time the three of us walked upstairs, our breakfast would be almost ready.

The cook said he was 18 years old, and during the festival period, he worked from early morning to late at night, without any days off. After completing his work, he told us, he went to the fair, where he spent most of the night hanging out with friends. I don't know how he managed to keep up that schedule; I expected him to keel over in exhaustion, but he never did.

When Ava and Salome went shopping, I did too – I found a tiny CD shop and sat down at the glass counter while the proprietor played different CDs for me. I bought a couple of discs, then went to the Internet café down the street, where I loaded the music onto my MP3 player. We sent some emails, and called home on the international phone from a shop near our hotel.

One evening, we walked down to the ghats to watch the pilgrims performing their bathing rituals. We took off our shoes and kept our camera packed in its case, as the signs posted on the wall advised. A man approached, telling us he was a priest and offering blessings on our behalf if we made a small donation. He looked decidedly un-priestly, and we decided not to play along. He followed us for a while, sounding almost threatening at times, as he cajoled us to make a donation. We opted to sit at the top of the steps and watch, rather than take a dip ourselves.

On the final day of the fair, preceding that night's full moon, the streets became so packed it was nearly impossible to walk. The police had erected rickety fences made of wooden poles that ran down the center of the main streets. The idea was that foot and scooter traffic was divided into two "lanes," one on each side of the fence, which traveled in opposite directions. When we emerged in the morning from the side lane where our hotel was located, the foot traffic was so dense that we could barely penetrate the solid column of people heading toward the fairgrounds.

Because we were almost out of cash, we needed to visit the ATM, which was down a side street off the main road to the fairgrounds. The only problem was, reaching the ATM meant crossing the barrier that blocked off the side road. Men in uniform – I wasn't sure if they were soldiers or police – stood guard at the barricades armed with sticks to prevent pedestrians from crossing the wooden barricade into the side road.

Luckily, the guards took pity on us foreigners and held up the barricade poles so we could scoot under. Indians who spied the opening and tried to follow us were not so fortunate – the guards yelled at them and poked them with sticks, forcing them back into the crowded road.

We went back to our hotel room to chill for a few hours, hoping the streets would clear by the afternoon.

That night, the frenetic activity in Pushkar reached a climax, as pilgrims carried out their rituals at the lake all night long, under the light of full moon. We were chickens, remaining in our room instead of thrusting ourselves into the mayhem. The noise flowing up the hill to our room was so loud that I had trouble sleeping, even with earplugs.

We had planned to stay on in Pushkar for a few days after the fair ended, hoping to get a feel for the town's quieter, more reflective side, and we weren't disappointed. Our friends at the hotel encouraged us to stay, assuring us that the nightly rate would decrease by "more than half."

Sure enough, in the morning we walked into town to see the people departing in droves, carrying the same meager possessions they had brought with them. By that afternoon, the town was noticeably quieter, a trend that continued over the next several days.

Near the end of our stay, as we were having breakfast on the roof of the hotel, we noticed a family of monkeys closely watching our every move. On impulse, Ava tossed a piece of toast covered with strawberry jam to the closest monkey, who snatched it up and began licking off the jelly.

We thought this was so cute we repeated the trick.

Each time, a monkey climbed down from its place on the wall and grabbed the toast. One other guest – a European woman – was on the roof, eating breakfast and reading a book at another table. We all laughed as we watched the monkeys daintily lick the jam off the toast, then stuff the bread in their mouths.

After a few minutes, though, we ran out of toast. This made the monkeys mad. A couple of the bolder ones jumped down on the patio and confronted us, baring their pointy teeth and hissing. Salome shrieked and ran behind a chair. "Daddy, do something!" she cried.

I had no idea what to do. I brandished a chair like a lion tamer in the circus, and shouted at the monkeys. "Shoo! Go away!" I yelled.

The monkeys held their ground, and we were at a stand-off until the cook limped up the stairs, scolding the monkeys. As soon as they saw him, they turned and ran through a hallway at the rear of the patio.

The European woman wailed, "They're going into the hotel, they're going into the hotel!"

"Don't worry, madam, there is no problem," said the cook. "The monkeys will not go in your room."

Salome's Journal

11/17/05 Pushkar, India

Hello. We have been in Pushcar for about a week and we leave tomorrow and we are going to Jipure. Today I talked to Grandpa and Aunty, Fred (the cat) and Aunt Fran. It was nice. Today we went for breakfast on the roof and there were so many monkeys running and playing all over. There were some right by us and I put a piece of toast there and he grabbed it and ate it. It was funny so I put another out and he ate it again. Finally I put one more piece out and they started coming tords us and I got scared and hid behind the chair and they do have sharp teeth so we did not know what to do. So the guy from the hotel came up and they all ran. It was kind of funny. Later we went to call and when we were leaving there was the cutest little dog he was so sweet! Now we are going to the Internet. Salome.

In between the monkey encounters and camel rides, Ava had taken full advantage of Pushkar's many shopping opportunities. The town was a mecca for shoppers, particularly for those wanting to buy textiles: bedspreads, tapestries and all manner of clothing. Staying down the hall from us at the Paramount Palace was an Italian couple who ran a business selling imported clothes at festivals throughout Italy.

They were regular visitors to Pushkar to purchase shirts, dresses, skirts and scarves, and they dealt directly with the clothing factories to buy these items in bulk. During the whole time we were in Pushkar, they spent most of their time in their hotel room, repacking the clothing into smaller boxes to be shipped back to Italy in time for the Christmas festivals in Europe.

The couple explained there were several options for shipping items home from India, including sea and air transport. Sending items by ship was the cheapest and took the longest; air freight cost the most and was quickest.

We hadn't bought anywhere near as much as the Italian couple, but Ava's purchases included several brightly colored, ornate quilts, and a fur-trimmed suede jacket for Salome, which we wouldn't need during our travels in India. All together, the stuff she had bought in Pushkar filled a large cardboard box, which the quilt salesman had provided. We packed the items in the box, taped it up, and headed to the post office to send the box by sea cargo, the cheapest and slowest method of delivery.

Our friend the cook went down the street and came back with a man pushing a flat cart, who would carry our package to the post office, which was about a 20- or 30-minute walk from the hotel. Not only was the package too heavy to carry that far, but we would never have been able to follow the directions to the post office, which involved many twists and turns through the back streets of Pushkar.

By this time, the town had emptied of the throngs of pilgrims and fair-goers, and it was pleasant to walk along with the cart and check out the daily life of this little Indian town. Salome didn't even have to walk – the cart driver was nice enough to let her ride with the package. The highlight of the walk was seeing a pair of braying donkeys tied to skinny tree on a side street.

We had read that before a package can be shipped from India, it must be wrapped in white cloth, which is then sewn closed with needle and thread and sealed with hot wax. A few blocks from the post office, a man sitting on a stoop called to us, asking if we needed our package wrapped.

He took his time, measuring our package, sending a boy on a bicycle to get a larger piece of cloth, and then methodically sewing and sealing the box inside its cloth wrapper. By the time he was done, we nearly didn't make it to the post office by the 3 p.m. closing time. If we hadn't been able to ship the package that day, we would have had to carry it with us to on the train, because we were scheduled to leave Pushkar early the next morning.

That night, we dined on the roof of the Paramount Palace, enjoying the warm, quiet night and the twinkling lights of the buildings ringing the sacred lake.

A taxi took us from Pushkar to Ajmer the following morning, where we caught a train for our next destination, Jaipur, the capital of Rajasthan.

As soon as we stepped off the train, our ears were assaulted: "Taxi, taxi! You need a taxi?"

Tuk-tuk and taxi drivers called out to us and walked alongside us, entreating us to hire them as we exited Jaipur's train station into a warm evening. Outside the station, people packed the sidewalks and vehicles rumbled and buzzed on the busy streets. Shop lights twinkled in the dusk as I walked across the street to find a pay phone. Our hotel, the Umaid Bhawan Guest House, offered to pick us up at the station if we called on our arrival. I used a public phone at one of the shops fronting the station, a well-used handset that sat on the counter, connected by a thin strand of wire running up to the eave. A bare bulb shone over the counter.

In a few minutes, a gray-haired, thin man with a shy smile pulled up in a tuk-tuk. We loaded our bags into the back, found places to wedge our bodies, and took off for the short, lurching ride to our hotel. Traveling through India, we never ceased to be amazed at how many people and things could fit inside a tuk-tuk, a wonder of transportation efficiency. American college students packing themselves into Volkswagen Beetles have nothing on India's tuk-tuk drivers.

The Umaid Bhawan was located on a quiet cul-de-sac several blocks from the main boulevard. I always felt down in the dumps when I arrived at a dingy, run-down hotel. But the guest house in Jaipur was lovely, and I felt the stress of the road fall away as we walked through the archway painted with floral patterns, scrolls and Rajasthani warriors.

The hotel was situated in a former historic Rajasthan mansion, and the exterior was decorated with carved wooden balconies and painted with traditional patterns and desert scenes.

A retired Indian Air Force doctor owned the hotel; it was managed by his two sons. Every interior and exterior space was stylishly decorated and furnished, and we found our room clean and comfortable, with a TV, air conditioning and antiques that could have graced the home of a maharaja.

The rooftop restaurant offered a nice selection of Indian food, and during dinner on our first night in Jaipur, we were treated to fireworks displays from the wedding parties taking place across the city.

At 1,900 rupees per night for the three of us, or about $40, we felt like we were getting a bargain. There was even a swimming pool in the courtyard, which Salome had eagerly looked forward to since we booked this hotel from hot and dusty Pushkar.

I was also eagerly anticipating a cold beer or two after enduring nearly a week of abstinence in Pushkar's arid environs.

I asked the front desk clerk if there was a market or liquor store nearby, where I might be able to buy beer.

"Not a problem, sir, just ask your room boy."

The Umaid Bhawan marked our first encounter with

India's ubiquitous hotel staffers – always male – who not only cleaned the guest rooms, but catered to the guests' personal needs, such as delivering alcoholic beverages and late-night snacks.

Our room boy had introduced himself when we checked in, and he appeared almost magically whenever we needed him.

"Can you get me some beer?" I self-consciously asked the room boy, who must have been at least in his 30s.

"Yes, sir, what would you like?"

"Three bottles?"

I handed him a couple of hundred-rupee notes, and he vanished.

In a few minutes he knocked on the door, holding several parcels wrapped in newsprint.

With a tiny thrill, I accepted the packages, which contained extra-large, ice cold bottles of Kingfisher lager beer that tasted, as an old friend used to say, "like honey dew vine water," after the long dry spell. While alcohol is legal and available in most parts of India we visited, there seems to be a certain stigma attached to it, and the consumption of alcohol runs counter to the mores of strict Hinduism. In one of India's many English-language newspapers, I had read an article about a mob of townspeople who looted a shop that had the effrontery to sell "spirits." (The article did not make it clear if the looters kept a few bottles for themselves.)

So, although beer and even hard liquor were relatively easy to find, there was always a whiff of shamefulness when I accepted my paper-wrapped bottles of beer from the room boy at the hotel where we were staying at the time.

The hotel arranged a city tour for us the next day, and after breakfast, a tuk-tuk was waiting out front. We squeezed into the back seat, and the driver kick-started the little engine, which chugged and whined as we pulled away from the hotel and onto Jaipur's busy roads.

We planned to cover a lot of ground: Jaipur's famous City Palace, a walled complex in the center of town that housed many of the city's best-known sites, from the Hawa Mahal, or the Palace of the Wind, to the palace museum and observatory, which displays a series of bizarre-looking structures used to take measurements of the sun and stars in ancient times.

The highlights of the palace included posing with the turbaned, mustachio'd palace guards, who asked for a tip afterward, and getting cozy with a basket of cobras that danced to the tune of a flute. The cobra trainer eagerly offered his turban and flute so I could pose for a memorable photo, but I kept close watch on the slithery creatures as they bobbed up and down in their basket.

The museum featured beautiful tapestries and clothing worn by Jaipur's maharajas, including an enormous coat and pants – made with raspberry pink silk and gold thread – worn by Madho Singh I, who stood 6 foot, 6 inches tall and weighed nearly 500 pounds.

From the front, the Hawa Mahal appears to be a palace several stories tall, fronted with delicate pink sandstone latticework and hundreds of windows. But from the back, where visitors enter, the "palace" is really a façade, with narrow, arched passages that run along its length. The Hawa Mahal is a great place to visit for its views of Jaipur, including the bustling streets and market right next to it.

We were told the family of Jaipur's last maharaja still lives in one wing of the palace, which is off limits to visitors.

After lunch in the very touristy and mediocre restaurant on the palace grounds, we set off for the rest of our tour, which included a stop at the Jaipur Zoo and the Amber Fort, another famous city landmark.

The zoo was a disappointment – a sign proclaimed that "foreigners" had to pay 100 rupees (about $2) to get in, compared to the entry price of 10 rupees for Indian citizens. The whole place was dusty and ramshackle, and we were horrified to see dozens of rats streaming through a monkey enclosure – although the monkeys didn't seem to mind. Another pen with a dirt floor held the scrawniest, most morose lion we had ever seen. The wretched cat, with its head hung low, paced around its 30-foot-long cage, once in a while making a pathetic attempt at a roar. The best exhibit in the zoo was a spotless cement cage where three gorgeous Indian tigers were housed.

We finished our tour with an 11-kilometer ride to the outskirts of town to see the Amber Fort. Ava hiked up the slanting ramp to the top of the hill where the entrance to the fort was located, while Salome and I walked down the road in search of elephant rides. On the way out to the fort, we'd seen a number of elephants lumbering along the side of the road. But it was too late in the day and the elephants were all back in their barns, so we were out of luck.

On the ride back, we passed what I think is one of Jaipur's most beautiful sights – a "floating palace" built on a lake. In the gentle reddish dusk, the palace seemed to glow above the dark water.

By this time, it was almost evening, and the tuk-tuk driver must have had somewhere he needed to be – he drove through the choked streets of central Jaipur with a vengeance, never letting up on the throttle or the horn. He beeped incessantly as we careened in and out of traffic, weaving between cars, taxis, buses, even horse and camel carts. How we avoided a crash, I'll never know, but he made it back to our hotel with the tuk-tuk in one piece. We were too stunned to complain.

That night, we had dinner with a Canadian couple who were in the midst of a five- or six-month trip through India. They were very cheerful and upbeat, and told us they'd been traveling nearly non-stop for the past four years. They kept their stuff in storage, occasionally going back home to hunker down for a few months before hitting the road again. We ended the very pleasant evening by trading paperback books and email addresses.

At this point in the trip, more than five months since we'd left home, I was feeling very stressed out. Part of it stemmed from my anxiety about traveling in India, with its dirt, crowds, poverty and noise.

We'd been in the country about 10 days so far, and I saw the next two months stretching out before us. Sometimes, it seemed that I would never be able to endure this country of paradoxes until our flight out of Bombay, or Mumbai, on Jan. 15. There were many things I liked, even loved, about India, but there were many other things I found tough to take. All of it was mixed up and jumbled together in my mind until I felt like I wouldn't be able to stand another day.

When I was awake, I worried about everything my

fevered imagination could concoct: would one of us catch some awful disease and waste away in a filthy, rundown hospital? Would we be robbed or injured in an accident? If we made it through our travels unscathed, would we be able to find jobs when we got back to San Diego? Would our tenants trash our house? And, even though we were trying to keep Salome on track with her schoolwork, would she be able to pick up where she left off in school, or would she suffer academically?

All these doubts and – admittedly – paranoid thoughts crept into my consciousness, day and night. When I fell asleep, things weren't much better. Night after night, I dreamed of finding myself in some strange place, wandering through narrow, crooked streets and buildings with slanting walls and floors, squalid rooms and strange characters lurking in the shadows, like funhouses in a horror movie.

To deal with the stress, I tried drinking, which didn't help much and always left me feeling lousy the next day. Then, I decided exercise would help chase away my demons, and began a daily workout regimen. The streets around our hotel in Jaipur looked hazardous for running: there were no sidewalks and vendors often lined up their carts along the dirt shoulder, within inches of the traffic streaming by.

So, I went back to the exercise routine I had devised in Pushkar, running in place for 30 or 40 minutes in our hotel room each morning while listening to music on my Mp3 player. I pulled a mattress onto the floor to cushion my joints and muscles, and pumped my arms and legs in time to the Beatles, Los Lobos or the Indian music I had added to my digital collection.

The workout wasn't bad, but it was boring to run in place in a darkened hotel room while Ava and Salome slept. So I asked at the front desk if there was a running path nearby.

The desk clerk surprised me.

"There is a nice park a few kilometers from here. You can run with us. We go just about every day. Be here in the lobby at 6 a.m."

The desk clerk (and son of the retired doctor/hotel owner) confided that he preferred to sleep in, but his father was a health nut and insisted his sons accompany him on his early morning runs.

It was still dark when the telephone rang in our room at 5:45 a.m. the next day. I dressed and went to the lobby, which was deserted. After a few minutes, the doctor came in. He was a trim man of medium height and build, with short dark hair dusted at the temples with gray. He wore a neatly trimmed mustache and a dark blue sweat suit.

"Let's go," he said, abruptly, but not unkindly.

"Are your sons joining us?"

"They are sleeping in. They stayed up too late last night," he said, sounding slightly exasperated.

I got into the front seat of his minivan and we set out through Jaipur's still-quiet streets. As we drove, the sky to the east began to lighten from black to gray, and soon, a thin band of pink spread across the hazy horizon.

As we drove, I asked him about India's new prosperity, and whether it had improved the overall quality of life.

The doctor shook his head as he swerved around a car that had shot out suddenly from a side street. "I can't say the quality of life has improved. Now, everyone owns a car, but they don't know how to drive!"

We turned into the entrance to the park, and took a spot in the near-empty lot. Around us, the entire eastern sky was colored brilliantly with streaks of orange, pink and red. A few other people in jogging suits and T-shirts were stretching or running past.

The doctor explained that the path ringing the park ran for five kilometers, or about three miles.

We stretched by a fountain that played loud instrumental music through speakers mounted in the grass. "Our new musical fountain," he said, with a mixture of pride and disdain.

We began to run along the path, but soon the doctor peeled off, heading away from me. "Just stay on the path," he called out, "and you'll be fine. You'll end up back where we started."

A little uneasy, I ran on by myself. I listened to music as I jogged, and looked around at the park, much of which was still shrouded in morning fog and gloom. In some spots, the path ran alongside open, grassy meadows; in others, it cut through forest. Occasionally, I came across encampments, where women squatted next to cooking fires and stared at me as I went past. I kept running on the dirt path, which was wide and easy to follow. Once in a while, I encountered another jogger, but mostly I had the path to myself.

After 30 minutes or so, I reached the parking area. The doctor was already back, and was in the midst of a full calisthenics routine on the grass near the fountain: pushups, situps, stretches, etc.

When he was finished, I followed him back to the van, where he stood ahead of me, hands on hips, studying the back end of the vehicle. I looked closer and realized what was the matter: we had a flat tire.

He cursed softly and began rummaging around in the back seat. Soon, he pulled out a tire iron, jack stand and the spare, which was small and resembled a rubber doughnut.

I tried to help out by handing him the items he needed, but the doctor ran the show. As he worked, some looky-loos gathered to watch and comment on his technique, which didn't seem to help his mood.

"Ah, must have hit a nail," one man commented as the doctor removed the offending wheel.

"Make sure to tighten those bolts. Don't want the tire to wobble," said another, giving the Indian side-to-side head wobble.

I busied myself with stashing the flat tire in the back of the van as the doctor finished up, and soon we were on our way, the minivan puttering along through the awakening streets.

On the way back, the doctor stopped off to show me the new hotel that his family would soon open. Like the Umaid Bhawan, the new hotel occupied a historic house that was under extensive renovation.

He also promised a surprise, something he said helped him stay healthy and fit. We drove down a leafy street, and suddenly the doctor pulled to the side, next to a street stand. He called out to the vendor in Hindi, and the man produced two bottles of pink liquid. He wiped off each bottle, popped the caps and handed them through the car window to the doctor, who passed one bottle to me.

"This is strawberry yogurt drink," he said. "It's very good for the digestion."

It was delicious. The drink was cold, creamy and sweet, and went down easily. Both of us had soon drained our bottles, handing them back to the vendor before the doctor put the minivan in gear and zoomed off.

He asked whether we'd had any stomach problems since we'd been in India. I shook my head.

"Just make sure that whatever you eat is very hot or very cold, and you'll be fine," he said, adding that we should drink only bottled water and avoid fresh fruits and vegetables.

We heeded most of his advice during our Indian rambles, except for the part about fruits and vegetables. We regularly ate salads and fruit and, luckily, none of us ever suffered more than a short-lived bout of stomach upset, which always cleared up after a day or two. Most of the time, though, we did try to stick to fruits and vegetables that can be peeled, such as cucumbers, oranges and bananas.

Before leaving Jaipur, we were determined to feast our eyes and ears on the spectacle that is Hindi cinema. We hadn't been in Mumbai long enough to visit a Bollywood studio or sample any of its cinematic offerings. But we had read about the Raj Mandir movie palace in Jaipur, one of the most opulent in all of India, and we took a tuk-tuk from our hotel with the hopes of catching an afternoon matinee.

When we got to the theater, the ticket line snaked around the side of the building. We noticed there were separate lines for men and women. Since the women's line was shorter, Ava got the dubious honor of trying to buy us tickets. A grim-faced matron armed with a stick kept the ticket buyers in their place. We were approached surreptitiously by a man who wanted Ava to buy his tickets as well. I managed to smuggle his folded rupee notes to her in line, and convey his request.

Art deco-style chandeliers hung from the ceiling of the theater lobby, and the place was all done up in white, pink and sky blue, leading one travel writer to describe it as looking like a wedding cake. We bought popcorn (no butter!) and walked up the curved ramp to the balcony, where we settled into our cushy seats.

The movie was called Kyon Ki, and it starred one of India's best-known screen hunks, Salman Khan. Like most Bollywood spectacles, the film was a crazy mix of melodrama, slapstick comedy and lots of over-the-top song and dance numbers. The basic plot was about a guy whose girlfriend tragically drowns in a swimming pool, causing him to be blamed for her death and committed to a mental hospital. There was even a dream sequence, when the hero and his girl find themselves suddenly in an unnamed European city, serenading each other as they drive around in a red convertible.

The crowd loved the movie, and shouted back at the screen, but the sound system was turned up so loud that neither the talking, crying babies or ringing cells phones proved much of a distraction.

As the story unfolded at maximum volume, we realized that the plot was almost identical to One Flew Over the Cuckoo's Nest, down to the main character's efforts to cheer up and rally the other mental patients, and the ending, in which he is smothered with a pillow in his bed after undergoing a lobotomy. We were all a bit queasy by the time the film ended. Whether it was the jarring on-screen action, the blaring soundtrack or something we ate, I'm not sure. It was definitely an experience, although I can't say it was completely enjoyable.

We used our time in Jaipur to plan our next few moves. Because I really wanted to see tigers in the wild, we read up on some of India's national parks and nature reserves, and decided to visit Ranthambore National Park, near the town of Sawai Madhopur, on the way to Delhi and Agra to see the Taj. We booked train tickets and a room at the Hotel Tiger Resort.

We also booked flights from Delhi to Darjeeling, in the Himalayan region in the northeast corner of the country, back down to Goa, on the southwest coast, where we planned to spend the Christmas holiday.

Our hotel recommended a travel agency; we arrived there just after lunch. Several excruciating hours later, we left the agency, tickets in hand. The division of labor in India can be fascinating to observe. In the case of the travel agency, a row of employees was stationed behind an L-shaped counter that ran across the back of the shop and down one side.

From our position at one end of the counter, we watched as nearly every staffer in the place got involved in our ticket purchase. One person wrote down our order, another punched the information into a computer terminal, another phoned the airline reservations desk, while still another began filling out our tickets by hand. When it was time to pay, the process was repeated: I handed my credit card to the man who sat across the desk from me and he passed it down the line to one man who swiped it in the card reader, while another tore the receipt off the printer.

Salome had been excited to learn that our hotel in Jaipur had a pool, which was at the rear of the hotel building, surrounded by a high wall. But in spite of the cool respite promised by the pool's blue water, she refused to dip even a single toe. Later, she sheepishly revealed why. Six months before we left on our trip, a tsunami generated by a massive earthquake had struck Indonesia, Thailand and India, wiping out entire villages and killing tens of thousands of people. Salome's imagination had run wild from the televised scenes of tsunami devastation, and during most of our time in Asia, she was afraid to go swimming, whether in the sea or in a pool in the desert state of Rajasthan.

We enjoyed our stay in Jaipur, and were sad to say goodbye to the Umaid Bhawan Guest House. But we were also looking forward to Ranthambore, a wildlife preserve midway between Jaipur and Delhi, where we hoped to "bag" our first wild Indian tiger. The train ride took only a few hours, and when we arrived in the town of Sawai Madhopur, we called our hotel, where the desk clerk promised to send a tuk-tuk for us.

"Watch for a Sikh in a turban," the desk man said.

The Sikh and his tuk-tuk putted up to us a few minutes later, and Ava eyed the small vehicle doubtfully.

"I think we may need two tuk-tuks," she said, pointing to our mound of luggage.

"No problem," said the Sikh. But what did we expect him to say? He began stuffing our bags into the back seat, and gestured for Salome and Ava to get in. I had the honor of sharing the narrow front seat with the driver; I had one cheek on the seat, and the other hung out into space. I clutched my heavy backpack in my left arm, holding on to the frame of the tuk-tuk above my head with all the strength in my right hand.

We lurched off into the city streets, and though the Sikh appeared to be a laid-back person with his droopy gray mustache, shorts and sandals, of course he drove like a madman. I gritted my teeth and held on as best as I could, while Ava and Salome looked on with a mix of fascination and horror from the back seat. The little tuk-tuk veered among traffic, swerved around potholes, and then hit a bump in the uneven road. I felt myself taking to the air, in what seemed like slow motion. But I managed to hang on with my right hand and pull myself back to my precarious perch on the seat. My heart hammered from the close call, and as soon as we had checked into the hotel, I headed to the rooftop terrace for a cold beer.

Ranthambore National Park is considered one of the best places in all of India for seeing a wild tiger. President Bill Clinton stopped off there during a trip to India just after he left office in 2001. Our guide told us, a bit scornfully, that the ex-president had indeed seen a tiger, but only after the park superintendent had closed the park to all traffic for several days preceding the historic visit, and utilized his network of rangers as tiger spotters.

Regular park visitors like us have a choice of taking a "canter," an open-air bus, for a few dollars apiece, or popping for a private jeep, which can cost more than $100 U.S. for a three-hour safari.

Tours of the park, which was located just a few kilometers from our hotel, were given twice each day, in the morning and evening. It was no problem lining up seats on the canters, but there were only a limited number of jeeps allowed in the park each day, so it took a little more finagling to reserve a jeep ride.

We chose the canter for our first foray into the park, and were treated to plenty of wildlife, from deer and antelope to monkeys and birds. The dirt roads that crisscrossed the park wound through forest, along lakes filled with crocodiles, and up on ridges to offer sweeping views. Ranthambore Fort, which gave the park its name, stands on a hill in the center of the park above red-stone ramparts. We didn't see a tiger, although our guide pointed out several tiger paw prints in the dusty shoulder of the road. Our one bit of excitement came when our bus stalled in a forest glade, and we had to summon help from another canter via radio.

Back at the hotel, we hung out drinking beer on the terrace with the other guests, mostly Europeans, some of whom showed off digital photos of the tigers they'd "bagged" on safari.

Not to be outdone by our European friends, I talked to the hotel manager, who promised to try to line up a jeep for us the next day. It felt like a black market transaction, as the manager said he would check with his contacts to get us seats in a jeep. Sure enough, for about 6,000 rupees for the three of us ($133 U.S.), we landed the coveted jeep seats for the afternoon safari. The jeep had both a driver and a guide, who seemed to know the trails extremely well. Ava, Salome and I sat in the middle seat, while a friendly, older Canadian couple rode in the rear.

As we set off, our guide said visitors were lucky enough to see a tiger about 30 percent of the time. We drove around for an hour or so, enjoying the scenery as the guide told us about the various species of plants and animals in the park and scanned the hillsides with binoculars. Suddenly, Ava pointed off to the side. "Tiger!" she shouted.

We all looked through the trees, and sure enough, we could see the familiar orange and black stripes between the tree trunks. The guide yelled a command to the driver in Hindi, and our jeep left the dirt road and began crashing through the brush in pursuit of the tiger. We held on, excited and fearful, since we were riding in an open vehicle.

The tiger began to walk slowly, and as we pulled to the edge of a clearing, it turned and advanced to within three meters of our jeep. The driver told us that as long as we remained inside the jeep, we would be fine, as the tigers were used to the vehicles and did not consider us either threat or dinner. We were close enough that we could hear a small cry as the tiger, a female that had recently given birth, yawned. We snapped pictures furiously, and after a moment or two, the tiger turned and headed through the brush.

We stalked the tiger for about 30 minutes, at one point watching as she appeared ready to chase a large male antelope grazing on the plain. The antelope caught her scent, stood up rigidly to its full height, and issued a warning bark to its friends. The tiger lay in the shade of a tree, waiting for its chance, but soon the antelope bounded away.

Salome's Journal

11/25/05 Near Ranthambore National Park, Rajasthan, India

Salome again and I saw one tiger she was so close only 3 meters away. It was kind of scarey! We saw lots of prints sloth bear prints, tiger prints and lepord prints, and hyena prints. We saw 1 jackle 1 tiger 2 owls and lots of deer and birds!!! We met some people who were very nice. Two of them 1 couple and one guy were German and one lady was from Argentina where we had been to both of those places earlier in the trip. But they all spoke English. The woman and the man live in London so they speak English but the couple from Germany spoke English too. They were nice and we got there eamail so we can keep in touch. Salome.

We were exultant; we had seen our tiger, and could now continue happily on our travels, proof of the encounter safely burned onto our camera's memory card. Of course, that evening, as we had dinner on the terrace with the Europeans, we let them to talk us into showing off our prized tiger shots, which were closer-up than any of theirs.

Sadly, we could be among the last visitors to have the thrill of seeing a wild tiger in India. Poachers have killed off the entire tiger populations at a number of famous sanctuaries and preserves, and even Ranthambore has not been spared. An article that ran in the newspaper during our stay in Sawai Madhoper announced the bust of a major poaching ring, which had reportedly killed 22 of the park's 48 adult tigers over a three-year period. The poachers had apparently bribed the park superintendent to overlook their activities.

The Thanksgiving holiday fell during our stay at the Hotel Tiger Resort, and we celebrated with omelets, pancakes, grilled cheese sandwiches and French fries. From our terrace, we could see a huge Hindi wedding across the road. They had set up a pavilion with colored lights, a dance floor and a sound system with massive speakers. The music was so loud that even in our hotel room with the windows closed we could barely hear each other talk. The wedding party arrived in a huge procession with horses, banners, lanterns and the bride in a chair carried by four bearers. To top it off, near midnight, they started shooting off fireworks. Indians sure know how to party!

We took a walk down the dusty road in front of our hotel one afternoon at my insistence, even though it was hotter than the inside of a tandoori oven. We were regaled by a couple of young boys driving a colorfully decorated camel cart, who wanted to give us a ride, and we posed for pictures with a group of giggling schoolboys. When we got hungry, we stopped at a restaurant whose outdoor tables were set on a pleasant green lawn surrounded by a hedge. As we waited for our food, we were disconcerted to see several rats scurry along the back of the building where the kitchen was located. When the food came, we were amazed to see that the cook had arranged our rice dish in the shape of heart, beautifully decorated with vegetable garnish. We couldn't get over the contradictions of a place where a cook can give so much care to the way his food is displayed on a plate, while rodents roam freely just a few feet away.

After the tranquility and open spaces of Ranthambore, I wasn't exactly thrilled at the prospect of traveling to Delhi, which I imagined to be crowded, hectic and polluted. And I wasn't far wrong. The train trip was only a few hours long, and we sat in one of the nicest "chair class" cars we had seen thus far in India, and enjoyed a hot lunch delivered to our seats. The car was jammed full of Indian businessmen and families, and as the train neared the outskirts of the capital, through the yellowish tint of the windows we could see row upon row of flimsy shacks and people in rags squatting along the embankments that ran next to the train tracks.

A middle-aged woman in an Indian pants suit stood next to us as we waited with our luggage in the corridor for the train to pull into the Delhi station.

"I'd love to wear jeans and T-shirts," she said, gesturing to my clothing. "But my husband won't allow me."

Railway workers had opened the doors before the train came to a full stop, and we were set upon by porters in red jackets who jostled for the right to carry our bags. It was easier to give in than to protest, so we allowed them to stride off with our bags into the seething mass of people coming and going at the busy station.

In what seemed like a few seconds, we found ourselves in the back of a taxi, pulling out into the busy Delhi streets.

The Maharani Guest House was in Sunder Nagar, a tree-lined neighborhood a few kilometers outside the city center.

We had no quarrel with the location, but the hotel itself left much to be desired. The carpet and furniture were shabby and marked with cigarette burns, the tiled corridor made sound carry into our room, and the staff was the pushiest and rudest we had encountered. After three bellmen helped us carry our bags up to our room, Ava stood at the doorway with a few folded rupee notes, ready to hand them out. The first man took the bill Ava extended with her right hand – then reached over and plucked the other bills from Ava's left hand!

"I will give it to them," he hastily explained before ducking out and leaving his disgruntled companions in the dust.

Each day when we returned to our hotel after sightseeing, one of the bellmen would stand by the door to our room as we inserted the key.

"Good afternoon sir," he would say. "I cleaned your room today."

We looked inside to see that the covers had been pulled up on the beds, and things had been straightened a bit. The man wouldn't leave until we had forked over some rupees.

In Delhi, more so than just about anywhere else in India, we felt like we stood out as targets for hawkers, vendors and beggars, some scrupulous, some not so much.

On our first day in the city, I made the rookie mistake of walking around Connaught Place, the heart of Delhi's commercial and tourist district, with my nose buried in my guidebook, as I sought the government tourist office.

The small map included in the book wasn't helping much, and a friendly young man approached, offering to help.

"I am a college student, and I want to practice my English," he said, explaining his generosity. This, in a country where nearly everyone speaks very good English. Delhi itself even boasts two competing English-language newspapers, the Times of India and the Hindustan Times.

He led us down a side street to a travel agency, which did indeed have the words "government sponsored" on its sign. He hustled us inside, where we were offered seats by an agent who no doubt hoped to sell us some high-priced tours.

We quickly realized we were in the wrong place, and beat a retreat. Nearby, we found the real government tourist bureau, where we booked a one-day trip to Agra and a Delhi city tour.

The people in the tourist bureau office were genuinely helpful, and one man even gave us his cell phone number, which turned out to be a lifesaver a few days later when Ava left her purse on the tour bus that brought us back from our visit to the Taj Mahal.

Although we didn't care much for our hotel, it was located in a quiet, residential neighborhood close to major thoroughfares, and just a short tuk-tuk or taxi ride from the city center. Down the street was a small commercial area with antique shops, a bank and several vegetarian restaurants. Soon after our arrival in Delhi, we went exploring, marveling at the wide boulevards (with landscaped medians) that led past the capital's government buildings and museums.

The city appeared to be laid out more logically than frenzied Mumbai and cleaner as well. We hired a car for a one-day whirlwind tour of Delhi, which included the services of a dour tour guide, a gray-haired, stern man who provided loads of historical facts, but rarely smiled.

We started out at Humayan's tomb, a monument built in honor of the second Mughal emperor in the 1500s, predating the Taj Mahal. We were pleasantly surprised to be the only people strolling the grounds at that early hour of the morning, and enjoyed walking around the reddish stone building and listening to the chattering birds.

Our tour included stops at such famous sites as the Qutub Minar, a 13th-century red sandstone tower more than 200 feet tall and covered with finely carved designs and quotations from the Koran; and the Lotus Temple, a stunning feat of architecture built by the Bahai community. After taking off our shoes, we walked inside the temple, awed by its soaring interior spaces and tranquility, in spite of the hundreds of people walking through with us. We also visited the Raj Ghat, the tomb of Mahatma Gandhi, a marble slab where the Indian leader was cremated. Today, the faithful set garlands of orange and yellow marigolds around the simple monument and its eternal flame, and pose for pictures in front of it.

Our tour ended at a brightly painted Hindu temple, a quiet oasis in the midst of the city's traffic and commotion. Our guide led us inside, paused to pray, and then briskly strode off to catch a bus home, leaving us to ride back to our hotel with the driver, who hadn't uttered more than a few words the entire day.

In spite of the advice of travelers we met in India, we opted to stay in Delhi and visit Agra, and the Taj Mahal, on a day trip from the capital. Many people say it is best to stay in Agra, both to avoid having to travel from Delhi and back on the same day, and also to allow time for visiting the famous "monument to love" when its white marble surfaces are painted pink and gold by the light of dawn and dusk. There are also a number of other ancient sites, some rated by travelers nearly as highly as the Taj, in and around Agra.

Wisely or not, we disregarded those tips and booked a day trip to Agra that departed at 6 a.m. on a Sunday. We rose early, and went outside into the dark morning to find a tuk-tuk. We had little margin for error; our tour bus was scheduled to leave right on time from the government tourist office in central Delhi.

A sleepy tuk-tuk driver climbed out of the back seat of his vehicle, still wrapped in a blanket. He looked like he was barely awake as he kick-started the engine to life, and then gestured for the three of us to climb in. We had traveled a few blocks when we came to a series of wooden sawhorses blocking the road. A man approached and exchanged heated words with the driver. The entire conversation was in Hindi, but it seemed we had been snared in some sort of checkpoint. After arguing for several minutes, while I became increasingly anxious in the back seat, the driver handed over the obligatory rupees, and we were allowed through the checkpoint.

A flower market had been set up by sleepy-looking vendors on the sidewalk in front of the tourist office. We rushed inside, and the tour guide was just gathering up the passengers to walk over to the bus. We barely made it!

Including our family, there were about a dozen passengers on the small bus, which probably seated 20 people. Our fellow passengers were Indian tourists, many of whom, like us, were visiting the Taj for the first time. The plan, according to the driver/guide, was to head toward Agra, and stop midway for breakfast. The one-way trip of about 200 kilometers (120 miles) would take four hours.

We took seats in the back of the bus, figuring to spread out across the back row. That proved to be a mistake because the suspension on the little bus was pretty much shot. Our seats were directly above the rear axle, and we felt the jolt of every pothole and bump as it was transmitted directly from the wheel to the frame, then to our spines and internal organs. And there were plenty of potholes.

The bus traveled through Delhi to the outskirts of the city, and then through a semi-rural area marked by agricultural fields. The four-lane highway seemed crowded for an early Sunday morning, and we jounced and bounced toward Agra, dodging cars, scooters and trucks.

Our breakfast stop was at a government-run tourist resort – we stretched our legs and walked the short distance to the dining room, where we were served hard-boiled eggs, white bread and tea. Ava and Salome both made a beeline for the bathroom: the two of them had needed to go nearly from the time we had left Delhi, but did not want to ask for a special stop. They gritted their teeth and endured the bouncing bus, suffering especially through the last few miles before our stop. As they rushed inside the ladies room, I stared with amazement as a sign taped to the door: "Caution – Dear Guests, Please Beware of Wild Monkeys."

And we did see the wild monkeys, who loitered near our bus and screeched at us for food scraps as we clambered back on board after breakfast.

Our first sightseeing stop was the tomb of Akbar the Great who was considered, appropriately, the greatest of the Mughal emperors who ruled vast swaths of northern India from the early 16th century to the mid-18th century.

Akbar was highly tolerant of diverse religious views for his time and sponsored debates by scholars of different faiths, even atheists. The tomb has four entry gates: one Hindu, one Muslim, one Christian and one representing Din-i-Ilahi, the religion Akbar founded.

By the time we left Akbar's tomb, it was near midday, and we were eager for a glimpse of the Taj Mahal, the reason for our trip south to Agra.

Either we were looking in the wrong direction, or the complex surrounding the Taj obscures it from view from the outside. In any event, we didn't catch even a fleeting view of the white marble structure as our tour bus wound through the choked streets surrounding the monument. We stopped at a corner and a dour man jumped aboard, who turned out to be the tour guide who would illuminate us about the wonders of the Taj.

From the back, it looked as though the man badly needed a haircut; great tufts of curly black hair sprouted from each side of his head. When we got a closer look as we disembarked from the bus in the parking lot of the Taj complex, we saw that the hair actually sprouted from the tops of his ears, which we found both unusual and strangely compelling.

Although he didn't smile much, the guide was very well-informed, telling us about the background of the monument as we fended off the souvenir hawkers who backpedaled in front of us, holding up their wares during our walk from the parking lot.

We paid our "foreigners" admission fee, then got in line for our bags and bodies to be searched and run through metal detectors. Once we had passed through this gantlet, we walked through a passageway where professional photographers besieged us. In spite of the hassles of getting to Agra, the jarring bus ride and the relentless vendors and beggars, when we caught our first sight of the Taj through the arched stone entranceway, all those cares fell away.

We gazed at the white marble edifice in wonder, hardly believing we were seeing it in person. Its gleaming dome and minarets shimmered in the bright sunshine, and we were captivated both by its famous outline and the aura of mystique that surrounds it.

The Taj is one of those sights included as a "must-see" stop on the itinerary of every traveler to India, and I half-expected it would fail to live up to the hype. But I was wrong. The monument, erected in the mid-1600s by Mughal Emperor Shah Jahan, was beautiful to behold. We were reluctant to take our eyes from it, so that we could turn our backs to the monument and have our pictures taken by the insistent photographer.

Shah Jahan, according to legend, was so distraught by the death of his favorite wife, Mumtaz, that he oversaw design and construction of the massive tomb as a monument to his beloved. Years later, when Shah Jahan died after being overthrown and imprisoned by his own son, Aurangzeb, he was laid to rest in the Taj next to Mumtaz.

Visitors are allowed to climb the stairs to the monument and walk inside to view the ceremonial tomb of Mumtaz and Shah Jahan under the Taj's white onion dome. But before setting foot on the white marble surface of the monument, everyone must put blue paper booties over their shoes. We shuffled along with the never-ending line inside the monument, where the air was stuffy and ripe with body odors, and circled the tomb, which was enclosed with white marble latticework. The earthly remains of the emperor and his bride lie in caskets one floor below the ceremonial tomb.

Soon, we moved with the crowd back outside into the warm, sunny day. We walked around to the back side of the Taj, where our guide showed us a cleared patch of earth across the river. Legend has it that Shah Jahan planned to erect a mirror monument to the Taj in black marble, where he wanted to be laid to rest. That second monument was never built.

The bus took us from the Taj to a touristy restaurant nearby for lunch, then to a "workshop" where we watched several men and women fashioning knick-knacks from white marble and small bits of semi-precious stone. The workers' faces were expressionless as they went about their monotonous tasks on a wooden platform just inside the front doors of the air-conditioned building.

Then we were led downstairs to a display room, where inlaid marble boxes, carved figurines, candlesticks and wall-mounted marble medallions were offered for sale. Ava bought a few trinkets, including a tiny box with an inlaid top.

The ride back to Delhi was uneventful, as we chatted with our fellow passengers, some of whom were from the capital, and others who had traveled to Delhi on business or pleasure, and signed up for the day trip to the Taj.

The bus was supposed to leave us at the tourist office near Connaught Place, but the driver was kind enough to drop a number of passengers, including us, near our hotels. It was about 9 p.m. when we finally stepped off the bus, tired, but pleased to be able to check the Taj Mahal off our list of travel to-dos.

We were walking to a restaurant near our hotel when Ava stopped suddenly.

"What's wrong?" I asked.

"You're not going to like this," she said in a small voice.

"What is it?"

"I think I left my purse on the bus."

I let out a string of curses that would have made a tuk-tuk wallah blush.

Ava has a history of forgetting her purse at strategically inconvenient times, and this was a doozy. Now, instead of relaxing over a nice dinner and reliving our visit to one of the world's most famous monuments, we had to figure out how to get her purse back late at night in strange, and very large, foreign city. Right at that moment, it seemed like a long shot.

There was one saving grace: although Ava had rarely heeded my advice to wear her money belt containing passport and emergency cash, and instead usually kept it in her purse, this time she had listened. While her lost purse did hold her wallet with her driver's license, ATM card and local currency, at least her passport was tucked safely in the money belt around her waist.

We went back to the hotel to plot out our next move: by now, it was about 10 p.m. and I was trying to figure out how we could contact the tour bus driver. Then I remembered that the man in the government tourist office had given me his cell phone number. Thanks to the handy cell phone we had purchased a couple of days earlier in Delhi, I was able to reach him easily in spite of the late hour.

While he would have been within his rights to be irritated by the late call, the man was very concerned and helpful. He immediately reached the driver, who was still at the bus yard, and confirmed that Ava's purse was on the bus. He then asked the driver to wait for us, and gave me detailed directions. I asked the hotel desk man to call a taxi, and soon I was riding in the back seat of a minivan through the surprisingly lively streets of a Sunday night in Delhi.

We pulled up to the bus yard, and the driver came out to meet us holding Ava's purse. I tipped him 500 rupees (on top of the 500 I had given him earlier) and, very relieved, rode back to our hotel. The contents of the purse appeared to be untouched, including the rupees in Ava's wallet, so we decided not to cancel the bank card. All was well.

The next day, I called the man at the tourism office to thank him again for his help, which had proved invaluable.

I had to say that in spite of my trepidation about visiting the Indian capital, the helpfulness and honesty of the tourism officials, the tour bus driver, and even the taxi driver, was impressive. I'm not so sure that if we had left a purse or wallet on a tour bus in New York City or Los Angeles things would have worked out so well.

With our remaining time in Delhi, we did what any intrepid tourist would do – we went shopping. Our acquisitive impulses took us to Connaught Place, where Ava perused the clothing at several tailor shops, and to Khan Market, an upscale shopping center where I bought a copy of Paul Theroux's The Great Railway Bazaar, about his train trip through Asia. To our delight, we found a tiny shop that carried American and English goodies, such as Pop-Tarts, Cheerios and shortbread cookies. We stocked up on a small bag of familiar food to staunch our homesickness, and paid dearly for our indulgence, more than $30 U.S.

By our last day in Delhi, we had covered most of the sights we had come to see, and found ourselves with a spare afternoon. Looking through the Times of India at breakfast, I saw that Harry Potter and the Goblet of Fire, the newest film in the series, was playing in English at a cross-town cinema. The theater turned out to be in one of Delhi's posher neighborhoods, where many international diplomats and their families live. We called the taxi driver who had transported me on my quest to recover Ava's purse, and we were on our way to visit Harry, Ron and Hermione at Hogwarts.

The next day we caught a flight to northeast India on Air Deccan, a relatively new "no frills" Indian airline dedicated to getting Indians out of their traditional train seats and into the sky. The plane was brand-new and immaculate, but we had to pay an extra charge because the combined weight of our bags exceeded the meager luggage allowance. Snacks such as curry-flavored Cup of Noodles were sold by the flight attendants from a cart they pushed down the aisle.

Our destination was the crossroads town of Siliguri in the Indian state of West Bengal. Siliguri was the jumping-off point for a tour of Jaldapara Wildlife Sanctuary (where we hoped to see rhinos) and the former British hill-station of Darjeeling at the foot of the Himalayan range.

Chapter 11

Where Do I Plug In My Blow-dryer?

Toothbrush. Check. Socks. Check. Passport. Check. DVD player. Huh?

In the months and weeks leading up to the start of our world trip, we went over our packing list again and again, trying to maximize the extremely limited space in our travel bags. Every item had to count – there was little or no room for things we didn't really need.

My vision of the trip was to travel low to the ground, moving around by train, bus, car and boat, or donkey if necessary. I wanted to travel light, which to me meant one bag apiece. I believed – and still do – that traveling with the minimum amount of luggage frees the traveler to experience the place he or she is seeing.

Rather than relying on all the things they know and love from back home, I think travelers should bring only essential personal possessions and fill in the rest on the road as the need arises. That way, whether it's toiletries or clothes, travelers get much more familiar with the customs and habits of people in other places. Finding what you need can be half the fun – I love browsing the aisles of a supermarket, drug store or clothing shop in a foreign country.

Being a lean, mean traveler also makes getting around

so much easier, whatever mode of transportation you happen to be using at a given moment. When you are in a foreign country where you don't speak the language, it's tough enough to find the right train, bus or plane, get on and find your seat without having to simultaneously wrestle with a mountain of luggage. Even better, I thought, would be a bag that could be carried on airplanes, avoiding the delay and hassle of checked bags, and the risk that our luggage would be sent on to some unknown destination.

One of the first decisions we had to make was what kind of bags to take. I voted for backpacks, which are compact, leave your hands free and make a nice pillow in a pinch. They also send a message that this is a serious traveler, who isn't loaded with cash, and is more interested in learning about the inner workings of a place than in finding a hotel with satellite TV and in-room whirlpool tub.

Ava and Salome, though, argued for bags that could be wheeled along a sidewalk or airport terminal. We compromised with a bag by Eagle Creek that featured wheels, a retractable handle and a set of padded shoulder and waist straps that could be tucked away behind a zippered panel. Another feature I liked was the zip-off day bag on the front, which had its own shoulder straps.

The bags had the added advantage of a lifetime guarantee on workmanship. During our world trip, the handle of my bag got tweaked, probably from all the gear I had been stuffing into it over many months on the road. When we returned, I sent the bag to Eagle Creek and they installed a brand-new handle for free. Early on, I had to scrap my one-bag-per-person dream because of

Salome's schoolwork. After meeting with her independent study teacher, who supplied us with a stack of textbooks, worksheets and educational forms, we realized we would need to take one bag designated strictly as a mobile classroom.

Because space was so limited, it was important that all of our clothing be as versatile as possible. I have come to love lightweight travel pants that can be converted to shorts by zipping off the legs. The pants also drip-dry nicely when hung over the shower curtain after being washed in a hotel sink.

Complicating our packing was an itinerary that would take us through a variety of climates and seasons. Our first international stop, Ecuador, was scheduled for late June, which is winter in South America. Thus, we had to be prepared for cold weather for the first several weeks of our trip, but then be ready to sizzle when we crossed the continent and reached Brazil.

I anticipated that – due to the budget nature of our trip – we would occasionally be staying in places that would never qualify for the Good Housekeeping seal of approval. So, I bought a set of silk sleep sheets for each of us, which were like a lightweight sleeping bag we could burrow into if we found the sheets at our hotel less than savory. While they were handy to carry – each set folded up into a palm-sized sack – I don't think we used them more than once or twice on the whole trip. The vast majority of places we stayed were neat and clean.

I also bought a travel towel for each of us. These are rectangles of highly absorbent material, much smaller and lighter than a regular terry-cloth towel, which dry quickly and take up little room when tightly folded. These towels did occasionally come in handy, such as when we went for a dip during our tour of the Galapagos Islands.

When it came to electronics, I spent a lot of time researching and thinking about what to take. Fairly early in the process, I decided not to bring a laptop. I figured that finding plug-in Internet access might prove difficult, and I anticipated – correctly – that Internet cafés would be easy to find on the road. At the time of our trip, Wi-Fi had not become as readily available as it is today. Add in the fact that the newest laptops are much lighter than the older models, and I very well might bring a computer on a future trip. I must admit feeling a stab of envy when I watched a traveler from New Zealand hook up a tiny satellite receiver to his laptop as he sat beside the pool in Goa, India.

We did bring a digital camera and found it quite simple and convenient to take our camera's memory card into a photo shop, have the pictures transferred to a CD, and then wipe the card clean to reuse. Unless the Internet connection at a café was particularly slow, it was quick and painless to email photos from the disc to folks back home. I kept all of the discs in a CD wallet in my backpack, which was one of my most closely guarded possessions.

The camera ran on rechargeable AA batteries, and I made sure before we left the charger worked on all international voltage systems. In fact, I found out that most new electronic gear is compatible with a wide range of voltages. This can be determined by looking at the back of the device, which should indicate a range, such as "Input 100–240V."

The other important thing regarding electronics is to bring a set of international adapters that fit the various plug configurations found around the world. Mine came in a handy cloth sack, and I think there were three or four different versions. In recent years, I have found that wall sockets in Asia, Europe and elsewhere are often designed to accommodate both flat and round prongs, meaning an adapter isn't always needed.

The other electronic gear we carried included an Mp3 player – I couldn't have survived without my Rio player, which carried about 1,000 songs in its memory – and a cell phone, which we purchased in India and used for the two months we traveled on the subcontinent. The original purchase price of $50 included 2,500 prepaid minutes, which could be used to call anywhere within the country. We were also able to purchase minutes that could be used for international calls.

The phone was incredibly handy to have, whether we were making hotel reservations, calling our friends and relatives back home or searching for a lost object. W still had about half of our minutes left when we flew on to Thailand. We gave the phone to an American traveler we met in Mumbai. As for the Rio, whenever I bought a music CD along the way, I would pop into an Internet café and load the music onto my player.

The only controversial item was the DVD player. Ava argued that we buy one before leaving the U.S. to keep Salome occupied during journeys and in countless hotel rooms where we would be bunking down along they way.

I resisted as long as I could, but eventually lost the argument. We carried a CD wallet stuffed with movies, and the portable DVD player, battery and charging cables in their own special backpack – another item we had to lug around.

But it did prove a Godsend for Salome, who was already dealing with a traumatic separation from her friends and familiar surroundings. She loved watching certain movies over and over, such as Miss Congeniality, starring Sandra Bullock. In most countries throughout South America and Asia, pirate copies of Hollywood blockbusters were readily available for a buck or two within days of the film's theatrical release. Sometimes the picture was dark and the sound obscured by echoes, and strangely enough, some of discs were overdubbed in Russian. But many of the movies were of very good quality, so we always had a fresh supply of films to keep us entertained.

We even learned how to hook up the DVD player up to the TV sets in our hotel rooms, which sometimes required a scavenger hunt through local electronics shops to find the proper cable. The device had the added benefit of playing music CDs and allowing us to view our photo CDs. And it really didn't take up that much room.

As we traveled, we accumulated souvenirs, clothing and other items that we didn't want to carry with us throughout our entire trip. So, several times along the way, we begged, borrowed or stole an empty cardboard box and found the nearest post office to ship our booty home. These packages would include the movies we no longer wanted to watch, the clothes that were too heavy or too light for the climate of the country where we happened to be, and anything else that we didn't immediately need. We must have sent at least a half-dozen packages (including a very large one from India containing three or four quilts) and all of them reached my in-laws' apartment in San Diego safely.

In my backpack, I kept a folder with important travel documents, such as copies of our passports, extra passport photos, vaccination records and prescriptions. I also printed out email reservation confirmations for hotels, flights and tours, and a phone and address list of friends, relatives and business contacts. Finally, I created a chart listing every country we planned to visit, with such key information as the local currency and exchange rate, telephone code, time zone in relation to Greenwich Mean Time, and electrical voltage. Along with carrying hard copies of the latter two documents, I also emailed them to myself for easy access at Internet cafes.

I am happy to report we never suffered any thefts or losses of key possessions during our travels. Sure, we spent an anxious night after an ATM in Rio de Janeiro swallowed Ava's bank card and refused to give it up. The next day, when the bank was open, a bank staffer graciously extracted the card for us. But we managed to maneuver our way through 19 countries over nine months without our baggage being rerouted, pilfered or purloined.

My notion of traveling light did take a bit of a beating, though. Ava and Salome are unapologetic shopaholic and missed no opportunity to pick up what they considered to be a prize, whether we were in a boutique, passing a street vendor, or waiting for a ride somewhere.

That meant we were constantly adding to our load, and soon after we hit South America, new bags started showing up in our luggage pile.

By the time we reached Brazil, we were toting several extra duffel bags along with our possessions. For Ava's birthday, I struck a deal – we would ditch the extra bags, and in exchange, I would buy her a large, new suitcase. My reasoning was that it would be easier to carry and track one big piece of luggage, than several small ones.

We visited a luggage store around the corner from our hotel in Rio, and Ava selected a large rectangular suitcase with wheels, a popup handle and a zippered expansion compartment on the front. Once it was fully loaded, the bag, which we nicknamed Big Bertha, became a force to be reckoned with. It was large, very heavy, and it was known to take on a life of its own on trains and buses, lurching down aisles and gaining momentum as we chased after it.

I pulled more than a few muscles hoisting it onto overhead luggage racks on buses and trains, which strained under the load.

I must admit I turned into a nag at times after Ava and Salome went on various shopping sprees. My constant litany became, "Let's ship it home!"

My advice? The creature comforts are nice, and can even help alleviate homesickness in a tiny, poorly furnished hotel room in an unfamiliar town far from home. But I still say, go light.

Chapter 12

India High and Low
From the Himalayas to the Arabian Sea

Our first impression of the Indian state of West Bengal was that of a fertile region dotted with palm trees and jungle foliage at the base of the Himalayan foothills. We planned to stop over for a few days to visit a wildlife sanctuary before traveling to Darjeeling and its tea plantations, Buddhist monasteries and breathtaking views of massive Kanchenjunga , the world's third-tallest peak behind Mt. Everest and K2.

The closest airport to Darjeeling is in Bagdogra, about 100 kilometers from the former British hill station. Our flight landed in the early afternoon, and we hired a taxi to take us the 10 or 12 kilometers to Siliguri, a crossroads town where we would spend the next few days.

I was ready for a change after the clamor and pollution of Delhi, and enjoyed the scenery on the road from Bagdogra airport, which wound through several villages, with their commerce and industry on full display in the fields and open-air shops. In spite of the technological revolution that has brought new prosperity and outsourced jobs to India, a large percentage of the country's billion-plus people still do things in the old-fashioned way, using brute strength and simple, mechanical equipment.

It is very common to see men pushing carts laden with all sorts of materials, from bricks and sections of concrete pipe, to cloth and agricultural goods. Workers in the fields irrigate their crops by dipping buckets of water from canals that run alongside planted areas, and bicycle rickshaws carrying both people and cargo can be seen on the streets of the largest cities and the smallest villages.

Those were the sights we encountered from the back of the taxi that drove us from Bagdogra to Siliguri, through green countryside with palm trees and lush foliage.

Our first view of Siliguri, though, was disappointing: the main drag through town – Hill Cart Road – is straight and long, with a metal railing down its center. Cars, vans, jeeps, bicycle rickshaws and horse-drawn carts streamed in each direction, separated by the barrier. The noise of revving engines and honking horns overpowered our conversation. We went straight to the Hotel Conclave, down a steep ramp to one side of the main road. The hotel was seven or eight stories tall, and its contemporary concrete-and-glass design made it stand out from most of the other buildings we saw, which were shorter and much more run-down.

The Conclave was only a year or so old, and turned out to be a great bargain – the rooms were 1,200 rupees per night, or $24 U.S., and were very clean and modern, with AC, satellite TV and spiffy private baths. The restaurant next to the hotel lobby was very good, and we ate almost all of our meals there. We enjoyed the Indian and Chinese dishes and the restaurant's signature dessert, fried ice cream.

We had arrived in Siliguri a couple of days before a scheduled overnight trip to the Jaldapara Wildlife Refuge, where we hoped to spot wild rhinos during an elephant safari.

Siliguri is a major crossroads and transit point for the northeastern section of India. It sits in the state of West Bengal, which abuts Bangladesh to the east, and is near the borders of Bhutan and Nepal further north. Along with the nearby Bagdogra airport is a major train station, and many bus and jeep stands, where people throng with their luggage for rides to such far-flung destinations as Kathmandu, Calcutta and Gangtok, the capital of the northernmost Indian state of Sikkim.

In spite of its hustle and bustle, there is very little to do in Siliguri. From the tiny balcony of our hotel room, the town looked dreary, dirty and devoid of color. A wide, sandy river bed bisected by a narrow band of gray water spread out next to our hotel, and we could see women squatting next to it, washing clothes, while children played nearby.

We walked up and down the streets a bit, but spent most of the time holed up in our air-conditioned room, watching TV, reading and (me) drinking beer. The hotel staff was happy to provide room service, so we often didn't even leave our room for meals. There were a couple of restaurants nearby, but nothing we liked very much. One evening I went across the street to a cluttered office where public Internet access was available. After reading and sending a few emails, I browsed through an online travel bulletin board, where one traveler called Siliguri a "horrible town."

We used the time to rest, do laundry and help Salome catch up with her schoolwork. I tried to talk her into walking next door to an English-language school. Each day, we would see the children coming and going in their red sweaters and dark pants or skirts. I thought she would enjoy meeting some local children and checking out their school, but she was too shy and refused to go with me.

I read the local English-language paper, the Statesman, which was published out of Calcutta. There were all sorts of interesting tidbits, including police briefs, some of them horrifying. One story told of a wild elephant rampaging through a village, killing several people. Another told of a mob chasing down and brutally beating a man suspected of molesting a child. The paper also carried political stories, most of which centered around local communities trying to secure more funding from the central government in Delhi for schools and health clinics. I found the classified ads fascinating, especially help wanted ads that included salary ranges. One ad for a position as an M.D. at a Calcutta hospital offered a salary of 20,000 rupees per month, or about $450 U.S.

After two or three days, it was time for our trip to the wildlife reserve. We showed up at the West Bengal Tourist Office, and in typical Indian fashion, were offered tea and told to make ourselves comfortable on the sofa. The tour was supposed to leave at 10 a.m., but things were running behind, as various officials conferred with each other, made a number of phone calls, and busily shuffled and stamped papers. The tour was a great deal – 2,500 rupees per person, including all transportation, overnight lodging, meals and entry fees.

We set out in late morning in a jeep. Ava, Salome and I were the only passengers; we were accompanied by several officials from the tourist office. Our guide was a friendly, entrepreneurial, young man. On the way back to Siliguri the next day, he made several stops to pick up furniture and other items, which he planned to sell in town. He showed us his house when we passed through his village, and told us he was getting married soon, and needed to build up his savings.

We rolled past fields planted with rice, and saw farmers spreading their rice crops along the edge of the road to let them dry in the sun. Later in the afternoon, after we had gained elevation, we drove past mile after mile of tea plantations. The green tea leaves grew on bushes two or three feet high, planted tightly together to create a carpet of green that stretched as far as we could see. Interspersed with the tea bushes were trees that provided dappled shade. Our guide explained that tea plants needed partial shade to thrive; just the right balance of sunlight and shade had to be achieved.

As it was not yet harvest time, there was very little activity in the tea fields.

By dusk, we were still driving, anxious to reach the Jaldapara Wildlife Reserve and the national park lodge where we would spend the night.

The last hour or so of the drive was one of the most harrowing times we spent on India's highways. We were traveling through more agricultural fields interspersed with small villages, and the highway was one lane in each direction, with very little shoulder.

The evening air was hazy with smoke from countless

cooking fires, and a steady stream of hand carts and bicycle rickshaws, loaded with goods, moved along each side of the road. We weren't sure if the jeep driver was trying to make up for lost time, but he barreled along the road, beeping his horn and swerving each time he came upon a cart, rickshaw or pedestrian. In the gloom, people on foot and in small vehicles seemed to suddenly materialize, out of nowhere. Each time we passed a rickshaw rider or pedestrian without a collision, we breathed a sigh of relief. The only time the driver braked – suddenly – was when a goat appeared in the road before us. The cliché that Indians hold animal life more sacred than human life held true on that particular ride.

Just after dark, we turned onto the dirt road at the entrance to the wildlife reserve. We bumped along through the forest for several kilometers, and came across the lodge, a rustic building lit with a few naked bulbs. We were shown to our room, which had two large beds shrouded in mosquito netting. The walls were rough-hewn boards, and the uneven floor was covered with dark, stained carpet. The bathroom was large and needed a thorough cleaning. Since we would only be spending a few hours in the room before our 5 a.m. wakeup call, we didn't worry about its shortcomings.

The best part of the lodge was a second-floor lounge furnished with well-used, upholstered sofas. At one end of the room was a large window that opened outward. Next to the window was a powerful, handheld spotlight that we could shine out through the window, past the neatly trimmed garden and the fence around the compound, to the edge of the forest. A waiter brought large bottles of ice cold beer, and we moved the spotlight beam around until we saw shiny red dots in the darkness, which turned out to be the eyes of wild bison. Next, we were astonished to see several rhinos amble up and begin feeding on the low vegetation. We were in heaven!

After dinner in the bright, cheery dining room, it was off to bed for the three of us. It seemed like our heads had just hit the pillows when we heard a sharp knock on the door. It was 5 a.m., time to rouse ourselves for an elephant safari.

We joined a few other guests for a cup of tea in the dining room, then we were led to a clearing, where we climbed the steps of a wooden platform that had been painted green, maybe to blend in with the surrounding forest.

An elephant stood next to the platform, a padded seat strapped to its back. The seat was large enough for four passengers, sitting back to back, two facing out to either side of the elephant. A metal handrail ran around the seat at waist level. The driver sat on the elephant's neck, guiding it with spoken commands and constant movements of his bare feet just behind the animal's ears. The driver also carried a thick iron bar, which he put to use later during the safari.

We took off just after 6 a.m., along a narrow path through the jungle. Our party consisted of two full-grown elephants, each carrying four passengers, and two baby elephants, who apparently came along to keep their parents company at work.

We could not have imagined a more exotic setting for our elephant ride. A thick layer of mist hovered over the ground, making it appear that the trees in the distance rose up from a pool of ghostly white. The trees around us dripped with dew-covered vines, and the path soon led to a stream, which the elephants crossed easily, stepping gingerly down and back up the banks with their enormous feet. From our perch, we gently swayed from side to side in time with the pachyderm's heavy footfalls. We sat comfortably on the thick padding, our eyes peeled for the preserve's famous rhinos.

The forest was very quiet at this time of the morning; other than the crunching of branches and twigs as our elephant convoy tramped along the overgrown path, the only sounds were occasional bird calls, which echoed in the mist-laden air.

Suddenly, the driver perked up. "Rhino!" he shouted, pointing into the bushes. Sure enough, off to the side of the path, we could see a patch of rough, gray hide through the leafy undergrowth.

The driver began barking commands, and our elephant turned off the path and plunged into the brush. Another sharp order, and the elephant reached out with its trunk and uprooted a small tree that blocked our path. We lurched forward in pursuit of the rhino, which seemed to leisurely keep pace with our advances, moving a few feet every time we got too close for its comfort. I wondered if the rhino might get tired of this cat-and-mouse game and charge at us, but that never happened. Instead, after several minutes, the rhino picked up its pace and rumbled off across a clearing.

By this time, shafts of golden sunlight were scattered through the trees as the morning fog began to melt away.

When our elephant failed to respond quickly enough to

a command to suit the driver, he shouted and whacked the animal several times on the head with the iron bar. Ava, Salome and I were shocked, but the thick-skinned elephant merely shrugged off the blows as we might swat a fly.

After a couple of hours, the driver turned the elephant convoy back toward the lodge and our safari was over.

At the lodge, we joined some other travelers in the dining room. We chatted with two men from the San Francisco Bay Area who were on their way to Bhutan, a secluded mountain kingdom nestled between India's northeast corner and China's southern border.

The Bhutanese government allows foreign tourists to visit, but only as part of organized tour groups, which cost several hundred dollars per person per day. One of the men said he had traveled in India in the 1970s for a full year, getting by on a total of $750, nearly the amount he and his companion would spend for a single day of their Bhutanese tour. He said he had stayed in the cheapest places possible, often sleeping on the floors of ashrams, where he went to learn about India's spiritual traditions.

After breakfast, the jeep from Siliguri showed up to collect us, and we headed back to town. We stopped along the way at a leopard rescue center and a newly built facility where retired circus tigers were housed.

We spent one more night at the Hotel Conclave in Siliguri before catching a jeep to Darjeeling the next morning. We had considered taking the train, which ran on a narrow-gauge track and has been recognized as a world heritage site by UNESCO, the cultural arm of the United Nations. The railway, affectionately known as the "toy train," runs from the railway station at

New Jalpaiguri, or NJP, just south of Siliguri, to central Darjeeling, a distance of about 100 kilometers, or 60 miles.

The trip takes about eight hours: bicyclists have been known to pass the train on flat stretches.

Although we had read descriptions of the fantastic views from the train, and many people on the Internet urged visitors to ride the train if they had the time, we decided to take a jeep to Darjeeling and ride the toy train later.

On our last night in Siliguri, we met a family from Bangladesh who had a girl Salome's age. The family had traveled to India to find a school for their daughter, and were visiting campuses in Siliguri and Darjeeling. The family was concerned about civil unrest and violence in Dhaka, and had decided to move to Northern India.

Salome and the girl played for several hours and we exchanged cell phone numbers with her family, thinking we might get together in Darjeeling, since we were both headed that way.

All day long in Siliguri, jeeps packed with passengers and loaded with luggage tied to their roofs took off for the Himalayan foothills. Although it would have been cheap and easy to get seats in a public jeep bound for Darjeeling, we splurged and hired a private jeep for the three of us, figuring the mountainous journey would be more comfortable that way.

The next morning, we were on our way. As we drove out of Siliguri, we passed the toy train, which was chugging along next to the road.

Soon, the road began to twist and climb, and we were truly headed into the foothills of the world's tallest mountain range. The day was cool and overcast, and there were pockets of thick fog that blanketed the road in some spots, adding to the adrenaline from the hairpin turns and rutted road, which had sheer drops to one side.

As we headed into the mountains, the road passed through a number of small villages, and we enjoyed seeing the houses and shops and a slice of daily life.

While the road's uneven surface left much to be desired, the local government was concerned enough to have road crews patching and filling holes by hand, using shovels and wheelbarrows full of asphalt.

Safety-conscious government officials had also posted a series of yellow caution signs along the route from Siliguri to Darjeeling, which we found funny but creepy. "Enjoy the ride, don't commit suicide," "Go slow on earth so you don't speed into eternity," and "Give blood at the blood bank, not on the road," were just a few. My favorite was: "Don't gossip, let him drive."

There was plenty of traffic along the two-lane road, including packed buses and jeeps in both directions. We also saw schoolchildren in uniforms walking in groups along the side of the road.

It took us two-and-a-half hours to reach Darjeeling, and by the time we got there, we were thinking seriously about whether we should take the train back down the mountain when it was time to leave. But we had survived, and our next challenge was to find our hotel, the Classic Guesthouse, near the Chowrastra, Darjeeling's central plaza.

Our room was spacious, with one big bed for Ava and I, and a small one for Salome, a TV with satellite, a small electric heater, a private bathroom and both a picture window and small balcony with views of hilly Darjeeling. If we craned our necks, we could glimpse majestic Kanchenjunga, which stands just over 28,000 feet tall, some 900 feet shorter than its more famous Himalayan neighbor, Mt. Everest.

The three of us were immediately enchanted with Darjeeling: the weather was mostly sunny, and the air was crisp and much cleaner than in the other Indian towns we'd visited. The architecture had a decidedly Nepalese and Tibetan feel, as did the features of many of the people we saw on the crowded streets. As we walked around, we were treated to views of Darjeeling spread down the flanks of the foothills, and of course, Kanchenjunga loomed over everything. I never tired of the sight of its jagged, snow-covered peaks.

Throughout the town were many Buddhist monasteries, which were painted vibrant colors and decorated with fluttering prayer flags.

The food was also a treat, and there was no shortage of restaurants to sample, from dirt-cheap, family-run places, to upscale hotels that seemed to date back to the days of the Raj. On our first afternoon, we splurged for lunch at the New Elgin Hotel, a luxurious place whose lobby was filled with overstuffed chairs clustered around fireplaces.

We were the only guests in the formal dining room. The tablecloths and napkins were white linen, and two waiters hovered around our table, filling our plates with the day's special menu of Chinese dishes, and pouring tea from silver pots. We felt like big shots, and were pleasantly surprised with the bill came – the tab was only about $20 for the three of us.

After lunch, we joined a steady stream of people walking up to Observation Hill, a small peak behind the central plaza, where a Hindu temple and a Buddhist shrine are located. For a small donation, we were allowed to light incense and receive a blessing from one of the priests, who sat cross-legged inside the small building, chanting and singing. As we left the temple, a man standing near the entrance reached over and tapped each of us on the forehead, placing a dot of reddish powder between our eyes. This bindi, or tilak, can mean many things – one scholar called it a "symbol of worship of intellect."

The trees planted all around the hilltop were decorated with hundreds of Buddhist prayer flags of red, yellow, blue, green and white.

Although we didn't fully comprehend the meanings of either the Hindu or Buddhist rites and symbols we saw, we could tell that the worshippers who were streaming to the temple and a nearby Buddhist shrine were very devout, and we picked up on the spiritual vibe around us. Near the shrine, a group of people sat in a circle, pounding on drums and chanting. The air was very smoky from burning incense, and I was struck by the beauty of the sunlight streaming through the trees and fluttering prayer flags.

Along with prayer flags, the trees teemed with brown monkeys. Entire families of the primates hung out by the pathways, hoping for an edible offering.

We were well-situated in Darjeeling, with the entrance of our guest house just a few feet from the bustling central plaza, where I was pleased to find a liquor store, the first I had seen on our travels in India. I bought a small bottle of dark Indian rum called Old Monk, which we mixed with guava juice to create a sweet, syrupy cocktail.

By nightfall, the air turned very chilly, and we were back in our room early with the electric heater's fan whirring softly and providing a bit of warmth. Soon after settling in, we heard a knock on the door, and one of the hotel staff asked if we wanted hot water bottles. We weren't sure exactly what he had in mind, but we said yes. A few minutes later, he returned with three flat rubber hot water bottles, which he showed us were to be placed under the bed covers near our feet. From that night on, we looked forward to bedtime, when we could snuggle up to the bottles under the heap of thick wool blankets provided by the guesthouse.

The next morning, I established another tradition for our brief visit to Darjeeling: a morning run on the footpath around the base of Observation Hill. Each circuit took about 15 minutes, so I usually went around twice, slowing to ogle at the vistas of Kanchenjunga from viewpoints along the way. Sometimes I would stop at the viewpoints and do push-ups and sit-ups, joining the locals in their morning exercise. For once, I was not the only person out jogging in the morning. Lots of other folks, most of them locals, were also out on the path, briskly walking or jogging in their sweat suits.

After my run, I went to a small tea stand at the edge of the plaza, where I enjoyed a glass of steaming chai.

When I could tear her away from her comfy bed and still-warm water bottle, Ava would join me. Salome would stay in the room, sleeping or watching a movie on her DVD player.

After our workout, the desk clerk brought a breakfast

tray with coffee, boiled eggs, toast, fruit and juice to our room. On warmer mornings, we sat on the balcony with our breakfast, admiring the green hills spread out below and the snow-capped mountains in the distance.

Each day we took off on foot to explore different sights, and take care of errands – we walked to Darjeeling's small but attractive zoo, which featured Himalayan wolves and bears; we went to the post office for the ordeal of mailing a couple of packages home; and we prowled through the crooked, hilly streets of the Darjeeling market, looking for bargains. I left Ava and Salome in the shops and walked down a steep path to visit a monastery I had read about, perched on a hillside at the edge of town, with the ever-present Kanchenjunga dominating the horizon above. When I walked up to the front door, a monk in crimson robes called out, and a man who appeared to be an attendant came up and agreeably offered to show me around. He was skinny, with dark skin, and his ready smile showed ravaged teeth. He wore loose-fitting, smudged cloth pants and shirt, and skimpy sandals, which he took off when we entered the temple.

I admired the altar and colorful painted decorations on the walls, and a framed photo of the Dalai Llama propped up on a small shelf behind several candles. My tour guide pulled out an ancient book from a cabinet, and held it out for my inspection, not allowing me to touch it. The book was tall and narrow, although several inches thick, with wooden covers held together with leather bindings. The edges of most of the pages appeared to have been eaten away by moths, or decay.

He told me this was the Tibetan Book of the Dead, an

original hand-printed copy dating back hundreds of years. In fact, the Book of the Dead was reportedly written in the eighth century and, according to one description, "is a guide that is read aloud to the dead while they are in the state between death and reincarnation in order for them to recognize the nature of their mind and attain liberation from the cycle of rebirth."

My guide took me to the monastery's second floor and showed me one of the Spartan rooms where the monks slept, and I gave him a small tip for his time before walking back to town.

On our third day in Darjeeling, we visited Tiger Hill, a popular tourist attraction where nature puts on a spectacular show at dawn. Each morning, hundreds of people gather before daybreak at this famous lookout spot to watch the sun rise over the Himalayas.

We asked for a 3:30 a.m. wakeup call and at 4 a.m. sharp, the jeep we had booked at the tourist office pulled up at a pre-arranged meeting spot. Half asleep, we bounced in the back seat for the 45-minute ride to Tiger Hill. The final ascent to the hill took us up a very steep, winding dirt road barely wide enough at some points for one vehicle to pass. We kept waiting to meet an oncoming car, but fortunately, all of the traffic at that early-morning hour was headed up the hill.

Our driver recommended we pay a few dollars more for our tickets so we could sit in relative comfort in a large room furnished with stuffed arm chairs that were lined up in rows facing picture windows. Below, on the tarmac, we could see a crowd of people huddled near each other for warmth.

Since it was still dark, Salome, Ava and I tried to slouch

in our chairs and doze for a bit until daybreak. Only Salome was successful, so Ava and I helped ourselves to the offered cups of chai tea and waited.

Before us, we could just make out the dark mass of Kanchenjunga. Soon, the black night gave way to a pale gray, then blue, along the eastern horizon, which was to our right. The snow-capped mountains straight ahead of us turned a ghostly silver. Then, a pink glow spread out to the east, and the mountaintops caught the light, turning a soft, rosy red. Before long, the eastern horizon burst into a fiery, orange-red, and the mountains glowed as if lighted from within. We were lucky enough to visit Tiger Hill on a perfectly clear day; not a cloud could be seen on the horizon, and the world's tallest mountains spread out before us in a dazzling display. To our left, the tip of Mt. Everest poked above lower mountains. As dawn broke, the crowd on the tarmac burst into cheers and shouts, coming to life after suffering through the chilly morning.

Salome's Journal

12/10 & 12/12, 2005 Darjeeling, India

Hi Salome. We are going to a big market today so we get to shop oh ya but we can't by much! We love our hotel. We go on the balcony and see the Himalayas the 3rd tallest mountain in the world. Also we love the heater and every night they bring 3 hot water bottles for are feet now believe me that's paradise. We hope that unkey will come and meet us! Yesterday I got up at 3:30 a.m. to go watch the sunrise. It was amazing when the sun started to rise. The top of the Himalayas started to get red it was truly amazing!!!!!! Well we won't want to leave as I keep telling you but I think the rest of the trip will be as fun I hope!

Hi Salome. I am so lucky because I was going to call Rainnies but her mom told me it was hailey's birthday which I totally forgot. So I got to talk to Summer Rainnie and Hailey so that worked out just perfect. When Hailey answered and I said this is Salome she is like well actually this is what she screamed oh my god oh my god oh my god oh my god oh my god oh my god oh my god oh my god. But it was so good to talk to them and I can't wait to actually see them! Salome.

The days in Darjeeling rolled by pleasantly. We visited a tea plantation and got a peek inside the processing plant, which was dormant in the off-season. Salome, with the help of two guides, climbed a rock named after Tenzing Norgay, the famous Sherpa who was the first to summit Mt. Everest in 1953 with Edmund Hillary of New Zealand. We also visited a Tibetan refugee center, where the workers proudly showed off their handmade clothing and rugs.

Each night, we struggled with a burning question: where should we eat dinner? We quickly established a short list of favorites, all within walking distance of the Classic Guesthouse. One was the tiny restaurant run by a friendly Tibetan family. We ordered plates of "momos," steamed dumplings filled with pork, chicken and vegetables. The momos came with a tray of homemade sweet, spicy and pungent sauces for dipping. The bill at the momo restaurant was always less than $10 US for the three of us.

Another favorite haunt was Glenary's, a Darjeeling institution with a fancy dinnerhouse on the top floor, a bakery-café with Internet access at street level, and a casual restaurant and bar on the bottom floor. We spent a few evenings in the bottom-floor restaurant, where comfort foods such as spaghetti Bolognese and macaroni and cheese were served. One night we listened to rock tunes cranked out by a local garage band, and drank a few Kingfisher beers with our meal. In India, when you order a beer, you are usually asked if you want it strong or regular. I found out the hard way that the strong version carries a nearly lethal punch – after a couple of bottles of strong beer, I would find the next day that I could remember very little of the night before.

I got my first Indian haircut in a shop barely big enough to fit two barber's chairs side by side. The haircut was great, and I even had a shave with a straight razor. Afterward, the barber patted on powder and cologne, and the entire treatment set me back 50 rupees, or just over a buck.

Before leaving Darjeeling, I was determined to ride on the toy train, but it was starting to look like a long shot. We wanted to take the "joy ride," a short loop from Darjeeling to the nearby town of Ghoom, on the train powered by a coal-fired engine.

The ticket clerk at the train station told us the joy ride would only depart if there were at least 25 passengers on board. One day, there were 14 people, including us, who wanted to ride. We offered to buy another 11 tickets to reach the magic number. But the ticket clerk, after conferring with some other people in his office, refused.

Finally, we showed up on a Saturday morning, which we figured would be our last, best chance to ride the train. That day, a family of four from Calcutta, who were on holiday in Darjeeling, also wanted to ride, but together, we had only seven passengers. For whatever reason, the clerk told us we could ride the train. We happily bought our tickets, and watched as several men fussed with the engine, loading in coal and making adjustments as it simultaneously belched black coal smoke and white steam from twin smokestacks.

The Calcutta family had two little girls, and Salome sat with them as the train slowly rolled out of the station. It really did feel like a toy train, as the track ran beside the road, and we were traveling much slower than the cars. We chugged along on the sunny, cool morning, listening to the train's shrill whistle, and watching the vistas of mountains and colorful Buddhist monasteries. We created quite a stir; entire families watched, waving and smiling as we passed by.

The train's first stop was in a park that offered wonderful views of Kanchenjunga. Vendors set out trinkets on blankets beside the track, and a few enterprising guys offered to let us look through telescopes they had set up on tripods for a few rupees apiece.

At Ghoom, we had a short layover, and spent most of it looking through a small, unimpressive museum about the history of the Darjeeling railway. The Calcutta family opted to take a taxi back to Darjeeling, saying they wanted to make the most of their limited holiday time.

We rode back on the train, having the car to ourselves except for the conductor, and thoroughly enjoying our slow progress back up the hill.

Our plan was to spend eight days in Darjeeling and then take a jeep down to Bagdogra Airport, where we would catch a flight to Delhi, stay for one night, then fly on to Goa, the former Portuguese colony on India's west coast.

But on the day before we were planning to leave Darjeeling, rumors began circulating around town about a general strike set for the next day to protest wages and working conditions. As part of the strike, disruptive roadblocks would be manned by disgruntled workers, which could make it impossible for us to reach the airport for our mid-morning flight.

We were on the fence about whether we should leave the day before, or chance it and drive down on the morning of our flight. Ava went to a dress shop to pick up an Indian suit she had ordered, and the woman who worked in the shop advised us not to wait.

"You should leave today," she said. "If you wait, you won't get past the roadblocks."

That cinched it for us; I didn't want to miss our flight to Delhi, so I visited Mickey, the wheeler-dealer at the tourist office, to arrange a jeep while Ava and Salome headed to the hotel to pack.

Back at the Classic Guesthouse, I settled our bill, and the owner, a nice gentleman in his 50s, brought by some gifts for us, including several packages of Darjeeling tea and a stuffed animal and candy for Salome.

We pulled into Bagdogra, and Mickey and the driver dropped us off at our hotel, which was sparsely occupied, but had a nice big lawn with outdoor tables for dining. Our room had a sitting area with a TV set, a bedroom and a private bath, all a bit grubby and well-worn, but the price was right: we paid 500 rupees, or about $10 U.S. for the night, the cheapest room we rented in India.

We caught our flight to Delhi, spent the night at the well-run Blue Triangle Family YWCA, and the next morning flew to Goa, where we planned to spend the holidays and relax for three weeks.

As soon as we stepped off the plane from Delhi, we had a sense that things would be much more laid-back in this former Portuguese colony on the Arabian Sea south of Mumbai than we had experienced elsewhere on the subcontinent.

The sky was bright blue and the sun shone brilliantly as we rode in a taxi from Dabolim Airport to the small town of Colva, which would be our base for the next three weeks. Palm trees lined the road, and the air was soft and warm. Goa reminded me of other tropical destinations I have visited, such as Puerto Vallarta in Mexico, and the Bahamas. The scene at the airport reinforced this image, as tourists with big bellies and white legs poking out of Bermuda shorts shouted at their children amid piles of designer suitcases.

As I sat in the back seat of the taxi with Ava and Salome, I smiled with anticipation at the thought of three weeks of doing very little other than snoozing on a chaise longue by a cool blue pool, or lying on a sandy beach while gazing at the Arabian Sea.

This would be our longest stay in one place during the entire trip, and I for one was ready to settle down, at least temporarily. We arrived in Goa in mid-December, after being on the road nearly six months. During that time, we had touched down in four different continents and visited cities in 15 countries, including the East Coast of the U.S. Most of the time we packed our bags and moved on after two or three days; just four times, we had lived at the same place for a full week. After all that traveling, packing and unpacking, I think the three of us were ready for some serious downtime.

We chose Goa for our mid-trip recharge for several reasons – first, we had heard and read that it is one of the most scenic and tranquil places in all of India. Second, we would be there during the holidays, and Goa is one of the few places in the country where Christmas is observed on a large scale, due to the influence of its Portuguese-Christian heritage. Finally, its location, eight hours south of Mumbai by train, seemed perfect, since we needed to be in Mumbai by mid-January to catch our flight to Bangkok for the next leg of our trip.

Goa's relatively cheap prices were also a draw.

As we traveled around the world, the climate and the number of foreign tourists we encountered varied widely from place to place. We shivered in South America during the months of July and August, and arrived in the beach resort of Punta Del Este in Uruguay to find a virtual ghost town. It had been so "off season" in Punta that even the town's traffic lights were turned off, lending an air of loneliness to the nearly deserted streets.

In Brazil, though, the temperature rose to the 90s, and the streets hopped. By the time we made it to Europe in September, days were growing cooler and became downright frigid in Poland and the Czech Republic.

Goa in December, especially around Christmas, means holiday time, for both Indian and foreign tourists. I had worked our cell phone hard over the weeks preceding our Goan sojourn, trying to book a hotel, and we ended up cobbling together reservations at two different hotels to cover our three-week stay.

We began our stay in Goa at William's Beach Resort, and when the taxi pulled up outside, we knew we had made a good choice. We entered through a white stucco archway at the street to a courtyard with a dining room cooled by rotating ceiling fans on one side, and a small, friendly bar on the other.

Straight ahead was the front desk; the clerk, Anil, remembered my name from when I called to make reservations.

"Welcome, Mr. Tash," he said.

Anil spotted Salome, who was shyly standing behind me and peering around me at the desk man. I told him Salome was feeling a little homesick, and he beamed at her.

"You're going to love it here, you won't want to leave," he said.

After taking our passport information, Anil led us through a passageway to the pool and gardens, which were shielded from neighboring properties by hedges and towering palm trees. Along one side of the pool was the swimup bar touted in our guide book, and behind it was a two-story building that housed rooms with individual balconies.

While the room was very plain, it was clean, right next to the pool, and it cost just 1,000 rupees per night ($22 US), including breakfast.

Later, we decorated the room with a tapestry and a tiny artificial Christmas tree – complete with blinking colored lights – that we bought in the local shops. We also requisitioned a few other items of furniture, including a second bedside table that was missing one leg and had to be propped against the bed, and a mattress for Salome, which we slid under the bed during the daytime.

The hotel was in the perfect location, as far as I was concerned. It was a five-minute walk to the beach, which we found was lined with beach "shacks," restaurants where guests could while away entire days over rum and cokes, Kingfisher beers and platters of fresh seafood. The shacks had lounge chairs set up for their customers, so there was no need to bring much of anything besides a towel and our appetites for a long day at the beach.

Between William's and the beach was a strip of touristy shops and restaurants, and a handy Internet café with a phone booth where we could make international calls.

We quickly settled into the Goan lifestyle – I got up early each morning for a run along the beach. The Arabian Sea would be grayish-blue at that hour, and flat as a pool table for as far as the eye could see. Up and down the beach, crews of a dozen or so men and boys, and a few women, pulled long nets out of the water. Their catch, hundreds of shiny silver fish just a few inches long, thrashed in the nets. As I ran, I had to detour around the nets.

Each morning after working out, we trooped up to the dining room for breakfast, which consisted of coffee and toast with marmalade, plates of fresh papaya and pineapple, scrambled eggs, little Goan sausages and bowls of porridge. After eating our fill and coaxing Salome to take her malaria pills with her juice, we changed into our bathing suits to spend the rest of the morning around the pool. Before she could swim or play with the other kids, we made Salome do schoolwork for at least an hour.

Not a bad life for a kid, sitting by the pool in her bathing suit and doing a few pages of math, spelling, science or social studies, instead of spending six hours in a classroom for five days a week. But Salome failed to fully appreciate her good fortune, often balking when it was time to do her lessons.

After schoolwork was done, if we were feeling lazy, we would order lunch from John, the efficient waiter, and dine at one of the umbrella-shaded tables near the pool.

After a few days, we started getting to know our fellow guests at William's. Salome played in the pool every day with Simone, a girl of Indian descent who was on holiday with her family from London. We also met a couple from the U.S. who were in India to adopt a child, and were staying in Goa while they waited for the government to process their paperwork. Brenda, a 60-ish widow from England, was spending the entire winter in Goa, enjoying both the warm weather and the buying power of her pension. She called Salome a "cheeky monkey," and sat out by the pool most days.

Also staying at William's were a lesbian couple from the U.K. who decided during their holiday they wanted to move to Goa to get away from their jobs and the frigid winters back home, and a man in his late 40s or early 50s who spent each day tanning by the pool in the company of his two teenage daughters, who wore the skimpiest bikinis.

In the evenings, we would walk around town and decide where to eat dinner. Sometimes we would wander down to the beach, where the shacks were decorated with twinkling Christmas lights. The setting was magical; each shack had a covered dining platform, and guests reclined in cushioned chairs, with fabulous views of the beach and the sea beyond. One place actually set up a table for us right on the sand, and lighted it with a candle in a glass holder.

At dusk, the beach was packed with Indian tourists who came out to stroll or eat dinner. (Large crowds also gathered in daytime around power boats pulled up on the beach to offer rides to the tourists, and to gawk at paragliders that floated high in the sky, towed by a rope attached to a boat below.)

Salome begged to bring her DVD player with her to dinner so she wouldn't have to suffer through the boredom of our "adult" conversation. But I held out, insisting that at least for the evening meal, we could have some family time without the company of Miss Congeniality, or the other movies Salome watched over and over during our trip.

One night, we had dinner at our hotel, and at the next table, a European couple sat with their little boy, a blonde kid who looked a couple of years younger than Salome. Salome noticed right away that the boy was watching a portable DVD player while his parents ate. She poked me in the ribs and said, "See? Why can't I bring my DVD player?"

Still, I resisted on the grounds that family dinner time should be a "DVD-free" zone.

The next night, we went to a beach shack where we had eaten a couple of times before, and the same European couple happened to be dining there as well. This time we struck up a conversation, commenting that Salome was envious of their son watching movies at dinner.

We ended up spending the evening with the couple, Marcus and Caron, and their little boy, Harry. Salome, who had been starved for the companionship of children during most of our trip, was getting it in spades in Goa, between playing with the kids in the pool at William's, and her new friendship with Harry.

Marcus was in his 30s, heavyset but muscular, and the tank tops he wore revealed multiple tattoos on his arms and shoulders. He formed an unlikely pair with Caron, a brunette who liked to show off her shapely figure, and was at least 10 years older than Marcus. The couple was making their second visit to Goa, which they loved because prices were so reasonable compared with European beach resorts. Their younger daughter, who was Salome's age, stayed at home in England with Caron's older daughter from a previous marriage. According to Marcus and Caron, the girl had refused to come to Goa because she didn't like the poverty she had witnessed on their earlier trip.

Marcus ran a successful construction and interior decorating business, and Caron was a stay-at-home mom. Ava, Salome and I hit it off with the three of them, and we spent a lot of time with them during our stay in Goa. They would come over to our hotel in the morning and hang out with us by the pool while Salome did her schoolwork, then we would all head down to the beach, where the adults would talk, drink and eat at a beach shack while Harry and Salome played in the sand.

We intended to take things easy for our three weeks in Goa, and not worry too much about sightseeing or playing tourist. But there were a few sights we planned to see, including the famous market at Anjuna Beach, which became well-known to young people in Europe and

America in the 1960s and 1970s when it was a hippie haven, and later, Ground Zero for all-night Goan rave parties.

We hired a taxi for the one-hour ride to Anjuna. During our outing, we also planned to visit Beryl, a Bombay resident whom we had met in Oceanside when she was visiting a mutual friend. We called Beryl just after we arrived in India, and arranged to meet her in Goa over the holidays. She was staying with her daughter and son-in-law at their beautiful home on the outskirts of Anjuna, called Casa Esmerelda.

We wandered through the flea market, which is housed in a labyrinth of stalls set up on the sandy promontory above the beach, disappointed at how touristy it was. We had hoped for a more local feel, as in the days when the market was dominated by hippies selling used merchandise to finance their escape from 9-to-5 servitude in the States or Europe or wherever. But we managed to buy a few things: I picked up CDs of Goan electronic "trance" music, incense and embroidered T-shirts, and Ava and Salome conspired to buy Salome's first bikini. A highlight of our visit was a cow decorated in bangles that danced by bobbing its head when its owner played a flute.

The taxi driver then took us to Beryl's daughter's home, which was light and airy, with wood floors and graceful handmade furniture. They fed us a hearty meal of pasta, chicken curry and salad, and we enjoyed the conversation. One of the guests was Mike, a cousin who had just driven his four-wheel-drive jeep from London to Goa, traveling along the way through Turkey, Iran and Pakistan. His adventures made our trip seem tame. When he asked about our biggest disaster so far, we told the story of our scare on the flight to Mumbai, when the oxygen mask warning had been triggered. Mike – who appeared to be in his late 20s or early 30s and was "semi-retired" from real estate sales – said that for his next trip, he wanted to ship his jeep to South Africa, and then drive it to London.

Christmas was fast approaching, and the three of us finished up our shopping for each other, and wrapped our presents. We planned to have a quiet Christmas morning in our hotel room, opening gifts, then join in the big holiday party at the hotel in the evening.

Each night as we dined in the beach shacks, groups of young Indian boys would come by, dressed in red Santa suits and scraggly white beards, singing Christmas carols in exchange for rupees from foreign and Indian tourists. It was both touching and comical as the boys, their brown, skinny legs protruding from beneath their padded Santa jackets, sang "Jingle Bells," and "Silent Night" with pronounced Hindi accents.

Salome, who was very homesick at this point, tearfully told us that she wanted to go home for Christmas, and spend it in her own house, and see her friends. We told her this would be impossible, and that our Christmas in Goa, although much different than the holidays she was used to, would be one to remember for the rest of our lives. What we missed in being away from our home would be made up for by the special way we would celebrate in India, with the three of us together and the new friends we were meeting.

On Christmas morning, we woke up and opened our presents, which were piled under the tiny tree on the bedside table in our room. I gave Ava and Salome the necklaces, rings and earrings I had bought for them in Darjeeling, and I got a silver pinkie ring, a very cool antique sextant (to allow me to navigate a ship by sun and stars) and some Indian music CDs. Salome, of course, made out, with her bikini, clothes, jewelry and toys. To me, the celebration highlighted how our trip had brought us closer together as a family, since we could enjoy the holiday in our simple hotel room, far away from home, as long as we had each other's love and companionship.

By evening, William's Beach Resort was bustling. Along with a full house of holiday guests, the hotel was hosting a wedding party for the son of one of the hotel's owners. The hotel staff had set up a full buffet dinner next to the pool, with everything from roast beef and salad to rice and curry. Card tables and chairs were set up for the guests, and a trio churned out Western pop music and holiday numbers. After the feast, Seby, the manager, handed out sparklers to the kids, and began setting off rockets and Roman candles on the far side of the pool. We sat with Simone and her family. They told us school authorities are so strict in Britain that a family can be fined for taking a child out of school for a vacation.

Salome's Journal

12/26/05 Goa, India

Hi Salome. We are still in Goa and last night we had the big Christmas party. A big buffet and fireworks and dancing. We got to hold fire crackers and play with them. The music was great and there was dancing. It was a very nice party. The other day I got a lot of nice clothes and like I said my first Baquiney. Not like the usual Christmas but it was a Christmas to remember. I really miss my friends and bagels.

*I know that I will get both of those things soon but I don't
think I can wait much longer but I always know they will be
there when I get back. I think when we get back we won't be
traviling for a long time afterward. See ya soon. Bye.*

After Christmas we rented bikes from a little market
across the street from our hotel, and set out for Benaulim,
the next beach south of Colva. There wasn't any sort of
bike lane along the roads, but in most cases, there wasn't
much traffic, so we felt safe. The road was overgrown with
tropical plants and trees on both sides, and we enjoyed
looking at the houses, both large and small, along the way.

The ride through Goa's back roads was scenic and
relaxing, and when we turned toward the beach at
Benaulim, we rode past rice paddies and open fields.
Salome and I got separated from Ava, and the three of us
spent a couple of hours cycling around trying to find each
other. We finally met up, and after squabbling about who
caused the mishap, cycled back to Colva.

In an effort to embrace India's culture, we began taking
Yoga lessons at our hotel. The sessions were held on a
small patch of lawn near the pool, and included the three
of us, along with a couple of ladies who were also staying
at the hotel.

The instructor was a young man who was expert at
the various Yoga positions, but seemed to be new to the
concept of teaching Yoga to others, especially beginners.

Each of us was given a small mat, which we unrolled on
the grass, and then sat on cross-legged, as the instructor
showed us.

At first, the positions were very simple: lay back, with
one leg extended, and the other folded back, then switch

sides. Or, kneel, and slowly lean forward on your hands until the top of your head touched the ground. Quickly, though, the positions became both more complicated and more difficult for the least limber of us – anyone over 10 years old – to perform.

There were backwards and sideways bends, touching the soles of our feet to other body parts that were never intended to meet, and perches on one leg or the other while performing contortions with arms and torsos.

To Salome's delight, she was able to do virtually everything the instructor asked, while Ava and I found many of the positions painful, if not impossible, to perform.

We also hired a taxi for an excursion to the Dudhsagar waterfall and a spice plantation near the town of Ponda, one of the few sightseeing trips we made in Goa.

The taxi took us to a village on the outskirts of a nature reserve where the waterfall – reputed to be one of the highest in India – is located. From there, we were loaded into jeeps with other tourists for a 45-minute ride through the forest, over a rutted dirt track that crossed several streams. The jeep took us to a clearing, where the driver parked, and we got out for a short walk down a steep path to the waterfall. Along the way, we were swarmed by monkeys looking for a handout. We had brought along oranges, bananas and cashews for snacks, which the monkeys snatched from our outstretched palms.

The waterfall was more than 300 meters high and far more impressive than we had expected. At the bottom was a large, deep pool, and Ava, Salome and I quickly shed our shorts and T-shirts for a swim (planning ahead, we had worn swimsuits under our clothes). The water was ice cold and bracing, but felt exhilarating after the long, dusty ride in the taxi and jeep. Salome dipped her toes in the chilly water and decided to stay on the bank.

Our next stop was the spice plantation; we walked through the grounds with a guide, who pointed out the plants and trees that produce cinnamon, nutmeg, various kinds of peppers, and even bananas and mangos. We were then shown to a restaurant featuring rough-hewn wooden benches and tables under a thatched roof, where we loaded banana leaf plates with rice, fish and chicken.

After lunch, we had the option of walking along on paths through the spice farm, or taking a "bath" with an elephant. While Ava and I felt refreshed from our dip at the falls, Salome was ready to get wet.

We paid a modest fee of 500 rupees, and the elephant handler led a full-grown female to a nearby river. At the handler's order, the pachyderm sank to its knees, then rolled over on its side. Salome, in her bathing suit, waded into the knee-high water, and was given a large brush with a wooden handle to scrub the animal's side, which it seemed to enjoy.

Then, the elephant got back to its knees, and the handler helped Salome scramble up on its enormous back. The elephant dipped its trunk in the river, then arched its trunk back over its head and doused Salome with a spray of water. This was repeated a few times, until Salome was thoroughly soaked.

A huge grin on her face, Salome climbed down and waded to the edge of the river.

Salome's Journal

12/28/05 Goa, India

Yesterday I went to a spice plantation. I got to bath an elephant then I got on his back and he squirted me with water from his trunk which was kind of nasty because before I got in he pooped and peed. After (that) another little boy did it and said "I got elephant poo water in my mouth." Anyway later I went to the waterfalls and I fed the monkeys. The reason Harry did not come was because his dad was sick but today he is here and after this I get to go in the pool! Bye Salome.

New Year's Eve provided another opportunity to party – as if we needed one. We met the Hudsons (Marcus, Caron and Harry) at one of the beach shacks, where we had reserved a seafood platter including lobster, prawns and grilled fish. The entire beach was ablaze with colored lights and fireworks, thanks to a ready supply of pyrotechnics on sale at every shop in town.

We ate, drank and danced, and got more than a little tipsy as the evening progressed. My buzz was enhanced by a couple of Valium provided by Marcus, who had picked up a supply at a local pharmacy. A prescription was rarely necessary to buy drugs in India, and Valium was no exception.

By the time midnight rolled around, both Ava and I were well-lit. Although we had been enjoying ourselves, somehow things turned ugly and we ended up in a big fight. I tried to cool off with a swim in the Arabian Sea, clothes and all, which didn't seem to have much effect.

I don't remember what the fight was about, but soon after it started, the Hudsons beat a hasty retreat, leaving us to our argument. Poor Salome had no such option, and had to endure the worst of it, during which, she later told us, Ava and I drunkenly threatened to get divorced.

We stumbled back to our hotel, where we probably made the smartest move of the night, which was to pass out. By morning, both the festivities and the fight were hazy memories, faded in contrast with the sharp discomfort of our hangovers. During a morning walk on the beach, we realized we were better off than some: Ava came to the rescue of a huge, drunken Russian man who was attempting to stand up in the shallow surf. He kept falling over, planting his face in the water. It took several of us to haul him up on the sand. After a while, another Russian came along and helped him stumble away down the beach.

Goa's Russian connection was mysterious – for some reason, maybe its cheap prices, the place had become a haven for vacationing Russian businessmen. We saw numerous tourist brochures written in Russian around Colva, including in the lobby of our hotel. With the businessmen came "business" women, who hung out in the hotels, apparently offering their services to their countrymen. One morning, we noticed a striking blonde woman in a bikini, posing by the pool as another woman snapped photos of her. We asked around, and found out the pictures from the impromptu photo session would later be posted to a Web site, advertising the availability of the Russian call girl.

Our time in Goa was beginning to run short. We bought tickets for an overnight sleeper train to Mumbai (Bombay to the old-school types), our next destination. I really wasn't looking forward to returning there, because I hadn't much enjoyed our first stay when we were fresh off the plane from London.

This time around, though, we were a little more experienced in the ways of India, having traveled around the country for two months. We booked a room at the YWCA near Colaba, the most tourist-friendly section of the city, with the help of Seby, the manager of William's Beach Resort, who vouched for us in lieu of a deposit

On our next to last day in Colva, we rented bikes and rode up to the Hudsons' upscale beach hotel. We literally rode off into the sunset on our bikes after saying farewell to our new friends, and inviting them to visit us back in San Diego. Salome teared up when she hugged Harry good-bye.

Our train left for Mumbai in the late afternoon, so we packed during the morning and then hung out by the pool until it was time to leave. Salome stayed in the water until the last possible minute, then changed into her clothes, while Ava tried to wring out her bathing suit as much as possible. We said our good-byes to fellow guests, such as Brenda, the older Englishwoman, and the hotel staff, including John, our favorite waiter and guardian of the swim-up bar. He wrote down our address so that his son could contact us if he visited the U.S.

The train arrived in Mumbai before dawn, and we caught a taxi to the YWCA, hoping our room would be ready. It wasn't, so they put us up in the TV lounge near the lobby, where we rested for a couple hours before venturing out to scare up breakfast.

When we finally did go outside the YWCA, we found a

city that was just waking up on a sunny January morning. Newsstand workers were opening bundles of papers and shopkeepers were sweeping the sidewalks in front of their stores. We stumbled onto a busy café near our hotel, where the menu included French toast with maple syrup, eggs and sausage. We enjoyed a breakfast of Western-style comfort food, still dazed from our overnight train trip.

After breakfast, we went to the tourist office and train station to make arrangements for a side trip to Aurangabad, which we would use as a base for exploring the Buddhist and Hindu caves of Ajanta and Ellora, which date back to 100 B.C. We had just over a week left in India, and planned to split our time between Mumbai and the Aurangabad excursion.

Since January is one of the most popular times to travel in India, due to the relatively mild weather, trains were running pretty full. Luckily, we were able to take advantage of the quota of tickets set aside for foreign tourists. At the tourist office, we booked one-day tours for Ajanta and Ellora, and three nights at the Maharashtra Tourism Development Council's Holiday Resort. Reservations and tickets in hand, we headed back to the Y, where we hoped to get into our room for a nap and a shower.

Workmen were busy painting and tiling the hallways and rooms on our floor, and we were given a room that had just been renovated. The bathroom was sparkling new from top to bottom, including all fixtures, and everything in the room was in top shape, including the three single beds. For $50 a night, we were entitled to both breakfast and dinner in the hotel's dining room, served buffet style by friendly staff.

Everything we wanted was within walking distance, including the Oval Maidan, a large grassy park where cricket and soccer players practiced every day. A running path ran around the edge of the maidan, where I jogged each morning. Along one side of the maidan was a row of art-deco style buildings, while on the other side, the architecture was Gothic, including the 260-foot-tall Rajabai clock tower.

The hotel was also down the street from Mumbai's Prince of Wales Museum, which contains treasures such as ivory and jade sculpture, ancient Hindu carvings, and Tibetan and Nepalese art.

A movie theater on the corner was showing a remake of King Kong in English, which seemed to go on forever and was especially painful because the sound system was turned up so loud. Salome was delighted that a McDonald's was upstairs from a row of shops. Down the street was Leopold's Café, an atmospheric tourist hangout also popular with locals, where you could linger over a beer or coffee and almost always end up in a conversation with a fellow traveler or a curious Mumbai resident. (Three years later, terrorists shot up at least 10 locations in Mumbai, including Leopold's, the Taj Hotel and the central train station, killing 173 people. We read about the attacks with horror, made even more real for us because we had visited many of the locations where the terrorists had struck.)

When we weren't searching for our next culinary conquest – which usually occupied a lot of our time – we shopped for books at a row of stalls set up on the street facing the Prince of Wales Museum. We found all sorts of bargains by sifting through the piles of new and used books, from pocket-sized Archie Comics digests for Salome, to a bootleg paperback copy of Salman Rushdie's novel, Shalimar the Clown, which had just come out in hardback in the U.K. and U.S.

My search for a good cigar led us to the Mocha Café, on a trendy street near the Churchgate train station. There weren't any cigars – contrary to the advice offered by a bellman at the posh Taj Mahal Hotel – but they did have water-filled hookah pipes, which patrons could use to puff on a variety of fruit-flavored tobacco mixtures. Ava and I ordered coffee and a pipe full of orange tobacco. A waiter brought the pipe and set it next to our table, then laid a large ember on top of the bowl. We sucked on the mouthpiece, which was attached to the pipe with a long piece of plastic tubing. The sensation of breathing in the warm, humid, orange-scented smoke was pleasant, and the waiter told us the tobacco had a very low nicotine content, so even though I'm a reformed cigarette smoker, I wasn't too worried about getting hooked. As we smoked, the waiter would occasionally come by and put another ember on the bowl from a covered metal tray he carried.

After a while, though, the smoke made us feel queasy.

The next day, we went back to the Mocha Café, but skipped the hookah. Instead, we sat in an upstairs loft, where customers reclined on sofas or big stuffed pillows around low tables. While we drank our coffee, a group of Indian teens sitting near us played a boisterous game of "Truth or Dare."

In the late afternoon, we took a taxi along Marine Drive to Mumbai's famous Chowpatty Beach, a favorite gathering spot for local families. Although the water is reportedly too polluted for swimming or wading, the sand was packed with mothers and fathers, children running around, and couples holding hands.

At the insistence of a "massage wallah," Ava and I decided to get scalp massages. We sat cross-legged on the sand while the man dug his fingers into our scalps with enough force to bring tears to our eyes. Once the most intense pain had subsided, we were left with a tingling sensation that was almost enjoyable.

Scalps still smarting, we headed up the beach to a row of brightly lit stands selling bhelpuri, a snack made of puffed rice, crispy noodles and ingredients such as chopped tomatoes, potatoes, onion, coriander and chutney. We ordered a couple of large stryrofoam plates of bhelpuri, and three bottles of soda to wash it down. We dug in, savoring the exotic flavors as we watched the parade of people from rickety folding chairs set in the sand around a flimsy table.

When we finished eating, the sun had slipped below the horizon, and dozens of schoolchildren were lining up for rides on a Ferris wheel in the warm night air. Ava and Salome decided to join them but I opted to stay on the ground after taking a closer look at the ride, which had seen better days.

The Ferris wheel had no motor; instead, it was powered by teenage boys who climbed up the side of its frame to the top of the wheel, then grabbed on to one of the seats, propelling the wheel as they swung to the ground. These daredevils got the Ferris wheel moving at a surprising velocity, which made the uniformed schoolgirls squeal. I snapped photos of Ava and Salome, crossing my fingers in hopes that the entire structure wouldn't topple over.

We headed back to the YWCA early that night, grabbed a quick meal in the hotel dining room, and packed up for our journey to Aurangabad the next day.

Since our train trip was during the day, we booked seats in an air-conditioned chair car instead of sleeper berths. The trip to Aurangabad – about 430 kilometers northeast of Mumbai – was supposed to take seven or eight hours, so we expected to arrive at our destination in the early afternoon. As soon as we entered the car, we noticed something unusual – nearly every seat was full, and most of the passengers were elderly Asian men and women who wore surgical masks and white cotton gloves. This made us a little nervous, until we learned the reason behind the other passengers' strange attire: they were a tour group of South Korean Buddhists who were visiting various holy Buddhist sites throughout India, including the intricately carved and painted caves of Ajanta and Ellora.

Their guide, an outgoing and cheerful young Tibetan man, spoke pretty good English, and sat next to me for part of the ride.

He explained that many Korean Buddhists yearn to make a pilgrimage to India, the birthplace of their religion some 500 years before the birth of Christ. The tourists/pilgrims were extremely sensitive about germs and infections so they wore the surgical masks and gloves wherever they went. I wondered if this offended their Indian hosts. Also, while we ordered spicy Indian lunches from the train's kitchen, the Koreans brought their own special boxed lunches and bottled water to tide them over on the train.

When I helped the guide hoist some of the Koreans'
bags to the rack above their seats, to show their gratitude,
one of the ladies gave Salome a crisp $1 bill, the first
American money she'd seen in more than six months.
They also offered to share their lunches with us, which
included hard-boiled eggs and green squares that looked
like seaweed crackers.

We passed the time by chatting, reading and watching
Salome's portable DVD player.

When the train pulled into the Aurangabad station, I
said good-bye to the Tibetan tour guide, who was busy
shepherding his charges off the train while simultaneously
trying to retrieve their luggage.

The government tourist lodge was just down the street
from the train station, so we grabbed a tuk-tuk for the
short ride.

While the "resort" was on a nice, tree-shaded lot with
a playground in front, the buildings themselves were
ramshackle, in need of a coat of paint inside and out. The
lobby included the hotel desk and a tour desk, and smelled
faintly of urine. The hotel deskman was so subdued it
seemed like he might drop off into a deep sleep at any
moment. The room itself wasn't a whole lot better: the bed
was lumpy, the sheets threadbare and the bathroom in
need of a thorough scrubbing. A torn window screen let
blood-thirsty mosquitoes into our room when we opened
the window for air. We used one of our bath towels to plug
the hole in the screen and fend off the little buggers.

We opted to stay in spite of being less than thrilled with
the place; it was cheap, at only $15 or so per night, and
very conveniently located. The two full-day tours of Ajanta

and Ellora that we had booked in Mumbai departed each morning from right in front of our hotel lobby.

We had a free afternoon, since our first tour departed the next morning, so we spent a couple of hours hanging out in the shady yard of our hotel, where Salome played on the swings with a group of kids who stopped by on their way home from school. Then, we hired a tuk-tuk to drive us around the Muslim section of Aurangabad, a densely populated area with throngs of traffic and pedestrians packed into narrow streets. We walked around, and Ava shopped for clothes in some of the local stores, then had dinner near our hotel and called it an early night.

As promised, the tour bus was waiting for us the next morning, and we piled in for the two-hour-plus ride to the Ajanta caves. Among our group were two Americans, a college professor from Connecticut and her friend, who lived in L.A. Rarely had we encountered Americans during our travels in India, so we enjoyed talking with them.

As we stopped to pick up a couple of people at an outlying hotel, those of us on the bus watched a teenager dump a barrel of trash off a bridge into a ravine below. "That is the real India," a European tourist remarked.

The Ajanta site consists of 30 caves carved into a horseshoe-shaped rock cliff above the Wagurna River, about 100 kilometers from Aurangabad. The earliest of the caves dates back to roughly 100 B.C., while the rest were carved over the next 500 to 600 years. The caves were used by Buddhist monks as monasteries and prayer halls, and many surfaces both inside and outside the caves were carved and painted with murals, remnants of which can still be seen. One of the most dramatic of the caves contained a towering stupa, a monument carved out of the solid rock of the cliff.

The carvings and paintings inside and outside the caves provide tantalizing glimpses of daily life 1,500 to 2,000 years ago in this part of the world, including clothing, hairstyles, musical instruments, architecture and customs. In fact, experts say the artistic style of Ajanta served as the basis for Buddhist art in many other countries where the religion is practiced.

Reportedly, the site was rediscovered in the early 1800s by a group of British officers on maneuvers.

To reach the caves, visitors must walk up a steep, rocky pathway from the parking lot, which can be too strenuous for elderly tourists, especially on a hot, sunny day like the one on which we visited Ajanta. A group of men trying to make a living the hard way hovered near the beginning of the path, offering for a fee to carry visitors up to the cave in a wooden chair lashed to a pair of long poles. Salome pleaded to be allowed to ride up to the caves in royal comfort, but we walked with the members of our tour group (after paying a few rupees for the men to hoist Ava up in the chair while I snapped a photo).

We rounded a bend at a lookout point where we could see the entire cave complex spread before us. The tour lasted a couple of hours, and was exhausting due to the heat and the many sets of stones stairs we had to climb up and down. I tried to imagine what it would have been like to live and worship at Ajanta in the time of the monks, when days would have been long and filled with hard labor and devoted prayer and meditation. The carvings were so intricate and beautiful, it was amazing to think such work had been done with primitive tools in the isolation of the river valley.

Scholars have speculated that the monks used reflectors of some type to illuminate the interior of the caves for the benefit of the painters and sculptors. Although tons of rock must have been removed to carve out the caves, no evidence of the waste rock exists on the site, and it is believed the scrap material may have been floated away on barges or rafts on the nearby river.

The next morning, we boarded the same bus for the shorter ride to the Ellora caves, which, although younger than their counterparts at Ajanta, are considered by some to be the more impressive of the two. Both sets of caves have been designated as World Heritage sites by the United Nations Educational, Scientific and Cultural Organization, or UNESCO.

The 34 caves of the Ellora complex were carved between 600 and 1000 A.D., out of a rock face that sloped gently, in contrast to the sheer cliff where Ajanta was carved. Another difference is that, while Ajanta's caves all contain Buddhist imagery, Ellora's represent three religious sects: Hindu, Buddhist and Jain.

I found the Ellora caves more pleasant to visit because the grounds contained tree-shaded spots where visitors could rest. The views from the Ellora caves were gorgeous, with rolling green hills spreading out into the distance.

Once again, just wandering among the caves was like taking a tour back in time, and we tried to put ourselves in the mind-set of the monks who once called Ellora their home. One monastery was carved with several "stories" into the rock, each level containing large central areas for prayer and study, and small cells where the monks slept. Crawling inside these gloomy spaces, whose inhabitants slept on built-in stone bunks, made me feel claustrophobic.

The most impressive of Ellora's "caves" is the Kailasa Hindu temple, a marvel of architecture, artistry and logistics carved and sculpted out of solid rock more than 1,300 years ago. According to the Maharastra state tourism department's Web site, Kailasa is "the largest monolithic structure in the world," meaning that its exterior wall, inner courtyard and imposing temple building – not to mention the carved panels of Hindu gods and goddesses and freestanding sculptures, were all chiseled by ancient craftsmen from the same huge mass of basalt rock.

The temple was conceived to bring to mind Mt. Kailash in the Himalayas, the legendary residence of Lord Shiva. The temple complex covers an area twice the size of the Parthenon in Athens, and it took thousands of workers more than a century to build. Scientists believe more than 200,000 tons of rock was removed to bring the towering temple to life from the chunk of rock where it lay "imprisoned."

Since we were with a tour group, our time at Ellora and Kailash was limited. I lingered as long as possible, climbing the stairs to enter the upper story of the temple and trying to soak in the history that had been hewn from the rock centuries before. Soon, Ava, Salome and I were the only members of our group still inside the temple complex, and we scurried out through the gate as the bus waited for us, motor running. I snapped a few more pictures of the outside of the temple and reluctantly climbed on the bus, which immediately drove off.

The Ellora caves are much closer to Aurangabad than the Ajanta caves, so we were able to tour the caves in the morning and then take in some other sights in the afternoon. Our next stop was a 12th-century fort and palace whose royal occupant must have been a bit paranoid. The palace sat on a high hilltop, but to get there, visitors (or would-be invaders) had to traverse seven concentric walls, and a final underground passage with false turns, and a chute leading directly to the moat below. There was also a spot where palace guards could drop boiling oil on unwelcome callers. During our tour, the guide turned off the lights inside the passageway so we could experience its total darkness, complete with the squeaks and rustles of the bats that now live there.

When we emerged at the top of the fort complex, we were treated to sweeping views and grassy patches where monkeys cavorted in an effort to mooch snacks.

Later in the day, we visited Bibi ka Maqbara, also known as the "Baby Taj," a tomb for Queen Begum Rabia Durrani built in 1678 by her doting son. The edifice was designed to resemble its larger, more famous cousin, the Taj Mahal, with its central dome and four minarets. But we found its shabby grounds and grime-stained surfaces to be a poor imitation of the glorious Taj. Last, we visited the Panchakki, a water mill built in the late 1600s to grind grain into flour.

Salome's Journal

1/12/06 Mumbai, India

Hi Salome from Mumbai. I took a side trip to Aurangabad, Ajanta and Ellora both one full day of non-stop tour. I hated Ajanta and I liked not much but I liked Ellora. Our hotel

was icky and the people at the front desk were rude but the
restraunt people were nice. The Ajanta and Ellora by the way
are caves carved out of solid rock into a side of a mountain.
Each one was built for either a budest or hindi god. The only
mystery was what did they do with all the rock the carved?
The caves with dome celings were the temples and flat celings
were used as houses. Each cave was built in 200 B.C. before
the time of Christ. Later they left and left some of the caves
unfinished. It was very cool. Now we are back in Mumbai.
Our train arrived at 5:30 and we have been back for 4 hours.
I am looking forward to waking up at 12:00 in the morning. I
am tempted just to stay up! See ya bye. Salome.

After the long day, we returned to our hotel to shower
and pack. We had tickets for a night sleeper train back to
Mumbai, which would arrive in the early morning.

Our final days in Mumbai were spent perusing a couple
of different art museums, hanging out at the coffee shop
and dropping by Leopold's, which had become one of our
favorite haunts. On one such visit, we met two Mumbai
locals who worked on a cruise ship, and had been to
San Diego during their travels. We also ran into John
and Kathryn, the two American college professors from
the tour in Aurangabad. Kathryn planned to be in India
for several more months, so we gave her our Indian cell
phone, which still had a lot of prepaid minutes on it.

The day before our flight to Thailand, I opened the
Times of India at breakfast and was astonished to see
a familiar sight – a color photo of the Oceanside Pier at
sunset. For whatever reason, the newspaper's editors had
chosen the photo with a brief caption to fill space on an i

nside page. We took it as a good omen, although it caused a pang of homesickness, since the pier is only a few miles from our house in Southern California.

We had spent nine weeks in India, and the only thing I could say for sure was that our travels on the subcontinent were never boring. Even two years later, as I write this, my true feelings about India are conflicted.

When our plane touched down in Mumbai in November 2005, I was very anxious about what awaited us on our travels through India. Early on, I had serious doubts about the wisdom of spending more than two months in such a chaotic, unpredictable and turbulent place. I wasn't sure I would make it until our planned departure in January 2006, and I often thought about moving our flight up to an earlier date.

Even after our family had gotten over the initial shock at the poverty and squalor of India, I kept an ongoing mental log of the days elapsed and remaining before we flew on to Bangkok. My moods ran the gamut from homesickness to exhilaration to tranquil acceptance and eventually an embrace of the country's considerable charms as well as reconciliation with its shortcomings. There are aspects of India I could do without: the dirt, the beggars, the crippled people scooting around on crude wooden boards rigged with rollerskate wheels. I didn't care much for the habit of Indian men of spitting large wads of phlegm onto the sidewalk, or urinating in public.

As we prepared to take a 1 a.m. taxi to the airport for our 5 a.m. flight (worried whether our exit would be blocked by barricades set up for that day's Mumbai Marathon) I felt both relief and pride at having toured

India on our own for more than two months, with happy memories and no visible scars to show for it.

But I am certain I will return. The fantastic variety of life is one reason, whether it's the vast array of religions practiced with unrivaled devotion, the colorful clothes worn by men and women alike, or the delicate flavors blended to create foods I have never tasted anywhere else. Long after our trip, I sometimes wake up longing for a steaming glass of the spiced chai tea sold by street vendors in every Indian city and village.

We were privileged to see awe-inspiring sights, from the clamor of the Pushkar Camel Fair to the splendor of the Taj Majal to the mysterious religious caves of Ajanta and Ellora. We loved the shopping, from fancy clothing stores to teeming covered markets. And we got to do things we would never have been able to do in the U.S., such as sit in an open jeep just a few feet from a wild tiger, bathe with an elephant and track rhinos on an elephant safari through the jungle.

From the beaches of Goa to the foothills of the Himalayas, India is simply astonishing. On top of all else is the complexity of the Indian people. They are at once vexing, joyous, caring and aloof. They are quick to smile, slow to anger, and able to look right through you. People who had almost no material possessions exhibited enormous dignity and generosity of spirit.

Oh, and did I mention the chai?

Chapter 13

Angkor What?

Thailand, Cambodia, Hong Kong and Tokyo

"Escape the tiger and happen upon the crocodile."
Thai proverb

"Travel is the most private of pleasures. There is no greater bore than the travel bore. We do not in the least want to hear what he has seen in Hong-Kong."

Vita Sackville-West, English Novelist

O ur flight from India to Thailand transported us from west to east, but it felt more like a time machine, lifting us from the raw, teeming streets of Mumbai and depositing us in Bangkok, with its freeways, steel-and-glass skyscrapers and elevated light-rail system, called the Sky Train.

We arrived in Bangkok in mid-morning, tired from our midnight wake-up call in Mumbai, but excited both to be arriving in a new country, and in anticipation of seeing six friends from San Diego.

Not to disparage India, but after more than two months on the subcontinent, I was ready to walk the streets of a modern, up-and-coming metropolis, and at first glance, Bangkok delivered. Instead of the mildew-stained but majestic Victorian-era buildings of Mumbai, our eyes were treated to the high-rise office buildings, indoor shopping malls and luxury hotels of Thailand's capital. Judging from the steel cranes poking up between buildings, a construction boom was well underway. Even Bangkok's tuk-tuks, present in every corner of India, were larger and more powerful.

In Bangkok, we enjoyed the guilty pleasure of 7-Eleven convenience stores, which we hadn't seen since leaving the U.S. in June. The familiar red, yellow and green 7-Eleven signs seemed to be visible on nearly every block in Bangkok. We walked through the aisles of the tiny stores, the powerful air-conditioners cooling our skin as we looked greedily at the racks of chips, candy, soft drinks and magazines. We recognized many familiar brands, although the packages were also marked with Thai script.

The taxi from the airport brought us to the door of Wendy House, a small, cheerful hotel a couple of blocks from Siam Square, a popular shopping and dining district.

My friend, Michael J. Williams, had advised us by e-mail that Thai people actually appreciate attempts by foreigners to speak their language, even if the words are badly mangled. So, with the taxi driver as Guinea pig, I tried the only Thai words I knew, the address of our hotel, and "sa-wa-dee-kaa," which means both "hello" and "good-bye." (Michael had provided both phrases in his e-mail, with the help of his wife, O, a Bangkok native.)

The taxi driver's face opened into a huge grin in spite of my butchery of his native tongue.

"You speak Thai!" he cried with delight. Sheepishly, I tried to let him know that I had exhausted my entire stockpile of Thai words with that single sentence.

The rest of the way, he continued to talk in Thai, and all I could do was nod and smile.

Wendy House proved to be the perfect place for our family – the central location was within an easy walk of stores, restaurants, transportation and an ATM. Our room was clean, large enough for the three of us and included both a mini-fridge and TV, along with air-conditioning. The price of 1,250 baht, or $30 U.S., included a hearty breakfast of either Thai noodle soup, or eggs and bacon, along with fruit and coffee. The lobby doubled as breakfast room and Internet café, where, for a reasonable rate, we could check our email or surf the Web. Coolers stocked with cold beer – for late-night bull sessions – were the icing on the cake. The staff was helpful and friendly, whether we needed directions or to have our clothes washed at the in-house laundry.

Our friends were supposed to arrive late on our first night, so after checking into our room, we set out on foot to survey our new, temporary neighborhood.

Wendy House was on a side street with three or four other small hotels, a travel agency, a couple of low-key restaurants with covered patios, and a dental office. This last attracted my attention because a toothache I had been trying to ignore for several weeks as we traveled in India was growing more painful by the day. Along the narrow one-way street, several lunch carts parked, where office workers congregated at midday to sit on folding chairs under umbrellas to eat grilled chicken and beef skewers. The delicious aroma of cooking meat mingled with the car exhaust and faint odors of decomposing trash from nearby alleys. Also on the street were fruit carts, whose operators sliced up ripe pineapples, watermelon and papaya, and served them speared on wooden sticks for convenient snacking.

We were across town from larger, more established tourist areas such as Banglamphu and Sukhumvit Road, but that was just as well, because we had Salome with us, and had heard those enclaves of budget hotels and trinket shops were on the seedy side.

At one end of our street was a busy thoroughfare, where cars, trucks and tuk-tuks beeped their horns under the shadow of the Sky Train line. A block away, at a busy corner traversed by pedestrian bridges, were two high-rise malls, kitty-corner from each other. On a third corner, workers toiled on the early stages of a new skyscraper.

The newer of the high-rise shopping centers, Discovery Center, looked like any Western mall, with trendy shops (including an English-language bookstore) arranged around an open central core and served by glass-and-polished-metal escalators.

We came to appreciate the second mall, called MBK, because it had many department stores and even a multiplex cinema, but also featured several floors that were more akin to traditional Thai markets. On those floors, row after row of stalls sold everything from cell phones to touristy souvenirs to pirated video games, movies and music CDs. My favorite thing about the MBK mall, though, was the food court.

We didn't learn about the food court until two or three days after we arrived in Bangkok when O took us there for lunch. Customers first lined up at a cashier's booth to buy scrip before venturing out to the culinary wonderland that was the MBK mall food court.

A sprawling area filled with tables and chairs – nearly all full no matter what time of day – was ringed by food stalls offering a huge array of choices, from Chinese duck to Thai noodles to Japanese tempura and sushi to Italian spaghetti. All of the food was cooked on the spot behind polished glass dividers. Ava, Salome and I would buy $10 worth of scrip, stuff ourselves with hot entrees, soups, desserts and drinks, and still have scrip to cash in when we were done.

We stayed close to home as we got our bearings in Bangkok, exploring the busy Siam Square neighborhood, with its restaurants, beauty salons and music shops. We all felt a bit jet-lagged, since our 5 a.m. flight from Mumbai had required us to wake up about midnight the night before.

Our friends – Michael J. and O, Bill and Michelle, and Marty and Gabrielle – were supposed to arrive that night. While our trip to Bangkok went smoothly, our friends were not so lucky. They missed a connecting flight in Japan, and had to lay over for the night before catching a flight to Bangkok the next day. The three of us resigned ourselves to waiting another day before we would see our friends.

At one end of our street were the Sky Train, Bangkok's National Stadium, Siam Square and the high-rise malls; at the other end was one of Bangkok's many canals, or "khlongs," a network of waterways that link up with the Chao Phraya River. The canals serve as vital transportation links for Bangkok's residents. "Long-tail" boats – which were long and narrow, with powerful engines – roared up and down the canals, sending out wakes that slapped into the concrete channel walls. The boats made regular stops to pick up and drop off passengers; each time, crewman lowered plastic tarps used to keep passengers dry, then raised them back into place as the boats sped off.

On our first full day in Bangkok, we took our time over breakfast at Wendy House, then walked to the Jim Thompson house, a complex of Thai-style teak buildings exquisitely decorated with art and antique furniture, including paintings, sculpture and porcelain, set on a lushly landscaped property. Thompson was an expatriate American and former military intelligence officer who made a fortune by designing and marketing a line of clothing made of Thai silk. He disappeared mysteriously in 1967 while hiking on a vacation in Malaysia. Before Thompson vanished, he was credited with reviving Thailand's entire silk industry and providing good-paying jobs for thousands of Thai women. Thompson's body was never found, and people have speculated for years about what really happened. Some said he fell into a camouflaged pit used to snare tigers, while others were convinced he'd been the victim of a botched robbery or kidnapping. His strange disappearance only heightened his mystique, and his home, which is now a museum, remains a popular tourist attraction. His line of brightly colored silk clothing for men and women still enjoys strong sales in Thailand and beyond. The Thompson House, which backs up to a Bangkok canal, was only a couple of blocks from Wendy House.

Before our tour began, the English-speaking guide asked us to remove our shoes and place our backpacks and handbags in lockers stationed near the door. Our route took us up and down stairs, through various buildings and across the richly polished wood floors. The rooms were airy with lots of natural light, and it was fun to imagine being a guest at one of Thompson's legendary dinner parties, which included such luminaries as the writer W. Somerset Maugham. Even before his disappearance, thousands of people had visited Thompson's house to admire his collection of Asian art when he opened the place to the public to raise money for charity.

In the evening when we returned to Wendy House, we checked with the front desk for any word from our friends. They hadn't called, so we went to bed, leaving a message asking our friends to wake us when they arrived. The phone rang at 1 a.m. and we went down to the lobby to welcome the tired, tardy crew from Southern California.

Ava, Salome and I were groggy, but overjoyed to see our friends after being on the road so long, and the scene turned into a party as we dipped into the cooler full of Singha beer and gabbed. O's cousin, Ot, a tour guide from the resort area of Phuket (which had been hit hard by the 2004 tsunami), arrived soon after and began collecting cash and passports from the group. Ot was organizing our side trip to Cambodia, giving him one day to get our visas and finalize transportation and lodging details before our planned departure. We finally went to bed at about 3 a.m., after I agreed to go out the next morning on a walk with Bill, a newspaper photographer, so he could grab a few shots of the surrounding neighborhoods. Although he assured me he would be up by 7 a.m., I didn't really believe him.

But Bill was good to his word, and he rapped on our door just after 7. Bleary-eyed and head reeling from the beers I'd drunk just a few hours before, I went downstairs to find Bill, entirely too chipper for the early hour, swigging coffee and eating a full breakfast of sausage, eggs and toast.

I was going to have a cup of coffee and wait until later for breakfast, but Bill insisted I order food. I acquiesced and ordered breakfast, and when it arrived, I took about two bites before he set down his fork, wiped his mouth with a napkin and pushed back his chair. "Let's go!" he cried cheerfully, shouldering his camera bag.

I glared at him through half-closed lids, stuffed a couple more forkfuls of eggs into my mouth, and got up.

We walked out into the Bangkok morning. The sun was already shining and the air was rapidly losing its early-morning coolness, turning hot and humid. We walked to the end of the street, where it intersected with the canal, and then walked along the waterway. We came to a foot bridge and crossed over to what looked like a residential neighborhood of small shacks crammed together in densely populated blocks. We took some photos of the canal, which was overgrown with bougainvillea in some spots. Narrow sidewalks divided the blocks, and I followed Bill as he zigged and zagged into the heart of the residential area.

We saw the locals waking up, cooking breakfast and getting their children ready for school. These people's lives were on display through the open fronts of their modest homes, as if we were window shopping on 5th Avenue in New York City. Some smiled and waved as we walked by; others ignored us, perhaps still wrapped in the fog of sleep.

If something caught Bill's eye as we walked, he stopped to take a photo, and occasionally he asked permission of people we encountered if he could photograph them. Most smiled and agreed.

I also snapped a few photos as we went along. Intermixed with the homes in the neighborhood were small shops selling snacks and newspapers, and what seemed to be humble restaurants where people sat on stools and devoured bowls of noodles before heading off for work.

Eventually we came to a main boulevard and took our bearings, and headed back to the hotel.

By this time, the rest of our party was stirring, and the whole group (the seven who were staying at Wendy House, plus Michael J. and O) met in the lobby to plan the day's activities.

We decided to ride the Sky Train to the river, then catch a boat up to the Grand Palace Complex, which includes "Wat Phra Kaew," or the Temple of the Emerald Buddha. Although Ava, Salome and I had become seasoned travelers during the seven months we had been on the road, and had managed to navigate our way around many new and bewildering cities, it was a luxury to travel in Thailand with O because she speaks Thai and knows Bangkok so well. She served as our group's organizer and tour guide, helping us with directions, buying train and boat tickets and ordering from restaurant menus. We enjoyed letting someone else take charge, and her knowledge led us to try foods and see sights we probably would have missed on our own.

The Sky Train was a sleek, high-tech light rail that ran on an elevated track supported by huge concrete pillars in the center of some of Bangkok's major, and most congested, thoroughfares. Stops were announced in both English and Thai by a soothing female voice, and the cars were clean, spacious and air-conditioned. We rode the train to the end of the line, then followed O down to street level, and to the river boat station. Our boat ride took us past some of Bangkok's famous hotels and temples, and soon we were disembarking at a crowded market near the Grand Palace.

Because the temples in the complex are sacred to the Buddhist faith, the government imposes a strict dress code for visitors. At the entrance, a guard determined Ava's sleeveless blouse was inappropriate, so she was issued a short-sleeve white shirt to cover up. Men who showed up in shorts were given sarongs – a sheet of fabric worn like a skirt – to cover their legs.

The day was blazing hot, and we walked around the temples admiring the brightly colored figures and gilded, mirrored walls of the buildings. The steeply pitched temple roofs were covered with red, blue and green tiles, and golden spires poked into the sky, where huge puffy clouds played tag with the sun.

All of us took off our shoes before we entered one of the holiest buildings, the Temple of the Emerald Buddha, where the figure carved from precious stone presides from the top of a tall stupa inside the cavernous prayer hall. We sat on the cool stone floor; around us, Buddhists bowed to the ground in prayer. Several different robes have been fashioned for the Emerald Buddha, and each season, the king himself (hoisted by a crane) changes the Buddha's outfit.

By the time we finished exploring the temple grounds, it was late in the afternoon and our group was tired, hungry and thirsty. We found a small upstairs café – with air-conditioning – and settled down for snacks and beer.

Thirst slaked, we headed back out, where we encountered a street musician who played traditional Thai tunes wearing a get-up decorated with hundreds of tiny mirrors. I thought of him as the Thai Elvis; his short, dark hair was swept up in a point in front, sort of an Asian pompadour. He was gracious and allowed us to take his picture, and we ended up seeing him again at a nearby park where he was joined by a second musician on an acoustic guitar. Maybe he was actually more of a Thai Bob Dylan, since he strummed a wooden stringed instrument with an elaborate carving at the end of its neck, and played a small version of a can, a Thai instrument resembling a pan flute, held in place with a bracket around his neck.

With O's help, we hailed a couple of tuk-tuks for a thrilling ride through rush-hour traffic back to our hotel. Since we had to leave at 3 the next morning for Cambodia, we had a quiet dinner near the hotel and went to our rooms to pack.

As promised, Ot met us in the Wendy House lobby on Wednesday, Jan. 25, to escort us to the Bangkok bus station, where we caught a 3:30 a.m. bus to Aranyaprathet, a town near the Cambodian border. The road from Bangkok to Aranyaprathet is all paved and in good condition so the 300-kilometer drive took about four hours. We arrived around 8 a.m. and entered the Thai border immigration office to have our passports stamped. Next, with Ot guiding us like a mother hen, we walked through the throngs of pedestrians, motorbikes and carts piled high with goods at the busy frontier, to the Cambodian immigration office, where we again waited in line for the processing of our entry documents. Since Ot had already obtained our Cambodian visas, everything went very smoothly.

Soon, we were walking through the archway emblazoned "Kingdom of Cambodia," our luggage piled onto a cart pushed by a local porter. A minibus took us to a one-room bus station, where the van hired to take us to Siem Reap soon pulled up. Along with Michael J. and O, and the seven of us staying at Wendy House, was Rob, a musician friend of Michael's who had been traveling by himself in Thailand, and met us for the trip to Cambodia. That made 10 travelers, plus Ot and the driver, for an even dozen in the van.

Although the road to Siem Reap was only 90 miles, we had been warned that in the past, this trip had taken up to 12 hours due to atrocious road conditions, from yawning potholes to bridges and entire sections of road washed away by flooding during Cambodia's monsoon season.

When we were planning the trip, we discussed our two options: flying directly to Siem Reap or going overland by van. We had reached a group consensus for the latter form of transport after Michael J. convinced us an overland trip would be much more interesting and adventurous.

As we bumped over the rutted paved road leading out of Poipet, the Cambodian border town, I had doubts about the wisdom of this choice. According to several Web sites that detailed the Bangkok-Siem Reap journey, the road had been fixed up considerably in recent years, and the journey normally took three to four hours by taxi.

"At least the road can't get any worse," I joked about a half-hour into the trip.

Within a few minutes, I was proved wrong, as even the rudimentary asphalt ended. The van jounced and jostled over the graded dirt road, which would put our kidneys through their paces for the next several hours, all the way to the outskirts of Siem Reap.

Our group had a few things going for it as we settled down for the long ride: our van was air-conditioned, and we were all in high spirits, anticipating the wonders of the Angkor Wat ruins. The company of friends was a novelty for Ava, Salome and I, since we had been on the road by ourselves for so many months. Just in case, Salome had brought her trusty portable DVD player, which kept her occupied between naps.

The driver tried to increase his speed, but the way the van bounced when he hit a pothole caused him to constantly slow down. He finally compromised with a moderate pace that kept our heads from knocking into the roof of the van, but seemed likely to get us to our destination before sundown.

Most of the way from Poipet to Siem Reap, we saw rural countryside from the windows of the van, including rice paddies and small farms. The dusty road and surrounding fields, edged by low, bushy trees, reminded me of India. The work we saw was being done by hand, or with antiquated plows pulled by oxen or bullock. We also saw what appeared to be water buffalo grazing. We passed through a few villages along the way, and one mid-sized town, Sisophon, which was hectic and full of buzzing motor scooters.

A few times by the side of the road, we spotted wooden racks full of plastic bottles of various sizes holding a golden liquid. Our curiosity finally made us ask the driver to stop so we could check out one of these stands. They turned out to be very low-tech gas stations, where cars and scooters could pull over to top off their tanks! We were also stumped by contraptions standing in the middle of many fields along the way. A plastic sheet was stretched across a frame, with a trough full of water at the bottom, and a fluorescent light fixture at the top. We just couldn't figure out what the devices were used for, until our trip back to Bangkok, when the picture snapped into focus: the frames were designed to collect crickets, which the locals fried up and seasoned for a crispy snack.

By mid-afternoon, we arrived at the outskirts of Siem Reap and were pleased when the road again became paved, turning into a wide, smooth expanse of asphalt. Lined up along each side was the source of the city's recent prosperity: dozens of new tourist hotels. But as we entered the city proper, the Holiday Inns gave way to broad, tree-lined avenues and colonial-style buildings.

Ot had arranged for us to stay in a relatively new, smaller hotel a short distance from the city center. Some of the group decided to take a nap while Ava, Salome and I, joined by Rob, went for a walk. One casualty of the trip from Bangkok was my trusty Lonely Planet guidebook for Southeast Asia, which I had loaned to Bill on the bus ride. Unfortunately, Bill left it on the bus. So, as we walked around, I kept my eye open for a replacement. I soon struck pay dirt, spotting the familiar book cover in a shop window. The book was bound in shrink wrap and looked new. It was only $10, so I plopped my money down. When I removed the wrapping and flipped through the book, I realized I'd been had – sort of. It was the right book, but I had purchased a bootleg that had apparently been photocopied from an original. Laughably, the book even had scribbles in the margins that had been made by the traveler who owned the original copy. Also, the maps hadn't reproduced well and were very fuzzy. But I figured it was the best I would be able to do in Siem Reap, and it did have the info about Angkor Wat I wanted for our visit.

Ava and I also needed to get some local cash, since we hadn't been able to make it to an ATM before leaving Bangkok. It turned out that all of the merchants accepted U.S. dollars and Thai baht, but were reluctant to accept Cambodia's own currency, the riel, which had been severely devalued. (At the time of this writing, the exchange rate was $1 U.S. to 3,948 riel, making the battered greenback look like a monetary Rock of Gibraltar.)

Most of the prices were in U.S. dollars, which made things expensive by Asian standards, especially when compared to India or even Thailand. Rather than getting cash from an ATM as we were used to doing, we had to go to a currency exchange, where the money was charged to our Visa cards for a hefty fee.

All that high finance made us thirsty, so we looked for a café where Ava, Rob and I could have a beer – and Salome could get a soda – before we headed back to the hotel and met our group for dinner.

There weren't many choices, so we settled on a small restaurant that looked inviting because a cook was grilling meat on a broiler at the front window.

I stuck my head inside the door and asked to see a menu.

"No menu. Pig insides," the cook said, gesturing to the cooking meat.

Okay, I thought, good thing we're not staying for dinner.

"Do you have beer?" I asked.

"Yes, yes, come in," the cook said.

The four of us sat at one of the long wooden picnic tables. With the famous pig insides sizzling on the grill, I couldn't figure out why the place was empty, but we were the only customers.

The waitress brought us three large, icy bottles of beer, and a Coke for Salome. When the check came, we saw the beers cost $3 apiece, more than we were used to paying in Asia. But at least it was cold.

A van picked us up in the morning for the short ride to Angkor Thom, a walled city dating to the 12th century that served as the capital of the Angkor Empire. When Angkor Thom was built, the Cambodian empire's territory included most of present-day Cambodia, Thailand, Vietnam and Laos.

Our guide, Kim Lee, had planned a busy itinerary for us. First, we visited Bayon Temple which, from a distance, looks like a crumbling, mildew-stained heap of stone. But, as our van got closer, we saw that what had appeared to be mounds of gray rock were actually dozens of huge, carved faces gazing serenely, if inscrutably, in every direction. Some say the faces were modeled after a royal personage; others say they represent the Buddha. But either way, viewed from up close, they are awe-inspiring. The temple boasts more than 200 of the carvings, each of which stands five or six feet tall, and three or four feet across.

The exterior wall of the temple complex is adorned with intricate carvings of scenes of daily life, including battles and religious ceremonies. Next door was the Terrace of Elephants, a large stone platform decorated on its sides with carved processions of pachyderms. The platform was reportedly used by the king to view ceremonial processions and parades.

That morning, we also visited Ta Prohm, a temple that most closely matched my "mind's eye view" of how Cambodian temples would look. Of the major temples in the Siem Reap area, Ta Prohm has undergone the least amount of renovation. Giant banyon trees grew in and around the temple, their trunks and roots literally having become part of the architecture. On a low platform next to the path leading to the temple, a band composed land mine victims played Cambodian music. All of the musicians were missing one or more limbs, and the sight reminded us of Cambodia's troubled recent history, when millions died at the hands of the Khmer Rouge regime.

After lunch, we hopped in the van for a short ride to the centerpiece of Siem Reap's ancient temples, Angkor Wat. Kim Lee told us Angkor Wat is considered the largest religious building in the world. Built in the early 1100s and dedicated to the Hindu god Vishnu the Preserver, Angkor Wat stands three stories tall and is surrounded by a rectangular moat nearly a mile long. The center temple was built inside four sets of protective walls, and features gorgeous bas relief carvings and statuary. One of the most famous panels depicts "the churning of the sea of milk," a Hindu creation myth. Researchers have postulated that Angkor Wat was designed with the heavens in mind, as a sort of observatory where ancient astronomers could chart the positions of the sun, moon and stars. As we approached, the temple towered above the surrounding countryside, and conversation stopped as we gazed at Angkor Wat's stone towers.

The day was sunny and very hot: we moved slowly from the van to a bridge over the protective moat. Once inside the temple complex, we were able to find shady spots as we admired the carvings and architecture.

When we reached the central temple building, we were confronted with a wide stone staircase that ascended on a near-vertical trajectory. The steps themselves were quite tall, requiring effort to climb each one. I hate heights and was nervous both for myself and Salome as we set out to climb our way to Angkor Wat's inner sanctum. I leaned forward, holding on to the stone steps as my feet and legs propelled me upward. I positioned myself below Salome so I could catch her in case she slipped. I purposely avoided looking down as I made my way up the stairs, not wanting to make myself dizzy by looking at the ground below.

At the top of the stairs we were rewarded with a light breeze, and a great view of the flat, tree-covered land around the temple.

I enjoyed walking through Angkor Wat's chambers, but kept thinking about having to go back down those stairs at the end of our visit, which made me anxious. Fortunately, when the time came, we found that a stairway on another side of the temple had a metal handrail, rickety though it was, that enabled me to get back down to earth safely and with most of my dignity intact.

Our last stop of the day was Banteay Srei temple, which

was as tiny and delicate as Angkor Wat was massive and imposing. The miniature temple was carved from pink sandstone about 967 AD, and its name, in the Khmer language, means "citadel of women." Some consider the temple the jewel of Khmer art due to its diminutive size and intricate, beautiful carvings.

Banteay Srei is about 20 kilometers from Seam Reap, and it was getting near dusk when we finished our visit. Before the ride back into town, Kim Lee took us to a nearby monument, where we sat on a stone building overlooking the countryside, watching the sun set. A number of other people, most of them locals, had the same idea, and perched alongside us admiring the display of soft orange, pink and crimson light spread out along the horizon. Someone pulled a few cans of beer from their daypack and we toasted to Cambodia, the sunset and whatever else we could think of.

A young man approached, wearing what looked like a security guard's uniform. We chatted a bit, and he told us he was a police officer. From his pocket, he pulled out a badge made of gold-colored metal.

"Do you want to buy?" he asked, holding out his policeman's badge. "Twenty dollars."

We looked at each other and declined, trying to be as polite as possible, since the whole thing seemed pretty strange.

The young man was persistent. "Fifteen dollars," he said, pushing the badge toward us. Smiling, we shook our heads and walked back toward our waiting van.

Before we set out for more sightseeing the next day, several of us took a walk around the neighborhood where our hotel was situated. We saw a funeral procession, which consisted of many men and women dressed in white shirts and blouses, walking behind a sort of mobile shrine containing the casket. People on foot and motorbikes moved to the side of the street to make way for the procession; from there they stood and watched.

We also visited a clinic, because Michael J. was afflicted with a persistent stomach bug that nearly put him out of commission. He saw a pharmacist, who gave him two types of Chinese medications that did make him feel better. Luckily, Ava, Salome and I managed to avoid whatever sickened Michael J., O and other members of our group. We theorized that we had been traveling so long and had encountered so many different bugs that our immune systems had toughened up and would repel most common ailments.

Our first order of business upon leaving the hotel was an elephant ride. On our visit to Bayon Temple the day before, Salome had seen the pachyderms with their riding platforms fixed to their backs, and insisted that we take a ride. It was only fair; we had been dragging her along to see so many "old buildings" and temples. Most of our group good-naturedly agreed to go with us, although a couple friends stayed at the hotel and met us afterward.

The elephant driver took us on a loop around Bayon Temple, and we were treated to great views of the serene Buddha faces looking down from their perches above the ancient temple. Also, as we walked, fruit vendors fed their scraps such as coconut husks and palm fronds to the elephant, which snatched the greenery with its trunk and gobbled it up.

Kim Lee had one temple on our agenda that day, a very nice one: there were lots of shady spots among the crumbling stone walls and banyon trees, and we spent most of our time lolling around, trying to keep cool. I think we were all feeling a bit worn out from the heat and all the walking we had done the day before – and maybe even a bit of "temple overload."

He had saved what turned out to be one of the most fascinating and scenic spots for last: Tonle Sap, Southeast Asia's largest lake, and a body of water that provides a home and livelihood to as many as 10,000 Cambodians and transplanted Vietnamese, according to our guide. During monsoon season, the lake increases in size to cover some 20 percent of Cambodia, and its waters are a rich source of fish both to feed and provide economic sustenance for the population.

Our van bumped over a dirt road to the edge of the lake, where we climbed over a rickety wooden ramp to board a boat for our excursion. The boat chugged through the brown water along a narrow lake finger until we reached the vast open stretches of Tonle Sap. Along the way, we looked at the houses lining the shore. They had been built on platforms that floated on the water, and were painted in vivid hues of red, yellow and orange. Nearly every house sported a TV antenna. There were also smaller houseboats, and we were passed by many canoe-like craft piled high with firewood, and fishing nets and fish. Some of the workers lined up their boats into caravans as they rowed in with their cargo. There was even a Christian church adorned with a large wooden cross along the edge of the lake, which also floated on the water.

The boat reached a point far from the shore, and the captain cut the engine and lowered the anchor. Our group sat, either on the open upper deck of the boat or in the seats on the semi-enclosed lower deck, and enjoyed the stillness of the late afternoon. Soon, three little boys, maybe 8 or 10 years old, rowed up to check us out. Two were in a beat-up canoe, while the third was in a black plastic tub. They goofed around and mugged for our cameras, and we gave them some Thai baht notes, which they squabbled over.

The captain then started the engine, and we slowly trolled back to shore. We pulled up to the dock at a floating restaurant, which was a hit with Salome because it had a souvenir shop and crocodile pits crammed full of the toothy reptiles.

We enjoyed the sunset over the lake from the restaurant's rooftop deck, drinking canned beers and sodas and munching on snacks, such as peel-and-eat shrimp with hot sauce.

The evening was so cool and pleasant, we hated to leave the lake, but finally it was time to go, and we headed back to the hotel to pack.

Much too early the next day, we piled into the van for the ride back to the Thai border. The group seemed quieter as we absorbed the sights and sounds of the past three days.

In about four hours, we were back at Poipet, where we tried a new delicacy while waiting for a shuttle bus to take us to the border crossing – deep-fried crickets. A vendor's cart was parked in front of the station with trays of different kinds of sautéed bugs displayed under heat lamps. Marty pointed to the smallest ones, which were dark and oily looking. The vendor pulled out a small brown paper bag and poured a scoop of crickets into it. Marty sauntered onto the bus, munching on the bugs, and eagerly offered the bag to each member of our group. Ava flatly refused, but Salome took one. She hesitated, wanting to try the bug, but afraid to put it in her mouth. She finally tossed it out the window. I took one and cringed as I placed it in my mouth. My biggest fear was that the cricket's body would be full of foul goo that would seep out into my mouth when I bit down. Instead, the cricket was crunchy and seasoned with soy sauce. I washed the wings and legs down with a swallow of Diet Coke, proud of being adventurous enough to eat a bug, but having no desire to try another.

Salome's Journal

1/22/06 Bangkok, Thailand

Hi Salome. I have not spoke to you for a long time but I will make up for it. Anyways my friends are here. We have been together for about 4 days. We went to Angkor Wat for 3 days. It is a huge temple for the Budest gods. It goes back 1,000 years old. Later a hindi king came and cut almost all the Budest's heads off because Budest heads were wirth a fortune back then. Finally when the hindi died out 2 French explorers stumbled across this all covered by jungle and forest. Only ten years ago it was opened for tourism and we had a fun time. We also took an elephant ride around the temple which was a lot of fun! Now after 12 hours of traviling from Angkor Wat we are back in Bangkok. We arrived last night and this morning we are going shopping. Oh ya! I don't want to be a teacher now I want to be a buyer where you work for a big shop like Macey's and go buy the things that you think will

sell. I've heard you earn a lot of money. So anyway (I) want to
go do my shopping. Bye love Salome.

We had a few days left in Bangkok before we were
slated to go south to the beaches of Phuket, which had
been hit only a year or so before by a devastating tsunami.
Soon, our group of San Diegans would split up, most of us
heading to one beach or another in Southern Thailand.

The next morning was a Sunday, so a bunch of us
took the Sky Train to the Chatuchak market, a sprawling
place with hundreds of indoor and outdoor stalls, like an
American swap meet on steroids. As we walked to the
market along a sidewalk crowded with locals, I noticed
a young man in front of me whose black T-shirt carried
a very provocative – what many would call offensive –
slogan in large white letters across the back: "Jesus is a
cunt." I was flabbergasted and unsure what to make of the
words (maybe a really bad translation from Thai of a more
positive message, such as 'Jesus is the giver of life'?), and I
diverted Salome's attention until the man had disappeared
into the crowd.

Like just about anyplace in Thailand where someone has
a gas-fired flame, a cast-iron pan and cooking ingredients,
the air in the marketplace was scented with many wonderful
aromas. We wandered around intoxicated by the smells and
unable to make up our minds about what to try first. Having
O along was a big help, as she steered us toward her own
favorite dishes, which were invariably delicious. We tasted
skewers of marinated chicken with peanut sauce, and fried
shrimp curry balls. The Thai penchant for sweets was fully
in evidence, as we sampled various types of chilled tapioca,
candies and fried, donut-like concoctions.

The sounds of twangy country-and-western music caught my ear, and I wandered over to a booth where Western clothing and leather belts were for sale. Two Bangkok cowboys sat in front of the stall on wooden stools: one sported a long, wispy, gray beard and dark sunglasses; the other wore a flashy Western-style button-down shirt adorned with red flames, and a bolo tie. The bolo guy slapped metal spoons on his knee in time with the music.

Down a covered passageway, a fortune-teller was hard at work, predicting the futures of market-goers with Tarot cards spread out on a small folding table covered with a red tablecloth. I followed Michael J. down the corridors as he searched for a music shop where he could buy a can, like the one we had seen the street musician playing. The can is made of bamboo tubes lashed together and creates a sound somewhere between a harmonica and a pan flute.

I was intrigued by one tiny stall with antique items displayed in a glass case. Among the trinkets was what appeared to be an authentic tiger tooth: a curved, yellowish object about three or four inches long, which tapered to a point. The top of the tooth was covered by a silver cap attached to a thin metal chain. The shop also had a few pieces of carved ivory. The proprietor told me the price of the tooth was about $100 U.S. While the souvenir would not have severely taxed my budget, it seemed too much to pay for something that was likely to be confiscated by Customs when I returned home. When I told her about it later, Ava was aghast that I would even consider buying a tooth from an endangered animal. I wasn't bothered by the ethical implications; I figured the tooth and the tiger it belonged to had parted ways long before I ever came on the scene.

I picked up a couple of engraved silver boxes as gifts for Ava and Salome, and we joined up with the rest of our friends, who had been shopping for clothes, tapestries and decorative wood carvings.

That evening, I left Ava and Salome at the hotel as a group of us took a tuk-tuk across town for a "muay Thai" match, also known as Thai boxing. The fighters wear padded gloves like their counterparts in the U.S., Europe and Mexico, but the Thai version of the sport has an added twist – the two men in the ring are barefoot, and along with trying to punch their opponent, they are allowed to kick him and also strike him with elbows and knees.

Before we had even entered the arena to see the first punches and kicks, we took a beating of our own: as foreigners, or "falangs" in Thai slang, we had to pay a hefty surcharge to watch the Thai national sport. We paid 1,000 baht apiece, or about $25 U.S. for third class, the cheapest seats in the house. These seats cost locals only a couple of bucks. We followed the concrete ramp all the way to the top of the building, and it opened into the arena's top level. Our section consisted of several rows of concrete bleachers; only a handful of other spectators sat nearby. Between us and the action was a chain-link fence, apparently to keep the rowdies in the "cheap" seats from throwing objects at the fighters or the well-heeled spectators sitting in the more comfortable seats below.

The fight card included seven or eight bouts, and the fighters, at least in the early contests, could not have been more than 12 or 13 years old. A live band played Thai music as the fighters circled each other warily, attempting to land kicks and punches. We had our fill after watching several bouts, and made our way out of the arena and into the warm Bangkok night.

We had planned an excursion for the next day, our last before our group split up.

A van picked us up at the hotel in the morning and took us to a canal dock, where we boarded a longtail boat for a ride to Bangkok's famous floating market on the outskirts of town.

The market was very touristy, with a large indoor bazaar selling souvenirs and trinkets. The most interesting part was the fruit and vegetable vendors, who spread their wares out on the decks of their little wooden boats, which bobbed in the canal. A few intrepid women even cooked food, such as small coconut pancakes, on little gas-fired griddles right on their boats. The goodies were cooked to order and handed up to us on the wooden deck next to the canal, in banana leaf plates.

We piled back in the van for stops at a national park, where we got our feet wet in a pool at the base of a small waterfall, and enjoyed a lunch of Thai barbecue at a rustic, very local restaurant along the highway, which featured wooden picnic tables under a corrugated tin overhang.

Our last stop of the day was the town of Kanchanburi, near the famous "Bridge Over the River Kwai." The Academy Award-winning movie named after the bridge is loosely based on the true story of how the Japanese military forced prisoners of war to build bridges and a rail line from Bangkok to Rangoon, then the capital of Burma, during World War II.

First, we visited a scenic and serene Buddhist monument on a ridge overlooking the river. From that vantage point, we saw several large platform party boats float past, disco music thumping loudly. The boats are chartered for weddings, graduation parties and other special events.

Next, we visited the bridge itself, which was crawling with tourists in the dusk of early evening. As we walked across the bridge, we saw the lights of an approaching train and realized there were only a few spots along the span wide enough for us to avoid being run over. And there were no handrails on the bridge. We made it to a safe spot and watched the slow-moving train, which appeared to be carrying a load of tourists, pass by.

Marty and Gabrielle, and Bill and Michelle, headed south the next day to check out some of Thailand's world-renowned beaches. We planned to spend a few more days in Bangkok, then fly south to Phuket, where we would enjoy a week of luxury at the Marriott resort. This would be the last timeshare experience of our round-the-world trip.

Among the tasks we had to take care of in Bangkok was changing our onward airline reservations. By this point in the trip, Ava and I had agreed that we would travel to Hong Kong and Tokyo for a few days each before flying back to California. This meant we would be shaving a couple of months – time budgeted for China and Japan – from our original itinerary.

Our reasons were simple; Salome and I felt increasingly homesick, and our bank account was dwindling rapidly. Our money hadn't stretched as far as we had expected, especially during our two months in Europe. By mid-

February, we still had about $15,000 left, but I wanted to make sure we had money to get re-established at home. We would face some major expenses, from renting an apartment to buying a second car.

To be honest, I was also feeling travel-fatigued and could not summon the energy and enthusiasm to launch another new and challenging adventure. To travel in China, we would need to master a whole new transportation system and learn the immense country's geography while dealing with a steep language barrier.

Although Salome had been a great sport for so long, it was clear that her ability to roll with the travel punches and absorb new cultural challenges was also nearing its capacity. She also was weary of the road and wanted to go home.

So, we plotted out a new plan that would shave a couple of weeks off our stay in Thailand, skip mainland China entirely, and sharply curtail the time we had allotted for Japan. We would return to the U.S. in late February of 2006, about nine months after we set out on our journey.

I found an American Airlines office in central Bangkok, and the three of us went there to make what would be the final changes to our round-the-world itinerary.

Our new reservations meant we had just over three weeks left on our trip. While there was a bittersweet feeling about leaving our rambling lives behind, I must admit I felt excited and a touch relieved at the prospect of soon standing back on American soil.

We continued to explore Bangkok after our traveling group split up. Most mornings, I took an early-morning run around our "neighborhood." Generally, I ran to

Lumpini Park, an oasis of grassy fields and tranquil lakes surrounded on all sides by the frenetic streets of the Thai capital.

The park was a couple of miles from our hotel, and to get there, I had to run along busy streets, up and over several pedestrian bridges, and past a major university, just as the sleepy students approached on foot, by bus and motorbike.

At 7:30 a.m., when I usually got to the park, the place was jumping with joggers, bicyclists, fast-walkers and people practicing tai chi, a cross between yoga and transcendental mediation. The tai chi people – mostly elderly men and women – stood in groups of 20 or 30, moving slowly in unison with their arms outstretched. Soothing music sometimes played on a boom box.

I ran along the pathways, soaking up the atmosphere as Bangkok's citizens exercised in the cool morning before their work day. The asphalt jogging path curved around the lagoon and over bridges, giving me a great look at all the action in the popular park. Banners bearing the image of Thailand's beloved King Rama IX decorated the broad esplanade of the park's main entrance. The king appeared to be mild-mannered and benevolent in these portraits, with his wire-framed glasses, receding hairline and camera hanging around his neck. Photography is reportedly one of the king's passions, and he is shown with a camera in many of the pictures of him on display throughout Bangkok.

On our last night in the city before heading south, O invited us to dinner at her aunt's house, where she had lived as a child. We took the Sky Train to the Victory

Monument stop and met Mike and O for the short walk to her aunt's house. The house was a warren of rooms where O's aunt had raised a number of orphaned boys and girls, whom O considered her brothers and sisters. As the family prepared dinner, there was much laughing and joking, and we felt right at home. A huge feast of Thai dishes was laid out on the table and we fell in, gorging ourselves.

Then it was time to fly to Phuket for a week at the Marriott timeshare resort. Mike and O decided to spend a few days with us before heading back to Bangkok and on to northern Thailand to visit relatives.

At the airport, Michael J. pointed out a muscular man in a track suit walking past in the opposite direction. The man's name was Khaosai Galaxy and Michael J. called him the "Muhammed Ali of Thailand," because he was a former muay Thai champion who switched to Western-style boxing, then became a movie star after his retirement. He looked like a shorter, stockier version of Jackie Chan, with slicked-back dark hair. I asked for his autograph and he readily agreed, signing his name on a page of my pocket notebook. I gave the autograph to Michael J. so he could share it with O's relatives.

The Phuket Marriott was, hands down, the most luxurious hotel we stayed at during our entire trip. We were greeted in the flower-filled lobby by a hostess with a tray of cocktails, and driven to our condo in a golf cart. The grounds were lushly landscaped; at the rear of the resort was a pristine white-sand beach on the Andaman Sea. Very few visitors strayed down to the beach; instead, they packed the padded chaise lounges around the two large pools, one of which was equipped with a water slide and shallow play areas for kids. Attendants scurried among the reclining guests, handing out extra-large beach towels and bringing cold drinks and snacks.

The inside of our condo was just as nice as the resort's exterior – the unit featured a fully equipped kitchen, a living room with a large color TV and DVD player, and two bedrooms. The bathroom in the master suite included a huge whirlpool tub, and our balcony overlooked the gardens.

The only drawback to the place was its location – the resort was a 45-minute drive from the airport, in a remote area far from any town. Unless we wanted to rent a car, we were marooned in the lap of luxury. Sure, there are worse places to be stuck; each of us did have our own fluffy white terry-cloth bathrobes and pool slippers. There were several restaurants on site, and a deli-market that, to Salome's delight, stocked bagels and cream cheese. The resort also had a children's recreation center, which hosted daily arts and crafts programs and activities. They even had classes for adults such as cooking, flower-arranging and dance.

Although our accommodations were all paid for, the amenities cost extra, and they weren't cheap – a can of soup in the deli cost $6. Beer was priced by the bottle, never a good thing. Internet access in the resort's "business center" cost 195 baht, or $5, for 15 minutes. To stock our condo with groceries and beer, we hired a van for the hour-long ride to Phuket Town, where we raided a local supermarket. We filled our cart with every type of munchies our eyes came across, from chips to donuts. It had been a long time since we stayed at a place with a kitchen, and we planned to use ours, so we bought items for breakfast, lunch and dinner. Things were a little different from the supermarkets we were used to – I decided to buy a roast duck, but the cooked, plucked bird still was still had its head and webbed feet, which we found distinctly unappetizing. An obliging store worker took it to the back room and made the bird more presentable by chopping off the offending parts.

Although it was certainly nice to bask in the comforts of the Marriott, including its plush beds and down pillows and comforters, I felt very much cut off from the world and out of place among the well-heeled travelers. The resort was fully booked because our visit took place during Chinese New Year. Salome was happy to meet some English-speaking children to play with, including a brother and sister from the U.K. who had moved to Hong Kong because of their father's job.

I tallied up our hotel tab each day, and went for long runs along the beach and through a wooded area next to the resort. While little visible damage remained from the prior year's tsunami, government officials had helpfully posted shiny new "Tsunami Evacuation Route" signs in both Thai and English.

Salome was completely in her element, and said she wanted to come back to the Marriott for her "Sweet 16" and bring her friends to celebrate.

Salome's Journal

1/30/06 Marriott Resort, Phuket, Thailand

We are at the Marriot luxury like I expected. It is so nice and a lot of kids. They are all rich. The have to eat breakfast, lunch and dinner at the hotel. It is really expensive but we can cook our own meals ya! At the Marriot Café they have bagels can you believe that? I had two for dinner last night. The kids activities are very fun and the kid's room is really nice. Play Station. Big flat screen T.V. and pool and kids stuff. Next to it is a huge pool and one big slide it is so much fun. Well to bad we can't stay here for the rest of the time in Phuket because we still have ten more days after the Marriot. Well talk to ya soon bye.

On the second day of our stay, O's cousin, Ot, stopped by for a few beers and then took us for dinner to a place we would never have found on our own. A taxi drove us to a dock on the edge of an inland bay, where we boarded a small boat for a ride out to a floating restaurant. Several floating eateries bobbed gently in our wake, their lights twinkling in the darkness.

Our table was under a shelter like a gazebo, and we ordered fresh seafood dishes prepared Thai-style, such as crab – chopped up and stir-fried still in the shell – and shrimp with lots of red chilis. Of course, pots of white and fried rice and ice-cold bottles of beer completed the meal. A mild breeze kept us cool as we ate and looked out across the ink-black water at twinkling lights on other floating restaurants, and further away on shore. The customers were all locals, and the bill for six of us came to 800 baht, or about $20 U.S. When we weren't stuffing our faces, we admired the variety of sea creatures swimming in enclosures built into the restaurant's wooden deck. The proprietor reached into one of the tanks and pulled out a 3-foot-long leopard shark for us to see.

The five of us took a boat cruise on Phang Nga Bay the next day to see the famed "James Bond Island," where scenes from The Man with Golden Gun were filmed in the early 1970s. We cruised around rock formations, past caves, and stopped at Koh Pannyi, a small island on stilts where the mostly Muslim inhabitants subsist on fishing and the tourist trade. Luckily, we arrived at a slow time and the souvenir shops were mostly empty.

The day was sunny and warm with clear blue skies and a few white puffy clouds over the turquoise water of the bay. Giant rock formations loomed above us as we sped past in our longtail boat.

In the evening, we had drinks by the pool and watched the sunset. O and Ava both were suffering from a stomach bug, so we laid low the next morning as well. In the afternoon, Mike and O called a taxi for the ride to the airport, where they caught an evening flight back to Bangkok. As they drove off, it struck me how far from home we were.

We had three days left at the Marriott and enjoyed every last minute of our time at those luxurious digs. In spite of my aversion to timeshare presentations, we signed up for the sales pitch in order to receive free tickets to Phuket FantaSea, a dinner-and-show extravaganza at a theme-park-like setting 45 minutes from the resort.

Ava and I took a long walk the next morning, while Salome stayed back in the room and watched DVD movies. We talked about our plans for when we returned home, and she admitted she was feeling anxious as the end of the trip loomed. While I often stressed out about things that might happen on the road, her concerns were the opposite. She worried about how she would deal with going back to our "normal" working lives, and whether she would fall into a depression. I totally enjoyed our travels, but was looking forward to going home, seeing our friends and family, and settling back into a routine.

Among the amenities at the Marriott was a fully equipped workout center, which also offered mountain bikes for rent. On our last day at the resort, we signed up for a guided bike tour through the nearby villages. Salome grumbled, but finally agreed to go with us. Most of the route was flat, and our guide, a friendly young man who worked in the fitness center, chatted about the villages as we pedaled along.

We were on the way back when the overcast skies – which had been threatening rain all day – finally delivered on their promise. We were hit by a wind-driven torrential rainstorm that came at us in waves. Lightning bolts electrified the sodden air and thunder boomed and echoed around us as we rode. We were instantly drenched, but Salome was ecstatic. She shouted, whooped and laughed maniacally as she stood up and pedaled her bike into the warm rain. Rather than being bothered by the downpour, she rejoiced in it; the thunderstorm, for her, turned a monotonous bike ride into a wild adventure. We rode on toward the resort and just before we reached it, the clouds parted to let a bright ray of sunshine shoot through. The sunlight created dazzling rainbows all around us, which we admired as we pedaled over the soggy path back to the Marriott.

Then came the moment I was both dreading and eagerly anticipating – our week at the cushy Marriott ended.

A taxi took us south to Karon Beach, a modest enclave with both high-rise luxury hotels and budget beach hostels. We decided not to stay at Phuket's largest beach town, Patong, because we read that it was much more crowded and some of the streets were seedy with their open-air bars, tattoo shops and cheap hotels.

Our plan was to spend about a week at Karon Beach, then head back to Bangkok for a couple of days before flying on to Hong Kong.

We used the time to recharge our batteries, helping Salome with her schoolwork in the morning and ambling over to the beach each afternoon. While it wasn't as fancy as the Marriott, ambitious vendors had set up reclining chairs and umbrellas, which could be rented for a few dollars per day. Cold drinks and sandwiches were available from a snack shack. Ava and I took up our positions in the chairs while Salome played in the sand and collected shells and live crabs. The beach was wide, the sand soft and the water warm, and there were no waves, which made Salome happy. From our perch, we could also see small islands off-shore. All in all, Karon Beach was a beautiful, relaxing tropical paradise.

We explored the little town, finding a restaurant around the corner that served pancakes and maple syrup, another huge plus in Salome's eyes.

Karon Beach did have its less-wholesome side, although its small scale made it fairly easy to ignore. Lining the commercial streets were small, open bars where young Asian women sat on stools, smiling and calling out to the men who walked by. It was common to see gray-haired American or European men in the company of young Asian women around the town.

By the time we moved to Karon Beach, another problem that I had been steadfastly ignoring for weeks, ever since

India in fact, was becoming unbearable – a toothache in one of my rear molars.

Whether from laziness or a reluctance to climb into the chair of a foreign dentist, I had been putting off the moment of truth. At first, I felt only an occasional dull ache in my tooth, which flared into a brief, stabbing pain when I bit into something hard. By Karon, though, the dull ache had ratcheted up to become a raging inferno. Even the slightest pressure sent blasts of pain into my jaw and – it seemed – right into the center of my brain. The tooth ached constantly, and ibuprofen had stopped working.

I went to see a dentist. She peered in at my tooth and shook her head. She said I needed a root canal and should see her teacher, a more experienced dentist in nearby Patong. She gave me the dentist's card, antibiotics and pain pills. The pills did help a little, but I called the Patong dentist office and made an appointment for a couple of days later.

During our stay in Karon Beach, months of dogged bedtime reading brought us to the end of Harry Potter and the Half-Blood Prince, a 652-page tome and the sixth in the popular series. The book was much darker than earlier installments, and when Professor Dumbledore died at the end, Salome cried. The ending was a shock even to Ava and I, but we tried to console Salome as best we could. She was supposed to write a report about the book to send back to her teacher, but she was so upset by the ending that she didn't want to complete the assignment. After some cajoling, she did write the book report – including her dissatisfaction with author J.K. Rowling's decision to do away with the beloved professor. I later gave the book to a girl who worked at the hotel where we were staying, after I had seen her reading an earlier Harry Potter book in Thai. I figured our book might help her polish her English skills, and she seemed grateful to receive it.

We lounged at the beach in Karon for a few days, then it was time for a two-day excursion to the Similan Islands, off the coast of Phuket. O's cousin Ot had arranged the trip, so we packed our bags and left them with the hotel for safekeeping. Early on the appointed morning, a van picked us up for the two-hour ride to the docks where we would board a speedboat bound for the islands. Our tour group included a couple from Encinitas, less than 20 miles from our home in Oceanside, who were nearing the end of their own round-the-world trip. The speed boat whisked us out to the islands, then visited several snorkeling spots, where we were allowed to jump into the water and paddle about, oo-ing and ah-ing (mostly to ourselves) as we spotted many different varieties of brightly colored tropical fish.

The boat dropped us off at "Island 4," where the Thai park service operates a rustic lodge. We would stay on the island overnight; the boat was scheduled to pick us up the next afternoon. The three of us fell in love with the island, with its translucent, blue-green water and white powdery sand beaches. We spent the rest of the day snoozing on the beach and lolling about in the swells that gently lapped at the shore.

Salome's Journal

2/8/06 Phuket, Thailand

Hi Salome. The day before yesterday we went to Similan

*island. It is total paradise. First you took a van for two hours
to get to the boat. Then you take a boat for two hours to get
to Similan. It is really worth it. The water is turquoise and
the sand is white soft sand. When you come off the beach it
is like having baby powder on your feet. The room was very
nice with a sea view but the beds were a wood plank. I have
a very sore neck! The snorkeling was fantastic. We had an
underwater camera and there were the most gorgeous fish. I
really would like to go back but I hate the beds. Well now I am
going to Dino World a miniature golf place and have a lot of
fun. So talk to ya soon. Bye Salome.*

We walked the next morning to the other side of the
island, and Ava and I took turns climbing to a lookout
point on a steep jungle trail with the help of guide ropes
installed by park workers.

The boat came right on time after lunch. We made a
couple of snorkeling stops on the way back to the dock
and were back in Karon by evening. We moved from our
hotel to Tony's Home, a family-owned hotel right on the
beach, which was accessible via a dirt road at the north
end of town. Our room was very large and featured a wide
balcony with a 180-degree sea view. The price of the room
included a generous buffet breakfast, with trays of fresh
fruit, French toast, eggs, sausage and bacon. The dining
room was on the first floor, and was open on two sides, a
very pleasant place to spend each morning while Salome
did her schoolwork. The tables spilled out onto a patio that
was shaded by umbrellas.

On the day of my dental appointment, we hailed a
taxi to take us to Patong Beach. I was a little nervous, but
looking forward to finally getting some relief from

my aching tooth. The infection had been tamed by the antibiotics, but I knew I needed to keep my date with the drill.

The air-conditioned waiting room was full of patients, and I anxiously waited my turn. The office had cool tile floors, dark wood paneling, soft music piped through hidden speakers and a couple of quietly gurgling fountains. As soon as I was called into the inner office, however, I realized the tranquility was an illusion. When I sat down in the chair, a swarm of dental assistants scurried around me, draping me with a cloth, reclining the chair, arranging dental tools on a silver tray and positioning a powerful light to shine into my mouth. The dentist, a slender woman, came in, wearing a surgical mask and goggles, so I never saw her face, and with her accent, it was hard to understand much of what she said.

She got right to work, probing my sore tooth before injecting me with Novocaine. She left to allow the numbing agent to do its work, then came back, picked up her electric drill and got started. In a few minutes, she had drilled out the offending roots, packed the cavity with medicine and installed a temporary filling. Since I would be leaving for Bangkok in a couple of days, there wouldn't be time for me to return for the permanent filling, so I resigned myself to having the work completed when I returned home. The procedure cost $60 and, miraculously, my pain was completely gone. A couple of months later, I visited my regular dentist back in Oceanside. Since I didn't have insurance, the quote for finishing the root canal and installing a crown was $2,000. I ended up waiting several months longer, until I had insurance, to complete the job and kicked myself for not having the work done in Thailand or India.

From the dentist's office, we walked down to the beach, where we saw rows of lounge chairs and beach umbrellas stretching out in either direction. Although Patong Beach had suffered heavy damage in the 2004 tsunami, there were no physical signs of the disaster when we visited in early 2006.

Since it was still early in the day and none of us had brought our beach things, we fell back on our default activity – shopping. Patong was like a larger version of Karon – more shops, more traffic and more people. We came upon a salon where, for a few dollars, visitors could soak their feet in a tub of bubbly, scented water, and then enjoy a vigorous foot massage. Ava and Salome jumped at the chance, reclining on the padded chairs with their feet up, like princesses. I decided to find an Internet café and check email.

Our days in Thailand's beach paradise were ending. One afternoon, Ava hung out at the hotel while I took Salome to Dino World, a nearby miniature golf course. We walked the mile or so to the place, mostly uphill, in the sweltering sunshine. By the time we got to Dino World, I was sweating heavily and dripped my way through the 18-hole course, walking past the palm trees, and plaster T-rexes and stegosauruses. We were hungry after our round of mini-golf and grabbed a bite at Nasa Burger, a corner hamburger stand decorated in red, white and blue, and run by an expatriate Welsh-American who had come to Phuket for a vacation and never left.

The burgers were tasty, but the meat had an unusual

flavor I couldn't place, and the cheese was rubbery. We enjoyed sitting at the counter of the burger stand, though, watching the world go by while chatting with the talkative proprietor.

Each day in Karon Beach, we walked past a place near our hotel that rented scooters. Up until the final day, I had resisted the impulse to try one. For one thing, motorists drive on the left side of the road in Thailand, and I wasn't sure how difficult that would be for someone used to driving on the right. But on our last morning, I decided to take the plunge. Maybe it was the beautiful, sunny day, or possibly I was bored with the beach life.

The scooters were ridiculously cheap – a full day's rental cost only about $5 U.S. Gas was extra, but I figured the scooters would get excellent mileage. I filled out the necessary paperwork, picked up a couple of helmets, and soon I was buzzing down the street on a gold-colored model. The scooter had an automatic transmission, which meant I didn't even have to shift gears. I took a long ride down to the southern tip of Phuket, stopping off at a lookout point from where the Andaman Sea stretched out like a sparkling blue plateau. Later, I took turns giving Ava and Salome rides on the back. When the gas got low, I stopped off at a filling station, really just a shack, where the woman attendant used a hand pump to top off my scooter's tank from a 55-gallon barrel of fuel.

I cruised along up and down hills, with the road hugging Phuket's coast. I loved the sensation of the wind and sunshine on my face, not worried about the vehicles passing me to the right.

In the late afternoon, while Ava and Salome packed, I

sat on the balcony of our room at Tony House, my feet up on the railing as I scribbled in my journal and looked out at the sea. It was mid-February 2006, and in less than two weeks we would land at San Jose airport in California, completing our journey.

As I watched the clouds roll in above the sandy beach and shimmering blue water, I looked forward to being back in familiar surroundings. I was proud of our family for making it nearly around the globe, and just a tiny bit regretful that we were cutting the trip short. But overall, I was content with the decision we had made. I'm sure Ava felt differently. We had visited 19 countries; I was more than satisfied with our accomplishment. After all, the vast majority of the time, we had traveled through foreign and exotic lands on our own, guided by our curiosity and instincts. (And sometimes a guidebook.) I wondered what would await us when we returned home – would we be able to find jobs, and would Salome pick up in school where she left off? Strangely enough, I looked forward to going back to work. Maybe I felt guilty at having "loafed" for so many months. Both Ava and I had emailed our old bosses to let them know we would be returning soon if they had any positions available. We each received encouraging replies.

Salome, too, was excited at the prospect of going home soon and talked about it a lot. She seemed to have recovered completely from the severe mood swings she had experienced earlier in the trip, which we had attributed to a bad reaction to her medication. That's not to say we didn't squabble, but the arguments were the kind you'd expect between any child and parents.

We had come to relish our little corner of Karon Beach were sorry to leave it behind. A taxi took us to the Phuket airport for our flight to Bangkok, where we would spend two more days before flying to Hong Kong.

Salome's Journal

2/11/06 Phuket, Thailand

Today is our last day in Phuket. Tonight we go to Bangkok for 3 days. Hong Kong (we have a very fancy hotel) then Tokyo and then   HOME!!!!!!!!!! Well actually San Jose then HOME. I think that I will enjoy being home for 2 weeks then I'll be like "When is our trip to Irland!" But really I probably will not want to travel for 3 years after. Oh except for Marriot time shares. Well talk to ya soon. Salome.

When our plane touched down in Bangkok that night, we headed for Wendy House for the third and final time. The staff was just as friendly and welcoming as on our previous two stays, and the time passed quickly as we shopped at the MBK mall and tried out as many restaurants as we could. On our last day, we visited the snake farm, which is actually a medical center in downtown Bangkok, where snakes are "milked" for their venom, which is used to make serum for treating snakebites throughout Thailand. The center is also a tourist attraction, with several daily shows, in which snake handlers demonstrate how they extract venom and feed many varieties of highly poisonous reptiles. We watched the handlers as they faced hissing, rearing cobras, carefully snagging the snakes and forcing their jaws open so their venom could be drained into glass containers.

We learned that snakes tend to go on a hunger strike when they are not fed live animals, and watched as the handlers force-fed them with sausages. At the end of the show, audience members were allowed to pose for pictures with a large Burmese python draped across their shoulders. Both Salome and I jumped at this snake-bonding opportunity; Ava stood back and snapped the photos.

Then, our month in Thailand was over. Our friends from California had long since departed, and we celebrated Valentine's Day 2006 by boarding a Cathay Pacific Airlines jet bound for Hong Kong.

When we arrived in Hong Kong, we should have changed our nickname from the "Three Wanderers" to the "Three Squabblers." The three of us were snappish and impatient with each other.

I'm not sure whether we had been living too close together for too long, but minor disagreements were turning into heated arguments with lots of shouting and tears. These spats were triggered by the usual things: Salome's schoolwork, where to eat lunch, or something that Ava and Salome wanted to buy, but I thought was too expensive, too heavy to carry or just plain unnecessary.

I'll admit I was cranky. With our remaining time on the road down to just over a week, I was edgy about trading our life of leisure for the world of alarm clocks, rush-hour commutes and neckties.

But we tried not to let it spoil the last week of our trip, and generally, it didn't. The airport in Hong Kong was clean and modern, and we took the express train to Kowloon, which is just across Victoria Harbor from Hong Kong Island. Based on a tip from my brother, we had booked rooms at the Salisbury YMCA, a moderately priced hotel with the same harbor views as the posh and pricy Peninsula Hotel next door, for a fraction of the cost.

The train whisked us comfortably to Kowloon in a half-hour, and we had to transfer to a shuttle bus for the last mile or so to our hotel. The YMCA was everything we could have asked for, a high-rise hotel across the street from the water, with a ground-floor restaurant and Internet café, swimming pools and workout rooms, all of which we were free to hotel guests. We lucked out when the regular harbor view room we had reserved was unavailable, and for the same price, we were given a corner suite with floor-to-ceiling windows overlooking Hong Kong's harbor and famous skyline. The room had a desk where Salome could do her schoolwork, and the hotel staff left a complimentary basket of fresh fruit for us.

Our plan was to spend three nights in Kowloon, then move to the Disneyland resort on nearby Lantau Island, where we would stay for two nights at the resort's Hollywood Hotel. The Hong Kong Disneyland park had opened just a few months before our visit, and we had been promising Salome for months that we would spend the day there when we passed through Hong Kong.

From our hotel, it was an easy walk to the waterfront, where locals turned out in droves on warm evenings to stroll along the boardwalk and admire the dazzling views of Hong Kong's skyscrapers across the harbor. At 8 each night, the skyline blazed with lasers and searchlights, and the skyscrapers became backdrops for colorful laser lights during a multimedia show synchronized with music played from speakers along the waterfront.

We could also walk to Nathan Road, the main drag of Kowloon's shopping and entertainment district, which was lined with everything from souvenir shops to gourmet restaurants to high-end jewelry stores.

We spent a lot of time walking around Hong Kong's colorful, lively streets, checking out sights such as the bird and flower markets, the electronics district and the "Walk of Stars" along the harbor (like its more famous cousin in Hollywood, but think Jackie Chan, Bruce Lee and Chow Yun Fat instead of Marilyn Monroe and Clark Gable). We went to the Sweet Dynasty Restaurant, famed for its desserts, where we were the only non-Asians in the place. Although the menu was written in Chinese, it did have pictures. We ordered bowls of sweet, creamy almond soup.

We shopped for gifts for friends and family – and ourselves – picking up silk kimonos and Chinese dolls. We were constantly harangued by peddlers of everything from hashish to fake Rolexes, who melted in and out of doorways along Nathan Road. One evening, our curiosity got the best of us and we followed a Middle Eastern man into a corridor in the sprawling Chung King Mansion, a multi-story building with shops on the ground floor and cheap hotels and youth hostels on the upper floors. The man had offered to sell us a Rolex and we followed him into a shop whose windows were papered with posters of baby clothes and toys. Inside, though, there was no children's merchandise, only a plain metal desk and a couple of chairs.

"Look, here is a Rolex," he said, pulling out a heavy watch with a thick leather band and loads of buttons and dials sprouting from its sides. Its face indeed carried the famous logo, but there was no pretense on his part that we were looking at the genuine article. "Eight hundred, Hong Kong dollars," he said, or about $100 U.S.

Since I knew I couldn't afford a real Rolex, which sold at the fancy jewelry stores down the street for $4,000 or $5,000, I was tempted as I felt the heft of the watch in my palm. As I thought about it, Ava urging me on, the man pulled out a binder from a desk drawer and flipped through photos of different styles of Rolex watches. "What kind you like?" he asked, apparently able to get me the style of counterfeit time-piece that would suit my personal taste.

I was seriously considering making a deal, but then realized that if the watch stopped the next day, I'd be out a hundred bucks with nothing but a handsome hunk of metal to show for it. I handed back the watch.

As we walked back through the corridor to the street, I stopped to look at the DVDs in one of the shops. Included in the titles was Kyon Ki, the Bollywood flick we had seen in Jaipur, India. Apparently, Hong Kong has a sizeable population of Indian immigrants drawn by the island's booming economy.

Among the "must-see" sights in Hong Kong are a ride on the Star Ferry and a trip by tram to the top of Victoria Peak. We were able to do both on one late-afternoon excursion. The ferry ride was short, but provided a great vantage point for viewing both sides of the harbor. We walked to the tram station and settled in for the near-vertical ride to the top. The tram has operated along its current route since 1888, although the equipment has been modernized over the years, most recently in the late 1980s. The route is so steep it almost feels like riding an elevator.

The payoff, of course, is the view from the top.

We arrived around dusk, and the lights of Hong Kong's dozens of skyscrapers were just beginning to wink on. A light mist was rolling in, enough to provide atmosphere but not too thick to obscure the view. We walked around, tried taking photos with different light settings on our digital camera, and bought gifts from an Indian shop inside the tram station. Although there were several restaurants, we opted to ride back down to the city for dinner.

We set out to find what our guidebook described as a moderately priced eatery favored by locals. Our search allowed us to experience Hong Kong's network of escalators and moving sidewalks, which shuttle people up and down the hill each day. Soon, we were thoroughly disoriented, but at least we got a good look at the city streets. Finally, we found the spot where the restaurant was supposed to be, but unfortunately, it had gone out of business. We ended up instead at a Mexican cantina, which was good, but it seemed strange to be wolfing down carnitas burritos and drinking Bohemia beer in Hong Kong. On the way back to the ferry terminal, I stopped in a cigar shop and bought a box of Cuban puros.

On our last morning at the YMCA, I went for my customary morning run along the harbor. This time, as I was finishing, I noticed a tai chi class starting in a space just off the boardwalk. There seemed to be a number of Westerners, and as I watched, the instructor beckoned to me and urged me to join in. I had been curious about this Asian meditation and exercise ritual since seeing groups performing it in Thailand, so I took a spot in the back row. We went through about a dozen different positions and exercises. Surprisingly, it took more out of me than I had imagined it would. I found it strenuous to hold the proper position with my body while following the arm and leg movements of the instructor. At the same time, it was very relaxing and peaceful, moving slowly to the music of the instructor's boom box while gazing at the harbor.

Reluctantly, we left the YMCA with its gorgeous view, and moved to the Disney resort's Hollywood Hotel, which was immaculate, brand-new and pricey. After lunch in the hotel's cafeteria, we set out to ride the subway and local bus to Po Lin Monastery, home of the largest outdoor, seated bronze statue of the Buddha in Asia, and perhaps the world.

We climbed more than 250 steps to reach the Buddha statue, which depicts the deity seated on a lotus throne, right hand raised, and wearing a serene expression. The statue was completed in 1993 and stands an imposing 34 meters, or about 100 feet, high, and weighs 250 tons. From the viewing platform that encircles the base of the giant Buddha, we could see the rolling green hills of Lantau Island under overcast skies.

We wandered around the monastery grounds, lighting incense sticks in the temples, and we eating a vegetarian meal that was included with our admission tickets.

We rose early the next morning to visit the Happiest Place on Earth, Hong Kong style. Ordinarily, I would steer clear of Disneyland during an international trip, since we live less than 50 miles from the original theme park in Anaheim. But we had promised Salome a break from museums and monuments, and I was curious to see how the park would differ from its stateside counterpart.

The park had only been open a few months when we visited, and everything, from the landscaping to the building decorations, was in pristine condition. As we entered the park and scrutinized the map, we saw that Hong Kong Disneyland was smaller and had fewer rides than the Disney parks in the U.S.

But there were a few of the most familiar attractions, such as Space Mountain, Jungle Cruise and It's a Small World. I'm not sure whether it was the season, or the cool, cloudy weather, but the crowds were sparse and lines for the rides were short. While such famous rides as Pirates of the Caribbean and Thunder Mountain were missing, the park did have several excellent live shows that are not available in the U.S., such as an extravagant production of the Lion King, and "The Golden Mickeys," a faux award show based on Disney characters and songs. All the shows alternated between English and Chinese.

The dining choices also showed a distinctive Asian flair, with noodle dishes offered at most of the restaurants and snack bars.

We were happy that Hong Kong Disney held the familiar fireworks, light and music show after dark, surrounding the trademark fantasy castle.

In all, we had an enjoyable time at the park, and Salome was happy, tired and ready to head back to the hotel after our full day's outing.

Very early the next morning, we caught a taxi to the airport for our flight to Tokyo, the last foreign stop on our world tour.

February in Tokyo means cold weather and although there was no snow on the ground, it was chilly outside.

We had heard and read that Tokyo is one of the most expensive cities in the world, and I was prepared for one last budget-busting assault on our fast-disappearing cash reserves. To my pleasant surprise, the Japanese-style guesthouse where we stayed, Kimi Ryokan, cost only about $70 U.S. per night.

The guesthouse was in Tokyo's Ikebukuro district on the west side of the city, almost directly opposite from Narita airport, which is on the city's eastern outskirts. The map provided on the guesthouse Web site showed that we would have to take two trains, and the trip would last about 90 minutes.

We got on the correct train, the Keisei Line, headed in the right direction, with the help of signs and maps that, thankfully, were written in both Japanese and English. We clutched our bags as the train bounced and jostled, sometimes above the city streets and sometimes below ground. As we rode, I felt like we had crossed another threshold toward the familiar Western world, since we passed a number of Little League baseball fields interspersed among apartment buildings and commercial blocks.

Throughout South America, Europe, India and Asia, we'd seen lots of youth sports fields, but they were all laid out for soccer, rugby and cricket. Baseball just isn't very popular outside the U.S., with notable exceptions of Mexico, Latin America and Japan.

The next leg of our trip called for us to take the JR Yamanote line to Ikebukuro station.

Japanese commuters eyed us curiously, but unlike in New York City or London, no one offered to help us carry our bags down the stairs, in spite of how pathetic we must have looked as we sweated, strained and stumbled our way down to the train platform.

The Ikebukuro station was an immense underground space, a small city really, inhabited by hundreds of hurrying Japanese and many shops and restaurants. The guesthouse's walking guide was like a treasure map, with a colored line and arrows leading from the station to the hotel. Landmarks were labeled in English and the guesthouse itself was shown as a bright red square. Our path would take us from the west entrance of the sprawling underground train station, past the KFC and something called the Big Echo (which turned out to be a multistory, neon-lighted karaoke palace), two pachinko parlors and a tobacco shop. We rounded the corner to the ryokan as dusk settled on the city, and the pulsing, bright lights of the buildings came to life.

Exhausted from our journey, we hauled our bags down a few steps to the ryokan entrance and found a soothing space with artfully arranged flowers and polished wooden floors. Just inside the door, guests had removed their shoes and lined them up neatly, so we did the same before approaching the check-in desk.

We found the Kimi Ryokan clean, friendly and well-located. Our room was tiny, with just enough floor space for three futons laid out on a tatami mat floor, which provided an amazingly comfortable night's sleep. There was a closet, and a small table, the only piece of furniture. We found robes for each of us, a good electric heater and the immaculate shared bathroom was down the hall.

The guesthouse also had a traditional cedar-lined Japanese bath, a large tub filled with hot, fragrant water, which available for use by guests. The only catch was, you had to shower before soaking in the tub. Two other innovations at the ryokan warmed my heart – and other parts – during our stay in Tokyo in chilly February. One was the heated floor in the lounge, where guests could watch TV or linger over a cup of green tea. The other was one of the best amenities I encountered during all of our travels – heated toilet seats. Little touches like these convinced me that Japan is among the most civilized of nations.

We had just two full days in Tokyo and spent most of our time on the go. The first night, we asked the hotel desk clerk to recommend a good sushi restaurant. Instead of simply giving us directions, he asked if we could wait a few minutes until he got off duty, then he donned his overcoat and scarf and led us to the front door of the restaurant, a good half-mile away.

The restaurant was a tiny hole-in-the-wall. Diners sat in a long row on stools before glass cases, where the fresh sushi ingredients were displayed and the sushi chefs worked. A conveyer belt brought the delicacies around for us to take. At the end of the meal, the waitresses counted up the empty plates and calculated the bill.

We sat next to a man who was eating and drinking alone. He spoke almost no English, but we gleaned that his wife was away on a trip and he was living it up as a temporary bachelor. He had been indulging in the saki and asked the waitress to bring cups for Ava and me. After he poured us generous portions of the hot rice wine, we all smiled at each other and held up our saki cups in repeated toasts. Sitting in the cozy restaurant and warming our insides with saki was very pleasant, even if we couldn't understand him, nor him us.

Once we had finished stuffing ourselves, we thanked the man profusely and headed out in the cold night.

The next day was cool and drizzly, so we rode the metro train to "Joypolis," an indoor, multi-level amusement center operated by Sega, the video game maker. Along with the usual video games were a half-pipe skateboarding simulator, virtual rides through jungles and river rapids, competitive video car racing and Aquarena, a "virtual aquarium" with fish swimming on interactive computer screens.

In spite of the wet weather, we covered a lot of ground, checking out some of Tokyo's glittery, neon-drenched shopping districts and ducking into a side street for bowls of steaming noodles and bottles of ice-cold beer in a place frequented by local business types, who hunched over their noodles with their shirt collars unbuttoned and ties loosened.

Kisaburo Minato, the bespectacled and ponytailed owner of the guesthouse, offered daylong excursions to his guests for a nominal charge, and we took advantage of this service on our last day in Tokyo.

Kibo, as he was called, was trim and wiry, of medium height, and quick to smile. He owned a truck with a camper on the back, and we piled in that morning for a trip to see Mt. Fuji, a Buddhist shrine and a Japanese bathhouse. Kibo provided us with a box breakfast which included seafood cake, but the meal didn't appeal to Salome. We sat in the back of the camper on comfortable seats with four other guests, all Europeans, while Kibo drove and played music from his i-Pod over the stereo system. His music collection included jazz, classical and blues.

Fog served as our nemesis for the last – but not the first – time on our trip, shrouding the famous mountain from view. Earlier in our trip, we had also missed views of such fabulous sites as Machu Picchu and Rio's towering Christo Redentor statue because of whiteout conditions.

But Kibo was undaunted and he took us to a shrine whose buildings and statues were draped in folds of snow. The setting was so peaceful that we could have remained there for a long time in quiet meditation, if not for the biting cold. We also lobbed snowballs at each other at the shore of a lake where, according to our host, Tokyo gangsters had reputedly dumped bodies in the past.

Lunch was at Kibo's favorite mountainside noodle house, and our last stop was at the bathhouse, where men and women headed into separate sections of the building. Before we could enter the steaming indoor and outdoor thermal pools, Kibo instructed us to wash our hair and bodies with a variety of scented soaps and shampoos. After the relaxing bath, we ate green tea ice cream and got back into Kibo's camper for the return ride to Tokyo. As we drove along the freeway, one of the Europeans excitedly pointed out the window and Kibo pulled to the side of the road. The shape of Mt. Fuji's peak was just visible through the haze, which had thinned in a burst of late afternoon sun. We all snapped photos, although the mountain's outline was too faint to be captured well on film or video card.

Then it was back to Tokyo, where our group split up. Ava, Salome and I headed to a karaoke palace down the street from the guesthouse. We booked a private room for an hour and took the elevator to the sixth or seventh floor.

Our room had sofas, a table and a powerful sound system and TV monitor. We ordered food and drinks by pushing buttons on an electronic menu and took turns crooning such oldies as "American Pie," "Hotel California" and "Paradise by the Dashboard Light." We were having so much fun that we ended up staying a second hour, and were finally ordered to leave by the exasperated staff.

Our voices hoarse and our heads full of beer (Ava and I, anyway), we went back to the guesthouse for one last night on foreign soil. The next morning we got up, packed, checked email at an Internet café, and I took a short, cold run around the neighborhood. This time, we opted for the express train to Narita airport, where we boarded an American Airlines Boeing 777 for a flight to San Jose. Since we crossed the international dateline during the flight, we landed in California the morning before we left Tokyo – February 22, 2006.

Full circle.

Salome's Journal

2/22/06 Tokyo, Japan

Today we are going to the airport. We are heading to San Francisco to go visit Sam and Emma. Then we get a flight to San Diego. I can't believe it today we are actually flying home! Yesterday we went on a trip to Mt. Fugi but we only got a glimpse through the clouds. Then we went to a Japanese bath and which is hot springs. They were very nice but we had to go naked but I did not care. Well talk to ya soon on my next trip. Oh PS. Last night we got crazy singing koroke. It was really fun!

Chapter 14

Home at Last

Re-entry, lessons learned

The sun felt good on my face as I walked out of the San Jose airport on a late February morning in 2006.

We were lucky to have had the opportunity to travel around the world independently, to go where we wanted, and see and do what we pleased. Few people in today's society are willing – or able – to put their lives on hold for such an adventure, although many probably fantasize about it.

That thought crossed my mind as we prepared to re-enter our lives in America, but still I was glad to be home.

Whether or not it was completely rational, I felt like a burden had been lifted from my shoulders. My anxiety about threats ranging from terrorists, robbers and insurrections to infectious diseases and poor medical care, which had been in the background of my thoughts throughout our travels, suddenly evaporated.

With a feeling almost like joy, I pulled out of the airport parking lot in our rental car, and onto the smooth, well-marked concrete ribbon of the interstate highway. We stopped at a fast-food place for lunch and enjoyed big fat burritos and giant soft drinks with free refills.

After visiting friends in the Bay Area for a few days,

we caught the last flight included on our round-the-world tickets, a commuter hop from San Jose to San Diego. As we walked from the tarmac into the terminal building, Salome snapped a photo of the huge "Welcome to San Diego" sign over the door.

The next days and weeks were a blur: we got our trusty Subaru out of storage, re-enrolled Salome in school and looked for a place to live. We weren't able to move back into our own house right away because our tenants still had a couple of months left on their lease. Workwise, I picked up where I left off, freelancing for local publications, while Ava interviewed for a nursing job.

We caught a break when our tenants asked to get out of their lease early because they had bought a house of their own. So, in April 2006 we left the beach condo we had been enjoying and moved our stuff from storage back into our Oceanside house. Within less than two months of our arrival at the San Diego airport, it was almost like we had never left – we were living in the same neighborhood, driving the same car, and Salome was back in her old school, finishing out the last couple months of fourth grade.

How had our "adventure of a lifetime" changed us? What had we learned? Were there "secret destinations" we discovered only after returning home?

I have pondered these questions since our trip ended, a period of time that has flashed by at meteoric speed.

I learned that the inner voice in my head, which has been known to shout dire warnings at the slightest hint of risk in any undertaking, can be my own worst enemy. I have learned that, in order to get the most from life, I must overcome my instinctive fears and constantly expand my horizons. I think I am now more likely to feel a sense of exhilaration when walking down the street of a bustling, foreign city, where I don't know anyone, than to feel anxious or apprehensive.

More than ever before, I relish the differences in how people live in other countries, as compared to the American way of life. My family's travel experiences changed my worldview by demonstrating that – while there are many things to admire about my country – the idea that America is inherently superior to all other nations on earth in every way is just plain silly.

The contributions of cultures around the world in areas such as religion, cuisine, art, fashion, science and education are too numerous to catalogue here, and I won't even attempt it. Suffice it to say that if more Americans deigned to travel overseas, our country would have a more realistic notion of our true place in the world. While we enjoy an unbelievably high standard of living when compared with many other countries, we can profit immensely by learning about the customs, traditions and values of other members of the international community.

I learned that traveling around the world is a terrific way to lose weight. During our trip, I lost about 20 pounds without even trying, getting down to a weight I hadn't seen since my 20s. I identified two key factors in my weight loss – during our trip, we traveled exclusively by public transportation, meaning we lugged our heavy bags along streets, up and down stairs, and in and out of airplanes, buses and trains. Second, the food in other countries is healthier than most of what's available in the U.S., especially in our fast-food joints. We ate heartily on the road, but mostly at mealtimes, and food was almost always freshly prepared, with a minimum of preservatives or processing.

Within six months of our return, I gained those 20 pounds right back, also without any conscious change in my eating habits.

I learned that living in close proximity over an extended period of time with your immediate family can be both extremely gratifying and deeply frustrating. Ava, Salome and I learned a lot about each other and became much closer as a family during our travels. We depended on each other for companionship, support and sustenance. I came to realize there is no one I would rather share a tuk-tuk, elephant safari or long-haul flight with than the two of them.

But it was certainly a challenge living with two other people for months on end in cramped hotel rooms. While we didn't have to limit ourselves to the most austere accommodations, such as $2-per-night bunks in cheap hostels, neither were we able to afford suites at the Ritz or the Taj. Instead, we opted for middle-of-the-road places where we could get clean, safe lodgings for a reasonable price. Sometimes, the rooms were small enough that we stepped on each others' toes – and we certainly trod on each others' nerves.

As I write this, several years after completing our epic journey, neither Ava, Salome nor I has a pat answer to the question we are most commonly asked: "What was your favorite place?" We visited too many wonderful cities and countries, and collected so many incredible memories, that it is next to impossible to rank them sensibly. I usually respond that I can't think of place I wouldn't want to visit again.

Also difficult is the larger question – which I ask myself – of whether I will ever again travel around the world.

In the final days of our trip, I was sure the answer was "no." More than anything, I looked forward to sitting in my recliner, watching my own TV in my own living room.

And, at first, I was content to stay put. But fortunately, the feeling was short-lived – many intriguing destinations call out to us.

We have continued traveling since our return. In 2007, at Salome's urging, we visited Scotland and Ireland, and the next year, we spent three memorable weeks in Thailand and Vietnam, traveling from Hanoi to Ho Chi Minh City (Saigon) by train. Our next adventure will be South Africa in the summer of 2010 during the World Cup soccer tournament.

Are there regrets, that most unhelpful of emotions? While I'd like to be able to say no, to be honest, I have a couple. Along the way, there were times when my anxieties took away from the pure enjoyment I should have felt. My overdeveloped sense of caution also caused me to miss out on experiences that I'm sure would have been memorable, such as the time I was invited to hear a band play indigenous music in a small town in northern Brazil. I declined because I was worried about walking alone through the town's deserted streets late at night, but I'm sure it would have been fine.

I can't say that I exactly regret cutting our trip short from our original itinerary; at the time it felt like the right decision for me and Salome, although, as I have noted, Ava was never fully convinced. But there are times when I ask myself if we shouldn't have just pressed on with our plans to travel in China and Japan.

Whenever that particular thought rears its head, I console myself by imagining new, future adventures. Maybe even another world trip!

By the time you read this, we may be steaming down the Yangtze River in China, or driving across the Australian outback in a rented jeep, places we missed on our last trip.

Who knows?

The world awaits.

About The Author

After Joe Tash left home at age 15, he supported himself by working as a janitor, traveling carnival worker, short-order cook, bartender and taxi driver. His earliest travel memory is of a trip to Florida with his parents when he was five or six years old, and his triumphant victory in a seashell-collecting contest. As a young adult, he found himself homeless for a short time, and while he was sleeping in an abandoned Cadillac in a vacant lot, the car was stolen. Luckily, the thieves let him gather up his belongings and get out of the car before they towed it away.

Deciding to make something of himself, he enrolled in college, and became an English major, greatly disappointing his parents. Following his graduation, he found work as a journalist, a profession many people consider less respectable than carnival worker or taxi driver.

He has worked at daily newspapers in California and Florida, winning awards from such organizations as the San Diego Press Club, the Society for Professional Journalists and the California Newspaper Publishers Association. He has also worked as a public-relations specialist at the County of San Diego and a private public relations firm.

Tash and his wife, Ava, have traveled extensively throughout the U.S., Mexico, South America, Europe and Asia. The couple and their daughter, Salome, traveled around the world in 2005 and 2006.

The family lives in Oceanside, California, with Charlotte the dog, Fred the cat and Mooshi the bearded dragon lizard.